KIDS LOVE MICHIGAN

A PARENT'S GUIDE TO EXPLORING FUN PLACES IN MICHIGAN WITH CHILDREN. . .YEAR ROUND!

Kids Love Publications
7438 Sawmill Road, PMB 500
Columbus, OH 43235

Dedicated to the Families
of Michigan

For the latest updates corresponding to the pages in this book visit
our website:

www.kidslovepublications.com

Although the authors have exhaustively researched all sources to
ensure accuracy and completeness of the information contained in
this book, we assume no responsibility for errors, inaccuracies,
omissions or any other inconsistency herein. Any slights against
any entries or organizations are unintentional.

ISBN# 09663457-3-8

KIDS ♥ MICHIGAN ™   Kids Love Publications

MISSION STATEMENT

At first glance, you may think that this is a book that just lists hundreds of places to travel. While it is true that we've invested thousands of hours of exhaustive research (*and drove nearly 3000 miles in Michigan*) to prepare this travel resource...just listing places to travel is not the mission statement of these projects.

As children, Michele and I were able to travel extensively throughout the United States. We consider these family times some of the greatest memories we cherish today. We, quite frankly, felt that most children had this opportunity to travel with their family as we did. However, as we became adults and started our own family, we found that this wasn't necessarily the case. We continually heard friends express several concerns when deciding how to spend "quality" and "quantity" family time. 1) What to do? 2) Where to do it? 3) How much will it cost? 4) How do I know that my kids will enjoy it?

Interestingly enough, as we compare our experiences with our families when we were kids, many of our fondest memories were not made at an expensive attraction, but rather when it was least expected.

It is our belief and mission statement that if you as a family will study and use the contained information to create family memories, these memories will grow a stronger, tighter family. Our ultimate mission statement is, that your children will develop a love and a passion for quality family experiences that they can pass to another generation of family travelers.

We thank you for purchasing this book, and we hope to see you on the road (*and hearing your travel stories!*) God bless your journeys and happy exploring!

George, Michele, Jenny and Daniel

Acknowledgements

We are most thankful to be blessed with our parents, Barbara Darrall and George and Catherine Zavatsky who helped us every way they could – researching, typesetting, proofing and babysitting. More importantly, they were great sounding boards and offered loving, unconditional support.

Our own young kids, Jenny and Daniel, were delightful and fun children during all of our trips across the state.

We both sincerely thank each other – our partnership has created a great "marriage of minds" with lots of exciting moments and laughs woven throughout. Above all, we praise the Lord for His many answered prayers and special blessings throughout the completion of this project.

We think Michigan is a wonderful, friendly area of the country with more activities than you could imagine! Our sincere wish is that this book will help everyone "fall in love" with Michigan!

In a Hundred Years...

It will not matter, The size of my bank account...
The kind of house that I lived in, the kind of car
that I drove... But what will matter is...
That the world may be different
Because I was important in the life of a child.
- author unknown

"Where to go?, What to do?, and How much will it cost?", are all questions that they have heard throughout the years from friends and family. These questions became the inspiration that motivated them to research, write and publish the "Kids Love" travel series.

This adventure of writing and publishing family travel books has taken them on a journey of experiences that they never could have imagined. They have appeared as guests on over 50 radio and television shows, had featured articles in statewide newspapers and magazines, spoken to thousands of people at schools and conventions, and write monthly columns in many publications talking about "family friendly" places to travel.

George Zavatsky and Michele (Darrall) Zavatsky were born and raised in the Mid-West. Although currently residing in Columbus, Ohio they have developed a strong affection for Michigan and have numerous family members living in the state. Along with writing and publishing a series of best-selling kids' travel books, each of them also own and operate a courier business and an internet marketing company. Besides the wonderful adventure of marriage, they place great importance on being loving parents to Jenny and Daniel.

INTRODUCTION

HOW TO USE THIS BOOK

If you are excited about discovering Michigan, this is the book for you and your family! We've spent over a thousand hours doing all the scouting, collecting and compiling (*and most often visiting!*) so that you could spend less time searching and more time having fun.

Here are a few hints to make your adventures run smoothly:

- ❑ Consider the **child's age** before deciding to take a visit.
- ❑ Know **directions** and parking. Call ahead (or visit the company's website) if you have questions *and* bring this book. Also, don't forget your camera! *(please honor rules regarding use).*
- ❑ **Estimate the duration** of the trip. Bring small surprises (favorite juice boxes) and travel books and toys.
- ❑ Call ahead for **reservations** or details, if necessary.
- ❑ Most listings are **closed major holidays** unless noted.
- ❑ Make a **family "treasure chest"**. Decorate a big box or use an old popcorn tin. Store memorabilia from a fun outing, journals, pictures, brochures and souvenirs. Once a year, look through the "treasure chest" and reminisce.
- ❑ Plan **picnics** along the way. Many Historical Society sites and state parks are scattered throughout Michigan. Allow time for a rural/scenic route to take advantage of these free picnic facilities.
- ❑ Some activities, especially tours, require **groups** of 10 or more. To participate, you may either ask to be part of another tour group or get a group together yourself (neighbors, friends, school organizations). If you arrange a group outing, most places offer discounts.

- ❑ For the latest updates corresponding to the pages in this book, visit our website: **www.kidslovepublications.com**.
- ❑ Each chapter represents an area of the state (*see map below*). Each listing is further identified by city, zip code, and place/event name. **The front index lists places by Activity Heading (i.e. Michigan History, Tours, Outdoors, Museums, etc.), the back index is alphabetical.**

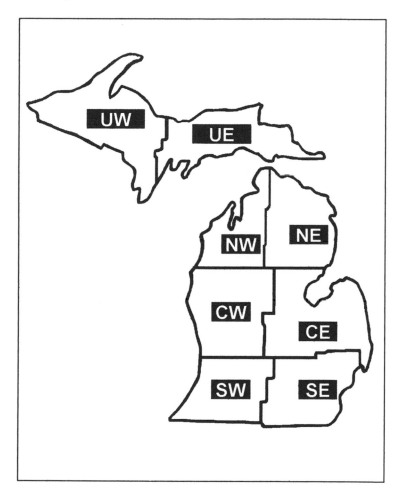

GENERAL INFORMATION

- Department of Natural Resources: www.dnr.state.mi.us. (517) 373-1220
- Fisheries Division - Lansing, (517) 373-1280
- Fishing Hotline - (800) ASKFISH
- Young Angler Program - (517) 373-1280
- Michigan Bicycle Touring - 3512 Red School Road, Kingsley (231) 263-5885, www.bikembt.com
- Michigan Charter Boat Association - Lansing, (800) MCBA-971
- Recreational Canoeing Association - Baldwin, (231) 745-4669
- Great Lakes Nordic Ski Council - Suttons Bay, (231) 271-6314 www.skinordic.org
- Snowmobiling, Skiing and Cross-Country Skiing - Livonia, (888) 78-GREAT, www.michigan.org
- Michigan Festivals & Events Association - Chesaning, (517) 845-2080
- Michigan Association of Recreational Vehicles and Campgrounds, MARVAC - Okemos, (800) 422-6478 www.MARVAC.org
- Michigan Association of Private Campground Owners (MAPCO) - Buckley, (231) 267-5089, www.michcampgrounds.com
- Farm Markets - Michigan Department of Agriculture - Lansing, (517) 373-1058
- Autumn Colors - (800) MI-4-FALL
- Snow Conditions - (800) MI-4-SNOW
- Oakland County Parks - (248) 858-0306
- West Michigan Tourist Assoc. - Grand Rapids, (800) 442-2084
- Travel Michigan - (888) 784-7328

GENERAL INFORMATION - PARKS

- SW - St. Joseph County Parks (616) 467-5519
- Missaukee County Parks, (231) 839-4945
- CW - Newaygo County Parks, (231) 689-7383
- SE - Washtenaw County Parks, (313) 426-8211

*Check out these businesses / services in
your area for tour ideas:*

AIRPORTS

Understand all the jobs it takes to run an airport. Tour the terminal, baggage claim, gates and security / currency exchange. Maybe you'll even get to board a plane.

ANIMAL SHELTERS

Great for the would-be pet owner.

BANKS

Take a "behind the scenes" look at automated teller machines, bank vaults and drive-thru window chutes. You may want to take this tour and then open a savings account for your child.

ELECTRIC COMPANY / POWER PLANTS

Coal furnaces heat water, which produces steam, that propels turbines, that drive generators, that make electricity.

FIRE STATIONS

Many Open Houses in October, Fire Prevention Month. Take a look into the life of the firefighters servicing your area and try on their gear. See where they hang out, sleep and eat.

HOSPITALS

Some Children's Hospitals offer pre-surgery and general tours.

NEWSPAPERS

You'll be amazed at all the new technology. See monster printers and robotics. See samples in the layout department and maybe try to put together your own page. National Newspaper Week is in October.

RESTAURANTS

DOMINO'S PIZZA

❏   Various locations

Telephone your local shop for tour status. Free. Usually ages 4+. Takes 15 – 20 minutes. Your children can be pizza bakers! While the group is instructed on ingredients and pizza secrets, they will get to make their own special pizza. After the custom made pizza bakes, your tour guide will take it out of the special oven, box it up and you get to take it home.

PIZZA HUT

❏   Many participating restaurants

Telephone the store manager. Best days are Monday, Tuesday and Wednesday mid-afternoon. Minimum of 10 people. $3.50 per person. All children love pizza – especially when they can create their own! As the children tour the kitchen, they learn how to make a pizza, bake it, and then eat it. The admission charge includes lots of creatively make pizzas, beverage and coloring book.

MCDONALD'S RESTAURANTS

❏   Participating locations

Telephone the store manager. They prefer Monday or Tuesday.
Free. What child doesn't love McDonald's food? This is your
child's chance to go behind the counter and look at the machines
that make all the fun food. You will be shown the freezer and it's
alarm, the fryer and hamburger flipping on the grills. There is a
free snack at the end of the tour.

SUPERMARKETS

Kids are fascinated to go behind the scenes of the same store where
Mom and Dad shop. Usually you will see them grind meat, walk
into large freezer rooms, watch cakes and bread bake and receive
free samples along the way. Maybe you'll even get to pet a live
lobster!

TV / RADIO STATIONS

Studios, newsrooms, Fox kids clubs. Why do weathermen never
wear blue clothes on TV?

WATER TREATMENT PLANTS

A giant science experiment! You can watch seven stages of water
treatment.   The favorite is usually the wall of bright buttons
flashing as workers monitor the different processes.

U.S. MAIN POST OFFICES

Did you know Ben Franklin was the first Postmaster General (over 200 years ago)? Most interesting is the high-speed automated mail processing equipment. Learn how to address envelopes so they will be sent quicker (there are secrets). To make your tour more interesting, have your children write a letter to themselves and address it with colorful markers. Mail it earlier that day and they will stay interested trying to locate their letter in all the high-speed machinery.

Index by Activity Heading (City, Place/Event Name, Page)

AMUSEMENTS

CE - Bridgeport, *Junction Valley RR,* 5

CE - Frankenmuth, *Bronner's Christmas Wonderland,* 10

CW -Grand Rapids (Kentwood), *AJ's Family Water Park,* 36

CW- Holland, *Dutch Village,* 40

CW -Muskegon, *Michigan's Adventure Amusement Park,* 47

NW- Interlochen, *Fun Country,* 77

NW- Petoskey, *Pirate's Cove Adventure Golf,* 80

NW- Traverse City, *Pirate's Cove Adventure Golf,* 81

SE - Farmington Hills, *Marvin's Marvelous Mechanical Mus,* 112

SE - Livonia, *Jeepers! Wonderland* 121

SE - Onsted, *Mystery Hill,* 128

SE - Onsted, *Prehistoric Forest,* 128

SE - Onsted, *Stagecoach Stop USA,* 129

SE - Shelby Twp*,Four Bears WP,* 133

SW- Battle Creek, *Full Blast & Battle Creek Youth Center,* 140

UE - St. Ignace, *Mystery Spot,* 172

UW- Ishpeming, *Da Yoopers,* 185

ANIMALS & FARMS

CE - Birch Run, *Wilderness Trails,* 4

CE - Pinconning, *Deer Acres,* 17

CE - Saginaw, *Children's Zoo,* 21

CW- Grand Rapids, *John Ball Zoo,* 33

CW- Remus, *Dreamfield Farm,* 49

NE - Grayling, *Fish Hatchery,* 59

NE - Mackinac Is., *Butterfly House,* 62

NE - Ossineke, *Dinosaur Gardens Prehistoric Zoo,* 68

NW- Beulah, *Platte River State Fish Hatchery,* 73

SE - Ann Arbor, *Domino's Farms,* 88

SE - Carleton, *Calder Dairy Farm,* 94

SE - Dexter, *Spring Valley Trout,* 111

SE - Hanover, *Childs' Place Buffalo Ranch,* 113

SE - Lansing, *Potter Zoo/Gardens,* 117

SE - Royal Oak, *Detroit Zoo,* 132

SW- Battle Creek, *Binder Park Zoo* 139

SW- Coloma, *Deer Forest,* 144

SW- Mattawan, *Wolf Lake Fishery* 151

UE - Naubinway, *Garlyn Farm/Zoo,*165

UE - St. Ignace, *Deer Ranch,* 171

MICHIGAN HISTORY

CE - Bay City, *Historical Museum,* 4

CE - Flint, *Crossroads Village & Huckleberry Railroad,* 8

CE - Frankenmuth, *Hist'l Mus,* 11

CE - Huron City, *Museum,* 14

CE - Port Sanilac, *Sanilac County Historical Museum & Village,* 20

CE - Saginaw, *Historical Society,* 22

CW- Hastings, *Charlton Pk Village* 37

CW- Holland, *Museum,* 38

CW- Ludington, *White Pine Village* 42

CW- Muskegon, *County Museum,* 44

NE - Cheboygan, *County Museum* 56

NE - Grayling, *Crawford Cty Mus,* 59

NE - Mackinac Is, *Ft. Mackinac SP* 62

NE - Mackinaw City, *Colonial Michilimackinac State Park,* 64

NE - Mackinaw City, *Mill Creek,* 65

NE - Rogers City, *Presque Isle Mus* 69

NW- Cadillac, *Wexford Cty Mus,* 75

NW- Manistee, *County Museum,* 78

NW- Petoskey, *Little Traverse Mus,* 79

SE - Dearborn, *Henry Ford Museum & Greenfield Village,* 98

SE - Detroit, *Historical Museum,* 103

SE - Lansing, *Michigan Hist'l Ctr* 117

SE - Lansing,*Michigan St.Capital* 119

SE - Monroe, *County Hist'l Mus,* 124

SE - Monroe, *River Raisin Battlefield Visitor's Center,* 125

SE - Plymouth,*Historical Museum,* 130

SW - Berrien Springs, *1839 Historic Courthouse Museum,* 142

SW - Dowagiac, *SW Michigan College & Cass County Mus* 146

SW - Hartford, *Van Buren Mus,* 146

UE - St. Ignace, *Father Marquette National Memorial,* 170

UW- Escanaba, *Delta Cty Hist'l Museum And Lighthouse,* 181

UW- Lake Linden, *Houghton County Historical Museum Campus,* 187

UW- Marquette, *County Museum,* 188

UW- Negaunee, *Michigan Iron,* 190

UW- Ontonagon, *County Museum* 191

MUSEUMS

CE - Bay City, *Delta College Planetarium,* 4

CE - Durand, *Michigan Railroad,* 6

CE - Flint, *Cultural Center,* 6

Index by Activity Heading (City, Place/Event Name, Page)

MUSEUMS (cont.)

CE - Flint, *Children's Museum*, 8

CE - Frankenmuth, *Memory Lane*, 13

CE - Midland, *H.H. Dow Museum*, 16

CE - Midland, *Center For The Arts / Hall Of Ideas*, 16

CE - Port Huron, *Lightship Mus*, 19

CE - Three Oaks, *Spokes Bicycle*, 23

CW- Baldwin, *Shrine of The Pines*, 27

CW- Grand Rapids, *Children's Mus* 30

CW- Grand Rapids, *Gerald Ford*, 33

CW- Grand Rapids, *Van Andel Ctr*, 34

CW- Muskegon, *Hackley Hose Co*, 44

CW -Muskegon, *W. Michigan Children's Museum*, 46

CW -Whitehall, *White River Light Station Museum*, 52

NE - Alpena, *Jesse Besser Mus*, 55

NE - Gaylord, *Call Of The Wild*, 58

NE - Gaylord, *Bottle Cap Museum* 59

NE - Mackinaw City, *Mackinac Bridge Mus, & "Mighty Mac"*, 65

NE - Presque Isle, *Lighthouses*, 68

NW- Traverse City,*Dennos Museum* 82

SE - Ann Arbor,*Hands-On Museum* 87

SE - Ann Arbor, *U/M Museums*, 89

SE - Belleville, *Yankee Air Force*, 91

SE - Dearborn, *Auto Hall of Fame*, 98

SE - Dearborn, *Spirit Of Ford*, 100

SE - Dearborn, *Fair Lane*, 101

SE - Detroit, *Museum of African-American History*, 102

SE - Detroit, *Children's Museum*, 103

SE - Detroit, *Science Center*, 105

SE - Detroit, *Dossin Great Lakes*, 106

SE - Detroit, *Motown Museum*, 107

SE - Detroit Vicinity (Bloomfield Hills), *Cranbrook Art And Science Museums*, 110

SE - Jackson, *Michigan Space Ctr*, 115

SE - Lansing,*Impression 5 Science* 118

SE - Lansing, *Michigan Women's Historical Center*, 120

SE - Lansing, *R.E. Olds Transport*, 120

SE - Livonia, *Greenmead Park*, 121

SE - Novi, *Motorsports Museum & Hall Of Fame Of America*, 126

SE - Okemos, *Meridian Township's Central Park*, 127

SW- Battle Creek, *Leila Arboretum & Kingman Museum*, 142

SW- Hickory Corners,*Gilmore Classic Car Club Of American*, 146

SW- Kalamazoo, *Valley Museum*, 149

SW- Kalamazoo (Portage), *Aviation History Museum (Air Zoo)*, 150

SW- South Haven, *Dr. Liberty Hyde Bailey Museum*, 154

SW- South Haven, *Maritime Mus*, 155

SW- St Joseph,*Curiosity Kids' Mus* 156

UE - Paradise, *Gr.Lakes Shipwreck* 166

UE - Sault St. Marie,*Soo Locks Pk*, 167

UE - Sault Ste. Marie, *Museum Ship - Valley Camp*, 168

UE - Sault Ste Marie, *River/History* 169

UE - Sault Ste Marie, *Tower/Hist.* 169

UE - St. Ignace, *Ojibwa Culture*, 172

UE - St. Ignace, *Totem Village*, 173

UW- Baraga, *Hanka Homestead*, 177

UW- Calumet, *Coppertown USA*, 177

UW- Caspian, *Iron County*, 178

UW- Iron Mountain, *Cornish Pumping Engine & Mining Museum*, 184

UW- Ishpeming, *US Nat'l Ski Hall of Fame And Museum*, 187

UW- Marquette,*Maritime Museum* 189

UW- Marquette, *UP Children's* 190

UW- Rockland, *Old Victoria*, 192

OUTDOORS

CE - Bad Axe, *Sanilac Petroglyphs*, 3

CE - Bay City, *Bay City State Park*, 3

CE - Burton, *For-Mar Nature Preserve & Arboretum*, 5

CE - Caseville, *Albert E. Sleeper SP*, 5

CE - Farwell, *Silver Ridge Resort*, 6

CE - Flint, *Genesee Recreation Area*, 6

CE - Freeland, *Apple Mountain Ski*, 13

CE - Ionia, *Ionia State Recreation*, 14

CE - Lakeport, *Lakeport State Park*,15

CE - Metamora, *Metamora-Hadley*, 15

CE - Midland, *Chippewa Nature Ctr*, 15

CE - Midland, *Dow Gardens*, 15

CE - Port Austin, *Port Crescent SP* 17

CE - Saginaw, *Shiawassee Wildlife* 22

CW- Cannonsburg, *Ski Area*, 28

CW- Grand Haven, *Grand Haven SP* 29

CW- Grand Rapids, *Fish Ladder*, 30

CW- Grand Rapids, *Blandford Ctr*, 32

CW- Grand Rapids, *Michigan Botanic Garden & Meijer Sculpture*, 35

CW- Harrison, *Wilson State Park*, 37

CW- Holland, *Holland State Park*, 38

Index by Activity Heading (City, Place/Event Name, Page)

OUTDOORS (cont.)

CW- Holland, *Saugatuck Dunes SP*, 39
CW- Holland, *Windmill Island*, 39
CW- Ludington, *City Beach*, 41
CW- Ludington, *Ludington SP*, 41
CW- Ludington, *Twin Points Resort*, 42
CW- Mears, *Hart-Montague Trail*, 43
CW- Mears, *Silver Lake State Park* 44
CW- Muskegon, *P.J. Hoffmaster State Park / Gillette Dune Center*, 45
CW- Muskegon, *Winter Sports*, 48
CW- Newaygo, *Little Switzerland*, 48
CW- Newaygo, *Newaygo State Park* 61
CW- N. Muskegon, *Duck Lake SP*, 48
CW- N. Muskegon, *Muskegon SP*, 49
CW- Pentwater, *Mears State Park*, 49
CW- Rockford, *AAA Canoe Rental*, 49
CW- Rothbury, *Double JJ Resort*, 50
CW- White Cloud, *Sandy Beach*, 52
NE - Atlanta, *Clear Lake State Park*, 55
NE - Carp Lake, *Wilderness SP*, 55
NE - Cheboygan, *Aloha State Park*, 56
NE - Cheboygan, *Cheboygan SP*, 56
NE - East Tawas, *Corsair Ski Area*, 57
NE - East Tawas, *Tawas Point SP*, 57
NE - Gaylord, *Ostego Lake SP*, 59
NE - Grayling, *Hartwick Pines SP*, 60
NE - Grayling, *Skyline Ski Area*, 61
NE - Harrisville, *Harrisville SP*, 61
NE - Harrisville, *Negwegon State Park* 61
NE - Indian River, *Burt Lake SP*, 62
NE - Onaway, *Onaway State Park*, 67
NE - Oscoda, *Iargo Springs*, 67
NE - Rogers City, *Hoeft State Park*, 69
NE - Rogers City, *Thompson's Harbor State Park*, 69
NE - Roscommon, *North Higgins Lake State Park*, 70
NE - Roscommon, *South Higgins Lake State Park*, 70
NE - Rose City, *Rifle River RA*, 70
NW- Bellaire, *Shanty Creek Resort*, 73
NW- Boyne Falls, *Boyne Mountain*, 73
NW- Cadillac, *Huron-Manistee NF*, 73
NW- Cadillac, *Mitchell State Park*, 74
NW- Cedar, *Sugar Loaf Resort*, 75
NW- Charlevoix, *Fisherman's Island State Park*, 75
NW- Charlevoix, *Young State Park*, 76
NW- Empire, *Sleeping Bear Dunes*, 76
NW- Harbor Springs,*Boyne Highlands* 77
NW- Harbor Springs, *Nub's Nob*, 77

NW- Interlochen, *Interlochen SP* 77
NW- Manistee, *Lake Michigan RA*, 78
NW- Manistee, *Orchard Beach SP*, 78
NW- Northport, *Leelanau State Park*, 78
NW- Petoskey, *Petoskey State Park*, 80
NW- Thompsonville,*Crystal Mtn.* 80
NW- Traverse City, *Clinch Park Zoo*, 81
NW- Traverse City, *Old Mission Peninsula Lighthouse*, 82
NW- Traverse City, *Sand Lakes*, 82
NW- Traverse City, *State Park*, 82
NW- Traverse City, *Yogi Bear's*, 83
SE - Brighton, *Mt. Brighton Ski*, 92
SE - Brighton, *Island Lake RA*, 92
SE - Brighton, *Brighton State Park*, 93
SE - Chelsea, *Waterloo State Park*, 96
SE - Detroit, *Belle Isle*, 106
SE - Dexter, *Delhi Metropark*, 110
SE - Fenton, *Seven Lakes SP*, 113
SE - Harrison Twp,*WC Wetzel SP* 114
SE - Holly, *Holly Recreation Area* 114
SE - Jackson, *Dahlem Environmental Education Center*, 114
SE - Jackson, *Phyllis Haehnle Memorial Sanctuary*, 115
SE - Jackson, *Cascades*, 115
SE - Laingsburg, *Sleepy Hollow SP* 116
SE - Lake Orion, *Bald Mtn. SP*, 116
SE - Lansing, *Fenner Nature Ctr*, 116
SE - Lansing, *Planet Walk*, 120
SE - Marine City, *Algonac SP*, 122
SE - Milan, *Heath Beach*, 122
SE - Milford, *Kensington Metro*, 123
SE - Milford, *Proud Lake SP*, 124
SE - Monroe, *Sterling State Park*, 125
SE - Mount Clemens, *Metro Beach* 125
SE - Northville, *Maybury SP*, 126
SE - Onstead, *Hayes State Park*, 127
SE - Onstead, *Lake Hudson SP*, 128
SE - Ortonville, *Recreation Area*, 130
SE - Pinckney, *Lakelands Trail SP*,130
SE - Pinckney, *Recreation Area*, 130
SE - Romeo, *Wolcott Mill Metro*, 131
SE - Somerset Ctr, *McCourtie Park* 133
SE - Sumpter Township, *Crosswinds Marsh Wetland Preserve*, 134
SE - Waterford, *Pontiac Lake RA*, 134
SE - Waterford, *Dodge No. 4 SP*, 134
SE - Waterford, *The Fridge*, 135
SE - Waterford, *Drayton Plains Ctr* 135
SE - White Lake, *Highland RA*, 135
SE - White Lake, *Alpine Valley Ski* 136
SE - Ypsilanti, *Rolling Hills Park*, 136

Index by Activity Heading (City, Place/Event Name, Page)

OUTDOORS (cont.)

SW- Albion, *Whitehouse Nature*, 139
SW- Augusta, *Fort Custer RA*, 139
SW- Augusta, *Kellogg Bird*, 139
SW- Bridgman, *Cook Energy Info Center And Dunes*, 143
SW- Buchanan, *Bear Cave*, 143
SW- Kalamazoo, *Echo Valley*, 147
SW- Kalamazoo, *Nature Center*, 148
SW- Middleville, *Yankee Springs*, 152
SW- Otsego, *Bittersweet Ski*, 152
SW- Saugatuck, *Mount Baldhead*, 153
SW- Sawyer, *Grand Mere SP*, 153
SW- Sawyer, *Warren Dunes SP*, 154
SW- South Haven, *Captain Nichols' & Captain Chuck's Perch Boats*, 154
SW- South Haven, *Kal-Haven Trail* 155
SW- South Haven, *Van Buren SP*, 156
UE - Escanaba, *Hiawatha Nat'l*, 161
UE - Garden, *Fayette State Park*, 161
UE - Manistique, *Indian Lake SP*, 163
UE - Manistique, *Palms Book State Park (Big Spring)*, 163
UE - Munising, *Pictured Rocks National Lakeshore*, 164
UE - Munising, *Wagner Falls*, 165
UE - Newberry, *Muskallonge Lake* 165
UE - Paradise, *Tahquamenon Falls*, 166
UE - Seney, *National Wildlife Ref*, 170
UE - St. Ignace, *Castle Rock*, 171
UE - St. Ignace, *Straits State Park*, 173
UW- Baraga, *Baraga State Park*, 177
UW- Brimley, *Brimley State Park*, 177
UW- Cedar River, *Laughing Whitefish Falls Scenic Site*, 178
UW- Cedar River, *Wells State Park* 179
UW- Champion, *Craig Lake SP*, 179
UW- Champion, *Van Riper SP*, 179
UW- Copper Harbor, *Ft .Wilkins SP*, 180
UW- Crystal Falls, *Bewabic SP*, 181
UW- Hancock, *McClain State Park*, 182
UW- Houghton, *Isle Royale Nat'l*, 183
UW- Iron Mountain, *Millie Bat Cave* 184
UW- Ironwood, *Black River National Forest Scenic Byway*, 184
UW- Ironwood, *Ottawa Nat'l Forest* 185
UW- Marenisco, *Lake Gogebic SP*, 187
UW- Marquette, *Great North Adv*, 188
UW- Marquette, *Marquette Mtn Ski* 189
UW- Marquette, *Presque Isle Park*, 189
UW- Ontonagon, *Mead Lake Mine*, 191
UW- Ontonagon, *Porcupine Mtn. Wilderness State Park*, 192
UW- Toivola, *Twin Lakes SP*, 193
UW- Wakefield, *Indianhead Mtn,* 193

SPORTS

CE - Flint, *Generals Hockey*, 7
CW- Grand Rapids, *Griffins Hockey* 31
CW- Grand Rapids, *Hoops Basketball* 31
CW- Grand Rapids, *Rumpage Football* 32
CW- Grand Rapids, *West Michigan Whitecaps Baseball*, 35
CW- Muskegon, *Fury Hockey*, 45
SE - Ann Arbor, *University of Michigan College Sports*, 89
SE - Auburn Hills (Detroit), *Detroit Neon Soccer*, 90
SE - Auburn Hills (Detroit), *Detroit Pistons Basketball*, 90
SE - Auburn Hills (Detroit), *Detroit Rockers Soccer*, 91
SE - Auburn Hills (Detroit),*Detroit Shock Women's Basketball*, 91
SE - Auburn Hills (Detroit), *Detroit Vipers Hockey*, 91
SE - Brooklyn, *Michigan Speedway*, 94
SE - Detroit, *Tigers Baseball*, 107
SE - Detroit, *Red Wings Hockey*, 108
SE - Lansing, *Lugnuts Baseball*, 117
SE - Milan, *Milan Dragway*, 123
SE - Pontiac, *Detroit Lions Football* 131
SW- Battle Creek, *Battlecats*, 140
SW- Kalamazoo, *Michigan K-Wings* 147

THE ARTS

CE - Flint, *Symphony Orchestra*, 8
CE - Saginaw, *Japanese Cultural Center And House*, 20
CE - Saginaw, *Art Museum*, 22
CE - Saginaw (University Center), *Marshall M. Fredericks Sculpture Gallery*, 23
CW- Grand Haven, *Musical Fountain* 29
CW- Grand Rapids, *Art Museum*, 31
CW- Grand Rapids, *Civic Theatre*, 31
CW- Grand Rapids, *Symphony*, 32
CW- Grand Rapids, *Youth Symphony* 32
CW- Grand Rapids, *Choir Men/Boys* 32
CW- Muskegon, *Civic Theatre*, 44
SE - Ann Arbor, *Wild Swan Theater*, 87
SE - Ann Arbor, *Youth Chorale*, 88
SE - Ann Arbor, *Young People's Theater*, 88

Index by Activity Heading (City, Place/Event Name, Page)

THE ARTS (cont.)

SE - Detroit, *Detroit Symphony*, 102
SE - Detroit, *Detroit Institute/Arts*, 104
SE - Detroit, *Detroit Youtheater*, 108
SE - East Lansing, *Greater Lansing Symphony Orchestra*, 111
SE - Lansing, *Riverwalk Theatre*, 121
SE - Northville, *Marquis Theater*, 126
SW- Coldwater, *Tibbits Opera*, 144
SW- Kalamazoo, *Civic Youth*, 149
SW- Kalamazoo, *Symphony Orstra* 149
SW- Three Rivers, *Carnegie Center of the Arts*, 157

THEME RESTAURANTS

CE - Lake, *Big Al's Restaurant*, 14
CE - Frankenmuth, *Bavarian Inn*, 9
CE - Port Huron, *Diana Sweet Shp*, 19
CW- Holland, *Queen's Inn*, 41
CW- Kentwood, *Kentwood Station*, 41
CW- Rockford, *Rosie's Dinerland*, 50
NE - Cross Village, *Legs Inn*, 57
NE - Grayling, *Stevens Family Circle*, 61
NW- Maple City, *Schoolhouse Café*, 78
SE - Auburn Hills, *Rainforest Café*, 90
SE - Detroit, *Lafayette Coney Island*, 108
SE - Rochester (Detroit), *Paint Creek Cider Mill Restaurant*, 131
SE - Williamston, *Rooftop Landing Reindeer Farm Restaurant*, 136
SW- Marshall, *Cornwell's Turkey*, 151
SW- South Haven, *Idler Riverboat*, 156
SW- St. Joseph, *Roxy's Depot*, 157
UE - Gould City, *Michihistrigan*, 162

TOURS

CE - Frankenmuth, *Cheese Haus*, 11
CE - Frankenmuth, *Riverboat Tours*, 12
CE - Frankenmuth, *Woolen Mill*, 12
CE - Port Austin, *Miss Port Austin*, 18
CE - Port Huron, *Blue Water Area*, 18
CE - Saginaw, *Johnny Panther Quests* 22
CW- Ada, *Amway Visitor's Center*, 27
CW- Coopersville, *Coopersville & Marne Railway*, 28
CW- Grand Haven, *Grand Haven/ Spring Lake Trolley*, 28
CW- Grand Haven, *Harbor Steamer*, 29
CW- Grand Haven, *Harbor Trolley*, 29
CW- Grandville, *Grand Lady Cruises* 36
CW- Holland, *Delft Factory And Wooden Shoe Factory*, 37

CW- Holland, *Wooden Shoe Facty*, 39
CW- Ludington, *SS Badger*, 42
CW- Mears, *Mac Wood's Dune Rides* 43
CW- Muskegon, *Port City Princess*, 46
CW- Muskegon, *USS Silversides*, 46
CW- Shelby, *Shelby Man-Made Gemstones*, 51
NE - Cheboygan, *Coast Guard "Mackinaw" Tours*, 56
NE - Fairview, *Michigan Ausable Valley Railroad*, 57
NE - Mackinac Island, *Horse-Drawn Carriage Tours*, 63
NE - Mackinaw City, *Transportation*, 66
NE - Oscoda, *Au Sable River Queen*, 67
NE - Charlevoix, *Beaver Island Boat* 75
NW- Petoskey, *Kilwin's Candy*, 79
NW- Traverse City, *Tall Ships "Malabar & Manitou"*, 80
SE - Blissfield, *Adrian & Blissfield*, 92
SE - Brooklyn, *Walker Tavern State Historic Complex*, 93
SE - Chelsea, *Chelsea Milling "Jiffy Mix"*, 95
SE - Chesterfield, *Lionel Trains*, 96
SE - Clinton Township, *Morley Candy* 97
SE - Detroit (Grosse Ile), *Diamond Jack's River Tours*, 109
SE - East Lansing, *MSU*, 111
SE - Walled Lake, *Coe Rail Train*, 134
SW- Battle Creek, *Kellogg's Cereal*, 141
SW- Douglas, *City of Douglas*, 145
SW- Douglas, *"S/S Keewatin"*, 145
SW- Grand Ledge, *J&K Steamboat* 146
SW- Saugatuck, *Dune Rides*, 152
SW- Saugatuck, *Star Of Saugatuck* 153
UE - Hulbert, *Toonerville Trolley & Riverboat Ride*, 162
UE - Munising, *Grand Island Shipwreck Tours*, 163
UE - Munising, *Pictured Rocks*, 164
UE - Sault Ste. Marie, *Soo Locks Trn.* 169
UW- Copper Harbor, *Lighthouse Boat Tours*, 179
UW- Copper Harbor, *Delaware Copper Mine Tour*, 180
UW- Copper Harbor, *Keweenaw Bear Track Tours*, 180
UW- Greenland, *Adv. Copper Mine* 182
UW- Hancock, *Quincy Mine Hoist*, 182
UW- Ishpeming, *Tilden Mine Tours*, 186
UW- Marquette, *Country Tours*, 188
UW- Vulcan, *Iron Mtn. Iron Mine*, 193

Table of Contents

General Information..…....Preface

Index By Activity...…...Preface

Chapter 1 - CENTRAL EAST AREA (CE)...........…...…...…....1

Chapter 2 - CENTRAL WEST AREA (CW)......................…...25

Chapter 3 - NORTH EAST AREA (NE)............................…...53

Chapter 4 - NORTH WEST AREA (NW)...........................71

Chapter 5 - SOUTH EAST AREA (SE)............................…...85

Chapter 6 - SOUTH WEST AREA (SW)...........................137

Chapter 7 – UPPER PENINSULA – EAST (UE) 159

Chapter 8 – UPPER PENINSULA – WEST (UW)................175

Chapter 9 – SEASONAL & SPECIAL EVENTS..................195

Master Index...232

Chapter 1
AREA - CE

Our Favorites...

- Crossroads Village & Huckleberry Railroad
- Frankenmuth Cheese Haus
- Frankenmuth Woolen Mill
- H.H. Dow Historical Museum
- Huron Lightship Museum

SANILAC PETROGLYPHS

(M-53 to Bay City - Forestville Road Exit - East to Germania Road
South), **Bad Axe** 48413

- ❏ Activity: Outdoors
- ❏ Telephone: (517) 373-3559
  www.sos.state.mi.us/history/museum/musesan/index.html
- ❏ Hours: Wednesday - Sunday, 11:30 am - 4:30 pm (Memorial Day
  - Labor Day)
- ❏ Admission: Free
- ❏ Tours: Guided tours (45 minutes)

Take a 1 mile, self-guided walking trail through the forest along
the Cass River. Stop at the 19th Century logging camp or 100+
year old white pine tree. The main reason you probably came
though is the petroglyphs. In the late 1800's, forest fires revealed
chiseled sandstone etchings by Native Americans of an ancient
woodland people dating back 300 - 1000 years ago. Look for
figures like a hunter / archer or animals and birds.

BAY CITY STATE PARK

Bay City - 3582 State Park Drive (I-75 exit 168 east to Euclid
Avenue), 48706. *Activity:* Outdoors. (517) 684-3020 *Admission:*
$4.00 per vehicle. **www.dnr.state.mi.us/www/parks/plsb.htm#bc**
Lots of camping (tent and cabins) plus a swimming beach free
from sharp zebra mussels found in the area, make this an
attraction. Also find boating, fishing, trails, winter sports. Another
highlight is the Saginaw Bay Visitors Center, (517) 667-0717,
which focuses on the importance of wetlands to the bay. It's open
Tuesday - Sunday, Noon - 5:00 pm. A great spot for birding, you'll
also learn from the 15 minute video presentation, boardwalks and
observation trails.

DELTA COLLEGE PLANETARIUM & LEARNING CENTER

Bay City - 100 Center Avenue, 48708. *Activity:* Museums. (517) 667-2260. **www.delta.edu/~planet**. *Hours:* Call or visit website for schedule. *Admission:* Adults $3.50, Seniors $3.00, Children $3.00 (under 18). A wonderful place to teach children the fun of star-gazing. The planetarium is state-of-the-art and the rooftop observatory seats over 100 people. The audience actually gets to choose what to see in the solar system.

HISTORICAL MUSEUM OF BAY COUNTY

Bay City - 321 Washington Avenue, 48708. *Activity:* Michigan History. (517) 893-5733. *Hours:* Monday-Friday, 10:00 am - 5:00 pm. Saturday & Sunday, Noon - 4:00 pm. Free Admission. Bay County history featuring period rooms relating to American Indians, agriculture, fur trading, lumbering, and shipbuilding industries.

WILDERNESS TRAILS ANIMAL PARK

11721 Gera Road - M-83 (I-75 to Birch Run Exit)

Birch Run 48415

❑   Activity: Animals & Farms
❑   Telephone: (517) 624-6177, **www.tir.com/~wtapark**
❑   Hours: Daily, 10:00 am - 8:00 pm (Summer). Daily, 10:00 am - 5:00 pm (Spring, Fall, Winter) (Closed Wednesdays in Winter)
❑   Admission: Adults $6.00, Seniors $4.00, Children $4.00 (3-12)
❑   Miscellaneous: Picnic area. Playground.

One of the most popular privately owned animal exhibits in the state, Wilderness Trails offers over 50 acres and 60 different types of animals. See lions, a Siberian tiger and bear, bison, elk, black bears, and deer just to name a few. Two gravel walking trails wind through the park or a horse drawn covered wagon is available for a small charge. Kids can have fun touching and feeding the baby animals in the petting area.

JUNCTION VALLEY RAILROAD

7065 Dixie Highway (I-75, exit 144 south - Just before you turn to head into Frankenmuth), **Bridgeport** 48722

- ❑ Activity: Amusements
- ❑ Telephone: (517) 777-2480
- ❑ Hours: Monday - Saturday, 10:00 am - 6:00 pm., Sunday, 1:00 - 6:00 pm. (Memorial Day Weekend - Labor Day Weekend), Weekends Only (September & October)
- ❑ Admission: Adults $4.50, Seniors $4.25 (65+), Children $3.75 (2-12)
- ❑ Miscellaneous: Picnic area and playground. You'll pull into a business parking lot, but the ride into the woods is cute, especially over the trestles.

See and ride the world's largest ¼ scale railroad. Voyage on rides through the woods, past miniature buildings, through a 100 foot long tunnel, and over 865 feet of trestles (one has diamonds underneath).

FOR-MAR NATURE PRESERVE & ARBORETUM

Burton - 2142 North Genesee Road, 48509. *Activity:* Outdoors. (810) 789-8567 or (800) 648-7275. *Hours:* Weekdays, 8:00 am - 5:00 pm. Trails, 8:00 am - Sunset. Special programs Saturdays. A 380 acre preserve with 7 miles of trails. Visitor Center with Gift Shop. Cross-country skiing in winter.

ALBERT E. SLEEPER STATE PARK

Caseville - 6573 State Park Road (5 miles east of town on M-25), 48725. *Activity:* Outdoors. (517) 856-4411. *Admission:* $4.00 per vehicle. **www.dnr.state.mi.us/www/parks/sleeper.html.** Hundreds of acres of woods and beachfront with camping make this a fun park. Also featured are hiking trails, winter sports, modern cabins, fishing, and boating.

MICHIGAN RAILROAD HISTORY MUSEUM

Durand - 200 Railroad Street, 48429. *Activity:* Museums. (517) 288-3561. **www.shianet.org/%7Ediamond4/main.html**. *Hours:* Tuesday - Sunday, 1:00 - 5:00 pm. Visitors stop at the Durand Depot to study area history or maybe catch an Amtrak train roundtrip from Chesaning-to-Owosso. Learn about the Great Wallace Brothers Circus Wreck of 1903 or the Knights Templar Wreck of 1923. Do you know which presidents have made "whistle stops" here? There's a Railroad Days Festival celebrated in May each year.

SILVER RIDGE RESORT

Farwell - 1001 Mott Mountain (off Old US-10), 48622. *Activity:* Outdoors. (517) 588-7220. 9 runs, ski lessons, rentals, and night skiing. Restaurant overlooks the slopes.

GENESEE RECREATION AREA

Flint - (I-475 exit 13). *Activity:* Outdoors. (800) 648-7275. Admission per activity. This area includes Stepping Stone Falls on Mott Lake on Branch Road which are lit with color evenings between Memorial Day and Labor Day. The Genesee Belle sightseeing boat also docks here offering 45 minute cruises on the lake. You can also find Penny Whistle Place outdoor creative playground, camping, hiking, boating, fishing, swimming, bicycle trails, and winter sports.

FLINT CULTURAL CENTER
1221 East Kearsley Street (I-475, exit 8A)

Flint 48503

❑ Activity: Museums
❑ Telephone: (810) 760-1169, **www.visitflint.net**
❑ Hours: Tuesday - Friday, 10:00 am - 5:00 pm, Saturday & Sunday, 12:00 - 5:00 pm. Open Mondays in July & August (Closed Holidays)

❑   Admission: Adults $4.00, Seniors $3.50, Children $3.00 (5-12)
❑   Miscellaneous: Museum Store. Educational programs such as
    "Michigan's Prehistoric Peoples", "The Fur Trade", and "From
    Farm to Factory".

The SLOAN MUSEUM highlights include:

❑   "Flint and the American Dream" - 20th Century Flint beginning
    with the birth of General Motors, United Auto Workers, and then
    neon colorful advertising. Also 1950's - 70's typical household
    furnishings. Check out the 1950's station wagon (a Buick Super)
    that was available before today's vans and sport utility vehicles.
❑   "Genessee County History Gallery" - the area's early history with
    displays on fur trading, pioneer life, lumbering, and carriage
    making. Look for the 10,000 year old mastodon and Woodland
    Indian wigwam.

Also in the same complex (recommended for grade school and up):

❑   FLINT INSTITUTE OF ARTS - 1120 East Kearsley. (810) 234-
    1695. Tuesday - Saturday, 10:00 am - 5:00 pm., Sunday, 1:00 -
    5:00 pm. Free admission.
❑   LONGWAY PLANETARIUM - 1310 East Kearsley. (810) 760-
    1181. Monday - Friday, 9:00 am - 4:00 pm, Saturday & Sunday,
    1:00 - 4:30 pm. Free displays. $3-6.00 for light and astronomy
    shows.

FLINT GENERALS HOCKEY CLUB

Flint - 3501 Lapeer Road (IMA Sports Arena), 48503. *Activity:*
Sports. (810) 742-9422. **www.flintgenerals.com**. *Admission:*
General, $8.00-10.00. A UHL team.

FLINT SYMPHONY ORCHESTRA

Flint - 1244 East Kearsley Street (Whiting Auditorium), 48503. *Activity:* The Arts. (810) 237-7333 or (888) 8-CENTER. **www.visitflint.net**. Professional orchestra performs family concerts and a free summer park concert series.

FLINT CHILDREN'S MUSEUM

1602 West 3rd Street (I-475 to exit 8A - Longway Blvd, Left on Saginaw Street, Right on 3rd Street), **Flint** 48504

❑   Activity: Museums
❑   Telephone: (810) 767-5437
❑   Hours: Monday - Saturday, 10:00 am - 5:00 pm. Sunday, Noon - 5:00 pm.
❑   Admission: General $3.00, Seniors $2.50 (60+), Family $12.00 (ages 1+)
❑   Miscellaneous: Recommended for ages 3-10. Gift shop.

Over 100 exhibits focused on science, technology, and the arts. Kids' favorites are the Crazy Mirrors and the Lego table. Be sure to check out the different theme rooms: Grow Room, Grocery Room, Activity Room, Transportation Room, Playhouse, and News Room.

CROSSROADS VILLAGE & HUCKLEBERRY RAILROAD

6140 Bray Road (I-475, exit 13 - follow signs)

Flint 48505

❑   Activity: Michigan History
❑   Telephone: (800) 648-PARK,
     www.jonra.com/village/trainvlg.htm
❑   Hours: Tuesday - Friday, 10:00 am - 5:00 pm., Weekends & Holidays, 11:00 am - 5:30 pm (Mid-May - Labor Day). Weekends Only (September)
❑   Admission: Adults $9.25, Seniors $8.25 (60+), Children 6.25 (4-12). Village and Train Ride

❑   Miscellaneous: Mill Street Warehouse, Cross Roads Café,
    Concessions, Carrousel, Venetian Swing, Ferris Wheel and
    Wagon Rides (pulled by ponies) - additional charge. Seasonal
    events keep the village open throughout the year - see Seasonal
    Chapter.

The 1860's era living village is a collection of 30 authentic
buildings that were relocated here to form a village. Friendly,
costumed villagers fill you in on the events of the day and answer
questions. For example, the barber shop (still operational) staff will
share their charges for a cut, shave or bath. We learned that they let
a dental patient (yes, they were the town dentist then) take a swig
of vanilla extract (full tilt variety!) before they extracted a tooth.
The fellas at the cider and sawmill will remind you of characters
from "Little House on the Prairie" as they demonstrate their craft.
Be sure to buy a cup of cider there - all natural with no added
sugar. You'll also meet the town blacksmith, printer (try your hand
printing a souvenir off the "kissing" press), doctor, storekeeper at
the General Store (with cute, old-fashioned novelties for sale), and
toymaker (try your hand walking on stilts - we have a video and
George did it!). Before you leave, take a relaxing slow ride on the
Huckleberry Railroad. The original line went so slow that
passengers claimed they could get off - pick huckleberries along
the tracks (still growing plentifully today) and catch the caboose a
few minutes later. Watch out for the playful train robber skit -
(don't worry...even pre-schoolers won't be scared!).

BAVARIAN INN RESTAURANT

713 South Main Street

Frankenmuth 48734

❑   Activity: Theme Restaurants
❑   Telephone: (800) BAVARIA, **www.bavarianinn.com**
❑   Hours: Daily, 11:00 am - 9:30 pm

❏   Miscellaneous: City tours depart every hour at the Fischer Platz
     outdoor plaza (June - August). Adults $3.50, Children $1.50.

A famous Frankenmuth restaurant (established in 1888) offering family style dinners. An authentically dressed server (aren't their hats cute?) will help introduce your kids to all the menu offerings they will like such as potato pancakes, veal cutlets, baked chicken, etc. (except maybe the sauerkraut). None of the food is over-seasoned...all kid friendly...but the adults may want to use their chicken and all purpose seasonings that are available at each table. Also see the Glockenspiel Clock Tower (with performances telling the Pied Piper of Hameln story in music) and the Doll and Toy Factory (see dolls created before you eyes). Open evenings year round.

BRONNER'S CHRISTMAS WONDERLAND
25 Christmas Lane (I-75, northbound to exit 136, southbound to exit
  144 - follow signs off Main Street M-83), **Frankenmuth** 48734

❏   Activity: Amusements
❏   Telephone: (800) ALL-YEAR or (517) 652-9931
     www.bronners.com
❏   Monday - Saturday, 9:00 am - 5:30 pm., Sunday, 12:00 - 5:00
     pm. Open Friday until 9:00 pm. (January - May). Monday -
     Saturday, 9:00 am - 9:00 pm., Sunday, Noon - 7:00 pm (June -
     December). Closed Winter holidays.
❏   Admission: Free
❏   Miscellaneous: "Season's Eatings" snack area.

A visit to Michigan wouldn't be complete without seeing the "World's Largest Christmas Store" that hosts over 2,000,000 visitors each year! View nativity scenes, 260 decorated trees, and 200 styles of nutcrackers. As dusk approaches drive through "Christmas Lane" that sparkles with over 40,000+ lights. While you're there be sure to check out the "World of Bronners" (an 18 minute multi-image slide show) that highlights the design and production of their selection of trains. Visit "Bronner's Silent Night Memorial Chapel" - named after the famous song (the chapel was originally made in Austria). Kids seem to be most fascinated with the "It Feels Like Christmas" drive around the vast parking lot and the animated displays of seasonal bears, elves, and children playing around the upper perimeter of each theme room. Be sure to get at least one ornament to keep - but "oooh" - how to decide!

FRANKENMUTH CHEESE HAUS

561 South Main Street

Frankenmuth 48734

❑   Activity: Tours
❑   Telephone: (517) 652-6727
❑   Hours: Daily, 9:30 am - 6:00 pm., 9:30 am - 9:00 pm. (Summers)
❑   Admission: Free

L ots of tasting going on here! Ever tried "Chocolate" or "Strawberry" cheese? Not only will you sample some...you can also try cheese spreads (smooth, creamy and fresh tasting) or over 140 different kinds of cheese. Watch a video of the cheesemaking process, or if you time it right, actually see the ladies make it from scratch. They have giant photographs of each step of the process, so if the kids can't see it all they can still understand the process from the pictures. Yummy samples of cheese spreads in varieties from Garden Vegetable to Jalapeno! You will want some to take home (although this souvenir will soon be eaten with a box of crackers!)

FRANKENMUTH HISTORICAL MUSEUM

613 South Main Street (I-75 to Frankenmuth Exit - Next to the Visitor's Center), **Frankenmuth** 48734

❑   Activity: Museums
❑   Telephone: (517) 652-9701
      www.dtimmons.com/frankenmuthmuseum

- ❑ Hours: Monday - Saturday, 10:30 - 5:00 pm., Sunday, 12:00 -
  5:00 pm (January - April). Monday - Thursday, 10:30 - 5:00 pm.,
  Friday 10:30 - 7:00 pm, Saturday, 10:00 - 8:00 pm, Sunday
  11:00-5:00 pm. (May - December)
- ❑ Admission: Adults $1.00, Children $0.50 (under 13)
- ❑ Miscellaneous: Geschenkladen (Museum Gift Shop)

Exhibits depict the area's German ancestry and history from Indian mission days to a town called "Michigan's Little Bavaria". Begin with a scene from the immigrants' ship travel from Bavaria to the Saginaw Valley. They designed this museum along the trend of "hands-on" activities and there are a few interactive stations in realistic settings.

FRANKENMUTH RIVERBOAT TOURS

Frankenmuth - 445 South Main Street, 48734. *Activity:* Tours. (517) 652-8844. *Hours:* Departure 12:30, 2:30, 4:30 and 6:00 or 7:00 pm. (May - October). *Admission:* Adults $6.00, Children $3.00 (3-12). *Tours:* 45 minutes long. Board at Riverview Café. Riverview Queen sightseeing cruises narrated about the Cass River folklore and history.

FRANKENMUTH WOOLEN MILL

570 South Main Street (I-75 to Frankenmuth Exit - Follow signs to downtown), **Frankenmuth** 48734

- ❑ Activity: Tours
- ❑ Telephone: (517) 652-8121
- ❑ Hours: Daily, 9:00 am - 9:00 pm (Summer). Daily, 10:00 am - 6:00 pm (Winter)
- ❑ Admission: Free
- ❑ Miscellaneous: Video of wool processing plays continuously when workers aren't in, but the store is open.

W e've all seen freshly shaven sheep and probably own wool clothing. But how is it processed? Here's your unique chance to see how it all happens. They began here in 1894 and the mill has produced over 250,000 hand-made, wool-filled comforters since then. See the mill in action where you can begin by looking through a window of the wash basins (great viewing for smaller children) where they clean wool brought in from farmers. Washed fleece is then air dried (it gets really fluffy that way) and then put through a "carding machine". The wool passes through wire-spiked rollers until it is untangled and meshed together to form a sheet. Comforters are assembled according to Bavarian tradition (hand-tied). Throughout the tour, your guide will let you handle samples of wool at different stages of the process. The kids will find "raw" wool disgusting, but love the way that it turns out. This "hands-on" activity keeps their interest throughout the demonstration.

MEMORY LANE ARCADE

Frankenmuth - 626 South Main Street, 48734. *Activity:* Museums. (517) 652-8881. **http://memorylanearcade.com**. *Hours:* Daily, open at Noon (June - December). Open weekends, (Spring). Closed Winter Holidays. Pay 25 cents per game as you step back in time... for a good time. The collection spans 100 years of penny arcades including 3D movies, baseball, kissing machines, modern games and computer games.

APPLE MOUNTAIN SKI AREA

Freeland - 4519 North River Road, 48623. *Activity:* Outdoors. (517) 781-6789 or (888) 781-6789. **www.applemountain.com**. *Hours:* Daily, 10:00 am - 10:00 pm (mid-December to mid-March). 12 runs. Night skiing, equipment rental, and instructions are available.

HURON CITY MUSEUM

7930 Huron City Road (8 miles east of Port Austin on M-25)

Huron City 48467

❑ Activity: Museums

❑ Telephone: (517) 428-4123

www.tour-michigan.com/~hcmus/tours.htm

❑ Hours: Thursday - Monday, 10:00 am - 5:00 pm (July 1 - Labor Day)

❑ Admission: Adults $6-10.00, Seniors $5-8.00 (55+), Children $3-5.00 (10-15). Children 9 and under are Free. (Prices vary depending on tours chosen)

S how your kids Michigan's agricultural early days at this restored 19th century lumbering town. See a village inn, log cabin (that survived 2 fires and a family with 17 children!), town church (known for its passionate, spirit-filled sermons), carriage shed, general store and the Pointe Auxe Barques lifesaving station (was a predecessor of today's Coast Guard).

IONIA STATE RECREATION AREA

Ionia - 2880 West David Highway (I-96, Exit 64), 48846. *Activity:* Outdoors. **www.dnr.state.mi.us/www/parks/ionia.htm** (616) 527-3750. *Admission:* $4.00 per vehicle. Camping/cabins, hiking, boating, fishing, swimming, bicycle trails and winter sports.

BIG AL'S RESTAURANT

Lake - (south of US-10), 48632. *Activity:* Theme Restaurants. (517) 544-3502. *Hours:* Friday - Sunday, 8:00 am - 2:00 pm. Monday - Thursday, 11:00 am - 2:00 pm. Elvis lives in Michigan? "Big Al" Kuebler hosts you at his Elvis theme restaurant (he was even an Elvis impersonator) where you can enjoy good, reasonably priced food.

LAKEPORT STATE PARK

Lakeport - 7605 Lakeshore Road, M-25 north, 48059. *Activity:* Outdoors. **www.dnr.state.mi.us/www/parks/lakeport.htm**. (810) 327-6224. Admission: $4.00 per vehicle. Located along the shore of Lake Huron. Camping/cabins, hiking trails, boating, and fishing.

METAMORA-HADLEY STATE PARK

Metamora - 3871 Hurd Road (off M-24 south), 48455. *Activity:* Outdoors. **www.dnr.state.mi.us/www/parks/meta-had.htm**.(810) 797-4439. *Admission:* $4.00 per vehicle. Camping, hiking trails, boating, fishing and swimming.

CHIPPEWA NATURE CENTER

Midland - 400 South Badour Road, 48640. *Activity:* Outdoors. (517) 631-0830. *Hours:* Monday - Friday, 8:00 am - 5:00 pm. Saturday, 9:00 am - 5:00 pm. Sunday and most Holidays, 1:00 - 5:00 pm. *Admission:* Donation. 1000 acres and 14 miles of trails through the forest, meadows, ponds, and rivers. Pass an 1870's farm and log school. The Archeological District is the site of a territorial Indian battle. The modern Visitor's Center is full of interactive ecosystem displays.

DOW GARDENS

Midland - 18 West Main Street (corner of Eastman Avenue and West Street/Andrews Street, next to the Midland Center for the Arts), 48640. *Activity:* Outdoors. **www.dowgardens.org**. (800) 362-4874, *Hours:* 10:00 am - sunset, daily except Winter holidays. *Admission:* Daily. Adults $3.00, Youth $1.00 (6-17). These gardens were started in 1899 as landscaping around Dow's home. Now there are 100 acres of gardens featuring flowers, trees, rocks and water. Seasonal tulips and wildflowers are pretty to look at. No food or pets allowed.

H.H. DOW HISTORICAL MUSEUM

3100 Cook Road (US Business 10 into town. Head NW on Main
Street from downtown to Cook Road south), **Midland** 48640

- ❑ Activity: Museums
- ❑ Telephone: (517) 832-5319
- ❑ Hours: Wednesday - Saturday 10:00 am - 4:00 pm. Sunday,
  1:00 -5:00 pm. Closed all holidays.
- ❑ Admission: Adults $2.00, Children $1.00, Family $5.00

First of all, please purchase the Children's Guidebook and use it as you go through the museum. It's sure to keep the kids attention because each page has an activity for them to do. You'll want to start at the replica of Evens Flour Mill Complex - the original Midland Chemical Company. This is where young Dow pioneered experiments of separation of bromine from brine using electrolysis. See a prototype of his first lab. Wood scraps were used to build electrolysis boxes that feed onto "spread beds" that feed into a wood tower full of scrap metal. The metal catches the bromine liquid vapor. The museum has many clever interactive (holograms, manual, conversation) displays conveying why Midland, Michigan was an ideal spot to experiment, how Dow's parents felt about his work (proud Dad, worried Mom), and his supportive wife. See a scene where Herbert is running his business yet trying not to be a workaholic. We feel the exhibits will inspire cleverness, tenacity, association with other great wise minds, hard work, and, in some, a zest for making money with science.

MIDLAND CENTER FOR THE ARTS HALL OF IDEAS

1801 West Saint Andrews Road

Midland 48640

- ❑ Activity: Museums
- ❑ Telephone: (888) 4-MIDLAND or (517) 832-0881
  www.midlandonline.com/wwwroot/mol/tour/cftarts.cfm
- ❑ Hours: Daily 10:00 am - 6:00 pm except Holidays.
- ❑ Admission: Yes, varies with events.

❑   Miscellaneous: Art Gallery, Peanut Gallery (Theatre Guild's family division).

See, touch, hear, explore the world's natural wonders of science, history, and art. "Captain" a Great Lakes fishing boat or set off a mine blast! Ride a John Deere combine (cab of one with panoramic view of field in front of you). Create computer music, visit an old-time theater and say "hi" to an American mastodon skeleton with size 80 feet!

DEER ACRES

2346 M-13 (I-75 to exit 164, go north on M-13)

Pinconning 48650

❑   Activity: Animals & Farms
❑   Telephone: (517) 879-2849, **www.deeracres.com**
❑   Hours: Daily, 10:00 am - 6:00 pm (early May - Labor Day). Weekends Only, 10:00 am - 7:00 pm (after Labor Day to mid-October)
❑   Admission: Adults $8.50 (13+), Seniors $7.50, Children $6.50 (3-12). Additional fee for rides.

Watching your children's eyes light up as they see a deer eating out of their hand is something that you'll never forget. At Deer Acres, the deer are so tame that they even know to come toward you when they hear the food dispensers clicking! Additional fun attractions (small additional fee) include several amusement rides (antique cars, Ferris wheel, carrousel, moonwalk) and a narrated safari trip (don't miss the monkeys). Story Book Village brings all of your child's fantasy characters to life like "The Three Little Pigs", "Old Woman In a Shoe", "Old Mother Hubbard" and many others.

PORT CRESCENT STATE PARK

Port Austin - 1775 Port Austin Road (along M-25, 5 miles southwest of town), 48467. *Activity:* Outdoors. (517) 738-8663. **www.dnr.state.mi.us/www/parks/plsb.htm#pc**. *Admission:* $4.00

per vehicle. A unique feature is their undeveloped beaches and sand dunes contrasted with many forest hiking trails. Camping and cabins plus these activities are available: fishing, swimming, winter sports.

MISS PORT AUSTIN

Port Austin - (at M-53 in downtown), 48467. *Activity:* Tours. (517) 738-5271. *Hours:* Leaves dock at 7:30 am and 2:30 pm (starting in July). Call for other times and types of trips. *Admission:* $28.00 per person. 20% discount for families and weekday trips. A home town fishing expedition is what the summer is all about. Join Captain Fred Davis (and up to 20 guests) on a quest for perch. Once the captain finds you a school of fish, you'll "bait up" using the minnows that he provides and then it's all up to you! A great, casual way to introduce your kids to fishing (and how to tell a fish story...).

BLUE WATER AREA

(Off I-94, I-69 to Military to the Black River), **Port Huron** 48060

❑   Activity: Tours
❑   Telephone: (800) 852-4242 or (810) 987-8687
www.bluewater.org

To navigate through this area of the state you might want to tour via one of the following services:

❑   THE BLUE WATER TROLLEY offers a nostalgic, narrated tour of historic sites including the THOMAS EDISON DEPOT on the St. Clair River (under the Blue Water Bridge). Young Tom moved here at the age of seven and began his road to self-education here. Admission: 10c. Season: June-September.

❑   THE HURON LADY is an international sightseeing tour boat. Seating up to 100 people, it cruises along the St. Clair River viewing large freighters, bridges, Fort Gratiot Lighthouse and the Canada coastline. Admission charged. Season: daily in the summer. (888) 873-6726 or www.huronlady.com. Reservations recommended.

DIANA SWEET SHOPPE

Port Huron - 307 Huron Avenue, 48060. *Activity:* Theme Restaurants. (810) 985-6933. Open daily. 1920's décor with high-backed wooden booths, gooey hot-fudge sundaes, homemade entrees, and homemade candies. Two brothers still maintain old-fashioned creations started by their uncle and father. Moderate prices.

HURON LIGHTSHIP MUSEUM
(End of I-94 east - Moored at Pine Grove Park along the St. Clair River), **Port Huron** 48060

❑   Activity: Museums
❑   Telephone: (810) 982-0891
    www.oakland.edu/boatnerd/museums/huron
❑   Hours: Wednesday - Sunday, 1:00 - 4:30 pm (July - August).
    Weekends Only, (May-June, September). Closed Holidays.
❑   Admission: Adults $2.00, Seniors $1.00 (60+), Children $1.00
    (7-17)
❑   Miscellaneous: Admission includes the Port Huron Museum -
    1115 Sixth Street, that traces 300 years of local history,
    especially American Indians, marine, and Thomas Edison's
    Youth. Open the same hours except year round.

Your entire family will really enjoy the brief tour of this unique lighthouse. It is the last "floating lighthouse" to sail the Great Lakes (decommissioned in 1970) called the "Huron". Used where it wasn't practical to build a lighthouse, it was built in 1920 and was operated by a crew of 11 who took 3 week turns (16 days out, 5 days in). Board the boat that bobbed through thick fog and rode out heavy storms to warn passing freighters of treacherous shoals ahead in the channel. Listen to the fog horn's "heeeee....ooohhhh" deep sound that bellows that sound of the ship's heart. What has replaced the Huron? Find out with self-guided tours of the interior hull, mess hall, captain's quarters, and then experience a panoramic view of the Blue Water Bridge from the pilothouse on top of the boat. It was most interesting to hear stories of freighters like the famous "Edmund Fitzgerald" and to know the dangers of being in a smaller boat that is calling giant ships right to you!

SANILAC COUNTY HISTORICAL MUSEUM & VILLAGE

228 South Ridge Road - (M-25)

Port Sanilac 48469

❑   Activity: Michigan History
❑   Telephone: (810) 622-9946
❑   Hours: Tuesday - Sunday, 11:00 am - 4:00 pm (Mid-June - Early September)
❑   Admission: Adults $5.00, Seniors $4.50, Children $2.00 (under 13)

Start at the 1875 Victorian Home with original home furnishings, period medical instruments, original post office cancellation stamps, and an "American" sewing machine (later they changed their name to "Singer"). The Dairy Museum features cheesemaking equipment and you can wander through the Log Cabin where they used some charred logs from the tragic Thumb Area fire of 1881. See an old schoolhouse and stop at the General Store (really cute - try a bottle of old-fashioned "body splash" or some penny candy - lots of licorice!)

JAPANESE CULTURAL CENTER & HOUSE

527 Ezra Rust Drive

Saginaw 48601

❑   Activity: The Arts
❑   Telephone: (517) 759-1648

❑   Hours: Tuesday - Saturday, Noon - 4:00 pm. (Memorial Day -
     September). Gardens are open Spring through Fall.
❑   Admission: Gardens are free. (Tea House Tour), Adults $3.00,
     Students $2.00. Full tea ceremony is $6.00 per person.

S tudy the ritual and ceremony of Japanese culture by
participating in a tea service. Following a tour of the garden's
many bridges and stones (from Japan), tea and sweets are served.
Traditional full teas are offered every second Saturday.

SAGINAW CHILDREN'S ZOO

1730 South Washington (I-675 to 5th/6th Exit)

Saginaw 48601

❑   Activity: Animals & Farms
❑   Telephone: (517) 771-4966
❑   Hours: Monday - Saturday, 10:00 am - 5:00 pm. Sunday &
     Holidays, 11:00 am - 6:00 pm. (May 1 - Labor Day)
❑   Admission: Adults $3.00 (13-64), Seniors $2.50, Children $2.00
     (2-12)

T his "kid-sized" zoo features all the fun animals including:
monkeys, bald eagles, alligators, and farm animals. Take a
miniature train or pony ride and then see and ride a unique,
locally built carrousel. After choosing your mount (from horses,
rabbits, ponies or sea horses), enjoy the views of hand-painted
panels depicting scenes of Saginaw's history.

SHIAWASSEE NATIONAL WILDLIFE REFUGE

Saginaw - ELC is at 3010 Maple Street in town. (Refuge is 6 miles south of town, west of SR13), 48601. *Activity:* Outdoors. **http://midwest.fws.gov/shiawase**. (517) 777-5930 or (517) 759-1669 (Learning Center). *Hours:* Dawn to Dusk. The 9000 acre Refuge provides food and rest for a variety of birds and other wildlife. This includes 250 species of birds, 10 miles of observation trails to walk, two observation decks with scopes, and The Green Point Environmental Learning Center. The Center offers 2.5 miles of hiking trails, indoor exhibits and many displays. For Shiawassee Flats "Michigan Everglades" Boat Trips call (810) 653-3859.

SAGINAW ART MUSEUM

Saginaw - 1126 North Michigan Avenue, 48602. *Activity:* The Arts. (517) 754-2491. **http://members.xoom.com/SaginawArt**. *Hours:* Tuesday - Saturday, 10:00 am - 5:00 pm, Sunday, 1:00 - 5:00 pm. Closed holidays. *Admission:* Donations. Housed in an early 1900's mansion, you'll find 19th and 20th century American art mostly. The Visionary Hands-On Room is the best place to spend time with kids.

HISTORICAL SOCIETY OF SAGINAW COUNTY

Saginaw - 500 Federal Avenue, 48607. *Activity:* Michigan History. (517) 752-2861. *Hours:* Tuesday - Saturday, 10:00 am - 4:30 pm. Sunday, 1:00 - 4:30 pm. Closed holidays. *Admission:* $0.50 to $1.00. View the winding spiral staircase as you enter the old post office that now traces the industrial development of Saginaw County. Guided tours by appointment.

JOHNNY PANTHER QUESTS

Saginaw – 48607. Activity: Tours. (810) 653-3859. *Admission:* $80.00 to $120.00 per couple. $30.00 to $40.00 per additional person depending on trip scheduled. The Everglades in Michigan?

Just a few short moments from downtown Saginaw is one of the greatest examples of wildlife and wetlands that you and your kids will ever see. Take a private boat tour that is personalized for your family. A quiet day with nature...floating along...with a chance to see deer, beaver and maybe even a bald eagle. As owner Wil Hufton says, "Eliminate the stress...get out of the mainstream and go on a Quest!" **www.frankenmuth.org/jpquests.htm**.

MARSHALL M. FREDERICK'S SCULPTURE GALLERY

Saginaw (University Center) - 7400 Bay Road (M-84) (Arbury Fine Arts Center on Saginaw Valley State University), 48710. *Activity:* The Arts. (517) 790-5667. **www.svsu.edu/mfsm**. *Hours:* Tuesday - Sunday, 1:00 - 5:00 pm. Closed holidays. Free admission. Home to more than 200 sculptures by the same artist. Free-standing sculptures, drawings and portraits, and photos of international bronze pieces are displayed. There's a sculpture garden and fountain too!

THREE OAKS SPOKES BICYCLE MUSEUM

Three Oaks - 110 North Elm Street, 49128. *Activity:* Museums. (616) 756-3361. More than two dozen exhibits including a 1860's "boneshaker" to a "monster cruiser" (36 inch balloon tires). Available at the museum are maps of 12 area bike routes.

Chapter 2
AREA - CW

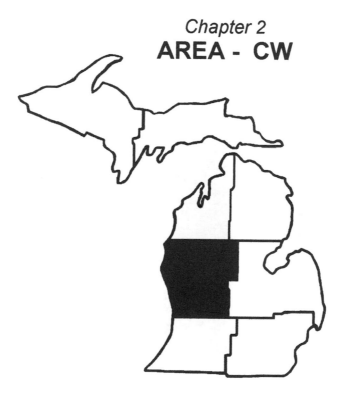

Our Favorites...

- Fish Ladder Sculpture
- Gerald Ford & Van Andel Museums
- Wooden Shoe Factories
- Dune Rides & Gillette Dune Center
- Rosie's Dinerland Restaurants

AMWAY VISITOR'S CENTER

7500 East Fulton Road

Ada 49355

❏ Activity: Tours
❏ Telephone: (616) 787-6701, **www.amway.com**
❏ Hours: Monday - Friday, 8:30 am - Noon, and 1:00 - 5:00 pm.
❏ Admission: Free
❏ Tours: To see the manufacturing operations, you must have at least 10 people in your group and pre-arrangements.

The famous Amway story comes to life through multi-media presentations, innovative technology and artifacts. A visual study of entrepreneurship and continued excellence in integrity and progress (i.e. The new spin-off sensation on the internet named Quixtar). Through displays, learn about the beginnings of the DeVos and VanAndel family businesses, setbacks (a valve that devastated the aerosol plant), and the introduction of many new or revolutionary products. Most kids marvel at the mile long facility and all the flags lining the circular driveway out front. It's guaranteed to spark any interest in business ownership from simple ideas.

SHRINE OF THE PINES

(M-37)

Baldwin 49304

❏ Activity: Outdoors
❏ Telephone: (231) 745-7892
  http://baldwin.localis.com/shrineopine
❏ Hours: Monday - Saturday, 10:00 am - 6:00 pm. Sunday, 1:30 - 6:00 pm. (May 15 - October 15)
❏ Admission: Adults $3.75, Seniors $3.00, Children $1.00 (6-18), Family $8.00.

It was Raymond W. Oberholzer's (a hunting and fishing guide) vision to create a shrine to the white pine trees that once covered Michigan. He began hand-carving and hand-polishing stumps, roots, and trunks (using the simplest of tools). Over 30 years of "works of art" are shown here including candlesticks, chairs, chandeliers, and beds. There is even a 700 lb. table with drawers carved from a single stump!

CANNONSBURG SKI AREA

Cannonsburg - 6800 Cannonsburg Road NE, 49317. *Activity:* Outdoors. (616) 874-6711. **www.cannonsburg.com**. Day and night skiing with 10 runs. Lessons and equipment rental are available.

COOPERSVILLE & MARNE RAILWAY

Train Departs from Downtown (I-96 to Exit 16 or 19)

Coopersville 49404

- ❑   Activity: Tours
- ❑   Telephone: (616) 837-7000, **www.coopersville.com/cmrr.html**
- ❑   Admission: Adults $7.50, Seniors $6.50, Children $4.50 (3-14).
- ❑   Tours: Saturday, 1:00 & 3:00 pm. (July - September)

A great way to introduce your children to rail travel at a relaxed pace. The summer rides offer a 5 mile tour though rural Michigan to the town of Marne and then returns on the same line. There are special theme rides that include The Great Train Robbery with Chuck Wagon Barbecue, The Pumpkin Train (in October), and The Santa Train (in December).

GRAND HAVEN / SPRING LAKE TROLLEY

Grand Haven - 440 North Ferry, 49417. *Activity:* Tours. **www.grandhaven.com/harbortransit/trolley.htm**.(800)303-4096 or (616) 842-3200. *Hours:* Daily, 11:00 am - 10:00 pm (Memorial Day - Labor Day). *Admission:* Adults $2.00, Seniors $1.00, Children $1.00 (3-12). A reproduction trolley that connects the towns of Ferrysburg, Spring Lake, & Grand Haven. See the sights or use it as a convenient means of transport.

GRAND HAVEN STATE PARK

Grand Haven - 1001 Harbor Avenue, 49417. *Activity:* Outdoors. (616) 798-3711. **www.dnr.state.mi.us/www/parks/holland.htm**. *Admission:* $4.00 per vehicle. The half-mile of beach and boardwalk is also the setting for campsites. There's also boating, fishing and swimming.

HARBOR STEAMER

Grand Haven - 301 North Harbor Drive (off US-31 - head West), 49417. *Activity:* Tours. **www.harborsteamer.com**. (616) 842-8950. *Hours:* Daily cruises at: Noon, 3:00, 4:00, 5:00, 7:00, 8:00, 9:00, and 10:00 pm. (Memorial Day - Labor Day). *Admission:* Adults $5-10.00, Children $2.50-5.00 (2-18). This cute replica paddlewheel boat offers tours of Spring Lake and the lower Grand River. Choose from a 45 minute waterfront or 90 minute scenic narrated lunchtime (or brown-bag lunch) tour.

HARBOR TROLLEY

Grand Haven - (Chinook Pier and points around town), 49417. *Activity:* Tours. (616) 842-3200. *Hours:* Daily until dark. (Memorial Day - Labor Day). Inexpensive, narrated tours of the Tri-Cities area. Any hotel or business can let you know pickup/drop-off spots.

MUSICAL FOUNTAIN

(Downtown Riverfront. Grandstand at Harbor and Washington Streets), **Grand Haven** 49417

- ❑ Activity: The Arts
- ❑ Telephone: (616) 842-2550, **www.grandhavenchamber.org**
- ❑ Hours: Summers at dusk – approximately 9:30 pm. Weekends only in September and May.
- ❑ Admission: Donations

❑ Miscellaneous: Tri-Cities Museum is in front of the grandstand and is open most evenings until the concert begins. It contains displays on railroading, shipping, pioneers, the lumber industry, Coast Guard and Maritime vessels in a former railroad depot.

The world's largest synchronized light, water and music show. For 30 years now, jets of water up to 125 feet high go through a series of pipes to create displays that change color to the beat of music. We thought some looked like angel wings and sunrises. The show lasts approximately 20 minutes.

CHILDREN'S MUSEUM

22 Sheldon Avenue NE

Grand Rapids 49503

❑ Activity: Museums
❑ Telephone: (616) 235-4726, **www.grcm.org**
❑ Hours: Tuesday - Saturday, 9:30 am - 5:00 pm, Sunday, Noon - 5:00 pm. Also Family Night on Thursday from 5:00 - 8:00 pm.
❑ General Admission: $3.00 (ages 2+). Family Night: $1.00

A well supported hands-on museum focuses on learning. The Lego Building Station leaves kids wanting to come back to make new creations (you never have that many Legos at home) and build cities with new friends. The Rapids is a unique area special to this Grand Rapids museum. The kids can try on waders to explore the rapids or design a bridge to cross the river.

FISH LADDER SCULPTURE

Grand Rapids - (US-131 East to exit 87 - turn right onto Front Street - On Grand River at junction of 4th and Front Streets), 49503. *Activity:* Outdoors. (800) 678-9859. *Hours:* Daily, 24 hours. Free admission. A concrete, 5 step ladder (actually a series of steps) was built by a local artist to assist salmon in jumping up a 6 foot dam to reach their popular spawning grounds further upstream. Leaping fish can be seen anytime, but the best time is late September to late October. If you spend about 20 minutes there you will witness at least one fish make it up all five steps! We sure are glad that Grand Rapids decided to help these pretty "fishies" out!

GRAND RAPIDS ART MUSEUM

Grand Rapids - 155 Division Street (US-131 to Pearl Street Exit), 49503. *Activity:* The Arts. **www.gram.mus.mi.us**. (616) 831-1000. *Hours:* Tuesday - Sunday, 11:00 am - 6:00 pm. Friday, 11:00 am - 9:00 pm. *Admission:* Adults $3.00, Seniors $1.00, Children $1.00 (ages 6-17). A nationally recognized art museum featuring work by local, state, and national artists. Call or visit website for current exhibitions.

GRAND RAPIDS CIVIC THEATRE

Grand Rapids - 30 North Division Street, 49503. *Activity:* The Arts. (616) 222-6650. **www.grct.org**. Children's Theatre with productions like Pinocchio or Teen Detective. The second largest community theatre in the U.S.. Season runs September-June. Downtown.

GRAND RAPIDS GRIFFINS HOCKEY

Grand Rapids - 130 West Fulton (Van Andel Arena), 49503. *Activity:* Sports. **www.grgriffins.com**. (616) 222-4000. Admission: $5.00 - 22.00. This IHL team plays in March and April.

GRAND RAPIDS HOOPS BASKETBALL

Grand Rapids - 130 West Fulton (Van Andel Arena), 49503. *Activity:* Sports. **www.grhoops.com**.(616) 456-3333 or (616) 458-7788. This Continental Basketball Association team plays in March. Admission charged.

GRAND RAPIDS RAMPAGE FOOTBALL

Grand Rapids - 130 West Fulton (Van Andel Arena), 49503. *Activity:* Sports. (616) 559-1871. **www.grrampage.com**. This Arena Football League plays mid-April through mid-July.

GRAND RAPIDS SYMPHONY

Grand Rapids - 169 Louis Campau Promenade, Suite One, 49503. *Activity:* The Arts. (616) 454-9451. **www.grsymphony.org**. Family and Lollipop Series available September-May. Summer season at Cannonsburg Ski Area. Admission charged.

GRAND RAPIDS YOUTH SYMPHONY

Grand Rapids - (DeVos Hall), 49503. *Activity:* The Arts. (616) 866-6883. Admission charged. Concerts featuring the 100 plus member ensemble, ages 12-21, performing classical favorites.

THE GRAND RAPIDS CHOIR OF MEN AND BOYS

Grand Rapids - 134 North Division Ave (St. Mark's Episcopal Church), 49503. *Activity:* The Arts. (616) 454-9423. Admission charged. Cathedral Classics Series.

BLANDFORD NATURE CENTER

Grand Rapids - 1715 Hillburn Avenue NW (US-131 to Leonard Street exit west to Hillburn), 49504. *Activity:* Outdoors. (616) 453-6192. **www.grmuseum.org/blnfrd.htm**. *Hours:* Monday - Friday, 9:00 am - 5:00 pm. Weekends, 1:00 - 5:00 pm. Closed major holidays. Trails are open from dawn to dusk. Free admission. The visitor center is probably where you'll start. Learn about their wildlife care program and then go out on the grounds along self-guided trails to see wildlife. A total of 140 or so acres of fields, forests, ponds and streams can be leisurely explored. The trails turn into cross-country ski areas in the Winter.

GERALD FORD MUSEUM

303 Pearl Street NW (I-196 to US-131 to Pearl Street Exit - East - on the West bank of the Grand River), **Grand Rapids** 49504

- ❏ Activity: Museums
- ❏ Telephone: (616) 451-9263
  www.grandrapids.org/fordmuseum
- ❏ Hours: Daily, 9:00 am - 5:00 pm
- ❏ Admission: Adults $3.00, Seniors $2.00 (62+), Children FREE (under 16)

This display of history through artifacts is outstanding to parents, but kids will gravitate to only a handful of displays. As you may have to race through some interesting exhibits, be sure to help your kids look for these (hey...tell them it's a scavenger hunt!): See Elvis' suit, James Dean's motorcycle, Bert and Ernie, A pole sitter, the first video game, Mr. Roger's sweater, and those "groovy" platform tennis shoes (since they are now back in style they may be wearing something similar!). The best areas for kids:

- ❏ <u>OVAL OFFICE REPLICA</u> - See the room that very few people ever see and listen as you eavesdrop on a typical day in the Ford Presidency.
- ❏ <u>HOLOGRAPHIC WHITE HOUSE TOUR</u> - Tour (using photographs taken by the Fords) up to 11 rooms usually off limits to the public. Attend a White House State Dinner or play in the Solarium.
- ❏ <u>CAMPAIGNS</u> - Deliver a speech like the President using a teleprompter or stand on the floor of a political convention. We have a great video of this memory!

JOHN BALL PARK ZOO

1300 West Fulton Street

Grand Rapids 49504

- ❏ Activity: Animals & Farms
- ❏ Telephone: (616) 336-4300 or (616) 336-4301
  www.co.kent.mi.us/zoo/animal.htm

❑   Hours: Daily, 10:00 am - 6:00 pm (mid-May to Labor Day).
    Daily, 10:00 am - 4:00 pm (rest of the year) Closed Christmas
    Day only.
❑   Admission: Adults $3.50 (14-62), Seniors $2.00 (63+), Children
    $2.00 (5-13). No admission is charged in December - February.

See more than 1000 specimens (you know…animals, fish,
amphibians, etc.) from around the world at the state's second
largest zoo. In addition to the usual lions, tigers, and bears there is
a special exhibit on Nocturnal Animals and a petting zoo with farm
animals for the young kids.

VAN ANDEL MUSEUM CENTER

272 Pearl Street NW (US-131 to Pearl Street, exit 85B)

Grand Rapids 49504

❑   Activity: Museums
❑   Telephone: (616) 456-3977, **www.grmuseum.org**
❑   Hours: Daily, 9:00 am - 5:00 pm
❑   Admission: Adults $5.00, Seniors $4.00, Children $2.00 (3-17)
❑   Miscellaneous: Planetarium and laser shows (additional charge).
    Museum Café. Curiosity Shop. Carrousel rides, $0.75.

Exhibits that depict heritage and manufacturers of the region. Best
picks for children might be:

❑   FURNITURE CITY - a partially operational reconstruction of an
    early 1900's furniture factory and displays of artistic and funky
    chairs.
❑   THE 1890'S DOWNTOWN - a recreated street with a theater
    and shops plus the sights and sounds of transportation and
    people's conversations as you wait with them at the train station.
❑   AMERICAN INDIANS - Anishinabe people were the first
    inhabitants of the area. Why do they re-tell the stories of their
    ancestry so much?

B e on the lookout for the 76 foot finback whale skeleton which greets you at the entrance in the main hallway. Also, you'll feel like you're in the movie "Back to the Future" when you see the Giant Clock taken from Old City Hall (it's transparent so you can see the mechanisms - and it's still keeping time).

MICHIGAN BOTANIC GARDEN & MEIJER SCULPTURE PARK

1000 East Beltline NE (I-96 to East Beltline exit - go north)

Grand Rapids 49525

- ❑ Activity: Outdoors
- ❑ Telephone: (616) 957-1580, **www.meijergardens.org**
- ❑ Hours: Monday - Saturday, 9:00 am - 5:00 pm. (until 9:00 on Thursday, June - August). Sunday, Noon - 5:00 pm.
- ❑ Admission: Adults $5.00 (14+), Seniors $4.00, Children $2.00 (5-13). Outdoor tram rides - Adults $1.00, Children $0.50 (5-13) - Weekends Only.

A 70-acre complex featuring indoor (5 stories tall) and outdoor gardens. See tropical and various plants from five continents on nature trails. The sculpture park offers 70 works by renowned artists. Gift shop and restaurant are available. A great virtual tour and current special events are available on their website.

WEST MICHIGAN WHITECAPS BASEBALL

Grand Rapids - US-131 & West River Drive (Old Kent Park), 49544. *Activity:* Sports. (616) 784-4131 or in Michigan (800) CAPS-WIN. **www.whitecaps-baseball.com**. *Admission:* Box $7.50, Reserved $6.00, Bleachers $4.00, Lawn $3.00. A baseball stadium with lawn seats? Show your kids the way that baseball used to be watched in the early days. Bleacher and box seats are also available too. The Whitecaps are the Class "A" farm team for the Detroit Tigers and always offer a great family fun value. Batter up! (April - September).

AJ'S FAMILY WATER PARK

4441 28th Street SE (I-96 to Exit 43A)

Grand Rapids (Kentwood) 49512

- ❑   Activity: Amusements
- ❑   Telephone: (616) 940-0400
- ❑   Hours: Daily, 10:00 am - 10:00 pm (Memorial Day - Labor Day)
- ❑   Admission: General $13.00 (48" tall and over). $11.00 (under 48" tall). Children under age 2 and Seniors 61+ are Free. Discounts offered after 4:00 pm.

A day of family fun awaits you at this indoor/outdoor family waterpark. We especially liked the fact that there is something for everyone. Attractions include 5 waterslides (you must be 48" tall to ride the straight speed slides) that can accommodate everyone's level of thrill. The wave pool was really "cool" since it could change from a calm lagoon to a ferocious whitecapped thrill every few minutes. The "Tad Pool" offers water just several inches deep with mini-slides and sprinklers. Other attractions include miniature golf, bumper boats, play tower, and arcades.

GRAND LADY RIVERBOAT CRUISES

Grandville - 4243 Indian Mounds Drive SW, 49418. *Activity:* Tours. (616) 457-4837. **www.river-boat.com**. *Hours:* Sightseeing tours on Saturday & Sunday (subject to prior charters). *Admission:* Adults $10.00 (for sightseeing tours). Call or visit website for tour schedule and options. Children ages 3 - 11 are ½ price except on Saturday Dinner and Happy Hour Cruises. Their cruise tells the story of sites you view and riverboat landings you pass between Grand Rapids & Grand Haven. Admission charged. Call or visit website for seasonal schedule of events. (May - October)

WILSON STATE PARK

Harrison - 910 North First Street (BR-27 one mile north of Harrison), 48625. *Activity:* Outdoors. (517) 539-3021. **www.dnr.state.mi.us/www/parks/wilson.htm**. *Admission:* $4.00 per vehicle. Camping/cabins, boating and boat rental, fishing and swimming.

CHARLTON PARK VILLAGE & MUSEUM

2545 South Charlton Park Road (2 miles South on M-37 then 4 miles East on M-79 - follow signs), **Hastings** 49058

❑   Activity: Museums
❑   Telephone: (616) 945-3775
❑   Hours: Daily, 9:00 am - 4:30 pm. (mid-May to September)
❑   Admission: Adults $4.00, Seniors $3.00 (55+), Children $2.00
     (5-15). Special events can have various admission fees.

A very authentic recreation of an 1890's rural Michigan town, this village offers 17 buildings that include a schoolhouse and a blacksmith shop. Also find a beach, boat launch, and playground.

DELFT FACTORY AND WOODEN SHOE FACTORY

12755 Quincy Street – US-31, **Holland** 49423

❑   Activity: Tours
❑   Telephone: (616) 399-1900, **www.veldheertulip.com**
❑   Hours: Monday - Friday, 8:00 am - 6:00 pm., Saturday &
     Sunday, 9:00 am - 5:00 pm. (April - December). Weekdays only
     (January - March)
❑   Admission: Free
❑   Tours: Of both wooden shoe and Delftware
❑   Miscellaneous: Veldheer Tulip Gardens. Colorful tulips, peonies,
     daylilies, iris, Dutch lilies, daffodils. Admission charged for
     gardens. Be sure to get at least one item personalized - we had a
     shoe magnet for the refrigerator imprinted with "Kids Love".

The Dutch began making wooden shoes as a replacement for leather which was too expensive and deteriorated quickly because of all the exposure to water in the Netherlands. Watch local craftsmen carve "Klompen" (wooden shoes) on machines brought over from the Netherlands. Sizes from Barbie (they really fit!) to Men's size 13. Plain or hand decorated they are great for gardening or decoration. Lots of sawdust! Delftware began being made by potters in the city of Delft in the 13th Century. It is known for its delicately hand-painted blue and white porcelain. This is the only U.S. factory that is producing replica Chinese porcelain and it's just beautiful! While you're having your wooden shoes burned with a special personalization, be sure to take the time to watch the artist use Delft colored paints to decorate plain pieces.

HOLLAND MUSEUM

31 West 10th Street, **Holland** 49423

❑   Activity: Museums
❑   Telephone: (888)200-9123, www.wowcom.net/commerce/museum
❑   Hours: Monday, Wednesday, Friday, Saturday, 10:00 am - 5:00 pm., Thursday, 10:00 am - 8:00 pm., Sunday 2:00 - 5:00 pm.
❑   Admission: Adults $3.00, Seniors $2.00 (65+), Students $2.00, Family $7.00

As you enter, you'll be mesmerized by the collection of miniature glass churches built by Dutch immigrants for a World's Fair.. Most all the displays are "no touch" but kids take an interest in the Dutch Fisherman's Cottage (kids sleep in bunks in the walls) and the carrousel made by a Dutch sailor for his kids.

HOLLAND STATE PARK

Holland - 2215 Ottawa Beach Road (west off US-31 on Lakewood Road), 49424. **www.dnr.state.mi.us/www/parks/holland.htm**. *Activity:* Outdoors. (616) 399-9390. *Admission:* $4.00 per vehicle. Drawn to the beaches and swimming along with the beautifully well-kept, bright red, lighthouse is the reason most come. 150 campsites, boating, fishing, swimming, and bicycle trails.

ORIGINAL WOODEN SHOE FACTORY

447 US-31 and 16th Street (I-196 West to exit 52), **Holland** 49423

- ❑   Activity: Tours
- ❑   Telephone: (616) 396-6513
- ❑   Hours: Monday-Saturday, 8:00am-4:30pm. Closed Winter holidays.
- ❑   Admission: 25 cents per person
- ❑   Miscellaneous: Gift Shop where you can get specially personalized shoes of all sizes.

The oldest wooden shoe factory in the U.S. still uses early 1900's European machines which turn out shoes one at a time. Using mostly poplar logs, you'll be able to see the bark removed and cut into lengths depending on shoe size and width. They are generally cut wide because most all who wear them must also wear heavy socks. Another machine shapes the block of wood as it spins around clamped to a rotating spit. Most interesting to the kids was the boring machine that uses a template to hollow out the shoe's guts - it always knows exactly how much to remove. The shoe is then sanded and painted and lacquer finished. Have an artisan paint your favorite design or saying on your new pair of souvenir shoes!

SAUGATUCK DUNES STATE PARK

Holland - 2215 Ottawa Beach Road (Off US-31 north), 49424. *Activity:* Outdoors. (616) 399-9390. **www.dnr.state.mi.us/www/ parks/saugatuc.htm#top**. *Admission:* $4.00 per vehicle. Over 2 miles of secluded shoreline along Lake Michigan. Hiking trails, swimming, winter sports, and dunes, of course.

WINDMILL ISLAND

7th Street and Lincoln Avenue,

Holland 49423

- ❑   Activity: Outdoors
- ❑   Telephone: (616) 355-1030, **www.windmillisland.org**

- ❑ Hours: Monday - Saturday, 9:00 am - 6:00 pm., Sunday, 11:30 am - 6:00 pm. (April, May, July, August). Monday - Saturday, 10:00 am - 5:00 pm., Sunday, 11:30 am - 5:00 pm. (June, September). Monday - Friday, 10:00 am - 4:00 pm., Saturday, 9:00 am - 4:00 pm., Sunday, 11:30 am - 4:00 pm. (October)
- ❑ Admission: Adults $5.50, Students $2.50 (5-12)
- ❑ Tours: Guided (May - October)
- ❑ Miscellaneous: Candle, sweets, and gift shop. Find every windmill product imaginable. Some activities are for summer only.

"DeZwann" (Dutch for the swan) is a 230+ year old, 12 story high, working, authentic Dutch windmill. It's the only one operating in the United States...they produce graham flour almost daily and sell it at the complex. Take a tour of all of the floors, learn how they change the direction of the windmill, see the mechanical wood gears turn (if there's at least a 15 MPH wind) and learn how the miller worked upstairs and sold product on the first floor at the same time. After your tour, Klompen (wooden shoe) dancers perform to organ music as those wooden shoes "klomp" to the beat. See a display of the Netherlands in miniature. The kids won't believe how many water canals are used as streets.

DUTCH VILLAGE

12350 James Street (US-31 and James Street) **Holland** 49424

- ❑ Activity: Amusements
- ❑ Telephone: (616) 396-1475, **www.dutchvillage.com**
- ❑ Hours: Daily, 9:00 am - 5:00 pm. (Mid-April - Mid-October)
- ❑ Admission: Adults $6.50, Children $4.50 (3-11)
- ❑ Miscellaneous: Café. Ice cream shop. Specialty shops.

You'll feel like you're in Europe (Netherlands) as you see the quaint Dutch Style buildings, canals and flower gardens. Klompen Dancers perform to the music of the Amsterdam Street Organ and wooden shoe crafters are working in their shops with old tools that shape logs into shoes. There are museums and historical displays plus the kids favorite spot (and Michele's when she was little)...STREET CARNIVAL - Wooden Shoe Slides,

Dutch Chair Swing, and antique Dutch pictured carrousel. There's also a farmhouse with "pet and feed" animals.

QUEEN'S INN RESTAURANT

12350 James Street (US-31 and James Street - Look for signs to Dutch Village), **Holland** 49424

❑ Activity: Theme Restaurants
❑ Telephone: (616) 396-1475, **www.dutchvillage.com**
❑ Hours: Daily, Lunch & Dinner

This restaurant is the only authentic Dutch restaurant in town serving authentic meals like Metwurst sausage and Dutch pea soup - everything meat and potatoes, everything with a mild flavor. Your authentically costumed waitress greets you in Dutch and serves your entrée with a Dutch suggestion (eat hearty!). The windmill-shaped, boxed high chairs are absolutely adorable - a little one in your party has to sit in one for a great photo opportunity - our son, Daniel still gleams when we show him the picture!

KENTWOOD STATION RESTAURANT

Kentwood - 1665 Viewpond Drive SE (East off Kalamazoo - 1 block south of 44th Street), 49508. *Activity:* Theme Restaurants. (616) 455-4150. *Hours:* Monday - Saturday, Lunch & Dinner. An early 1900's railway station has a "Soup and Salad Car".

LUDINGTON CITY BEACH

Ludington - North Lakeshore Drive, 49431. *Activity:* Outdoors. (231) 845-0324. *Hours:* Daylight (Memorial Day - Labor Day). Free admission. A great summer place to cool off featuring swimming and miniature golf.

LUDINGTON STATE PARK

Ludington - M-116, 49431. *Activity:* Outdoors.(231) 843-8671 or 843-2423.**www.dnr.state.mi.us/www/parks/plwc.htm#ludington** Admission: $4.00 per vehicle. Over 300 campsites or cabins, plenty of beaches (one with surfing waves), and extensive hiking trails are big hits here. Lots of dunes here and a great canoe trail, boating, swimming, and fishing. Many love the cross-country skiing and the nature center.

SS BADGER

701 Maritime Drive, **Ludington** 49431

- ❑ Activity: Tours
- ❑ Telephone: (888) 337-7948, **www.ssbadger.com**
- ❑ Hours: Depart times vary. Call for details. (early May - October)
- ❑ Admission: Adults $63.00, Seniors $58.00, Children $31.00 (5-15), Ages 4 and under are free. Vehicle transport fee $98.00. (All rates are per person, round trip and subject to change). Shorter cruises are available in mid-May and special select dates.
- ❑ Miscellaneous: Cafeteria, movie room, bingo, children's activities.

The 410-foot "SS Badger" is the only Great Lakes car ferry boat running today and can carry over 600 passengers and 180 vehicles. The current voyage is a 4-hour tour that travels from Ludington to Manitowoc Wisconsin. Kids will be fascinated at the thought of this all day cruise with plenty of activities to keep their attention. Be sure to call or visit their website for information on travel packages.

TWIN POINTS RESORT

Ludington - 2684 Piney Ridge Road (near Ludington State Park - off M-116), 49431. *Activity:* Outdoors. (231) 843-9434. A family friendly resort offering 10 cottages which vary in size from one to three bedrooms. Large beach.

WHITE PINE VILLAGE

1687 South Lakeshore Drive, **Ludington** 49431

- ❑ Activity: Michigan History
- ❑ Telephone: (231) 843-4808

- ❑ Hours: Tuesday - Saturday, 11:00 am - 4:00 pm. (Early May to mid-October)
- ❑ Admission: Adults $5.00, Seniors $4.50, Children $4.00 (6-18), Family $15.00. Slightly higher admissions for special events.

A reconstructed 1800's village that features over 20 buildings including a courthouse, hardware store, fire hall, schoolhouse, chapel, and logging and maritime museums.

HART-MONTAGUE TRAIL STATE PARK

Mears - 9679 West State Park Road (along US-31), 49436. *Activity:* Outdoors. (231) 873-3083. A paved, 22-mile trail passing through rural, forested lands. Picnic areas and scenic overlooks areas are available along the trail.

MAC WOOD'S DUNE RIDES
West Silver Lake Drive (off US-31), **Mears** 49436

- ❑ Activity: Tours
- ❑ Telephone: (231) 873-2817
- ❑ Hours: Daily rides, 9:30 am - Dusk (Memorial Day - Labor Day). Daily rides, 10:00 am - 5:00 pm (mid-May - Sunday before Memorial Day & Labor Day - early October)
- ❑ Admission: Adults $11.00, Children $7.00 (11 and under)

A "Model A Ford" with big tires, a big engine, and 2000 acres of rolling sand...a man's dream! Nearly 70 years ago Malcolm "Mac" Woods created the thrill of dune buggying with this vehicle. Today, your vehicle is a multi-passenger, modified, convertible truck "dune scooter". Hang on as you begin a fun and educational 40 minute, 8-mile ride that helps you understand the dunes and why people have come to love this sport. You even get to race along the hard-packed sand beach...just...not too close to the waves!

SILVER LAKE STATE PARK

Mears - 9679 West State Park Road (US-31 exit Shelby Road west), 49436. *Activity:* Outdoors. (231) 873-3083. *Admission:* $4.00 per vehicle. Lots of campsites along the dunes is one draw but dune buggy riding is considered the best here. Look for the Little Sable Point Lighthouse (great for pictures at sunset or dawn) and participate in swimming, boating, fishing, hiking trails on/off dunes. **www.dnr.state.mi.us/www/parks/plwc.htm#silverlake**.

HACKLEY HOSE COMPANY NO. 2

Muskegon - 510 West Clay Avenue, 49440. *Activity:* Museums. (231) 722-0278. Hours vary depending on pre-arranged appointments or special events. Call ahead. Tour a replica Fire Barn, complete with firefighting equipment artifacts, horses stalls, firemen's living room.

MUSKEGON CIVIC THEATRE

Muskegon - 49440. *Activity:* The Arts. (800) 585-3737 or (231) 722-3852. **www.visitmuskegon.org/frauenthal/muskegon_civic_theater_schedule.htm**. *Admission:* Adults $13.00-15.00, Seniors $11.00-13.00 (62+), Students $11.00-13.00 (under 18). Summer Children's Theatre and Christmas plays for children.

MUSKEGON COUNTY MUSEUM

Muskegon - 430 West Clay, 49440. *Activity:* Michigan History. (888) 843-5661 or (231) 728-4119. *Hours:* Monday - Friday, 9:30 am - 4:30 pm. Weekends, 12:30 - 4:30 pm. Closed major holidays. Free admission. History of Muskegon County with features of Lumbering, Industry and Wildlife, Native Americans, and a favorite kid spot - Hands On Science Galleries. Educational Gift Shop.

MUSKEGON FURY HOCKEY

Muskegon - 955 Fourth Street (L.C. Walker Arena), 49440. *Activity:* Sports. (231) 726-3879. **www.furyhockey.com**. *Admission:* Adults $8.50-10.00, Seniors $6.00, Children $6.00 (3-18). United Hockey League professional team plays here October - April. The Muskegon Sports Hall of Fame is located in the Arena.

P.J. HOFFMASTER STATE PARK
GILLETTE DUNE CENTER

6585 Lake Harbor Road (I-96, exit 4 west - Pontalune Road)

Muskegon 49441

- ❑ Activity: Outdoors
- ❑ Telephone: (231) 798-3711

  www.dnr.state.mi.us/www/parks/hoffmas1.htm
- ❑ Hours: Daily, 10:00 am - 5:00 pm. (Summer). Tuesday - Friday, 1:00 - 5:00 pm., Saturday & Sunday, 10:00 am - 5:00 pm. (Rest of year). Park is open 8:00 am - Dusk.
- ❑ Admission: $4.00 per vehicle
- ❑ Miscellaneous: 2 ½ miles of sandy shoreline, towering dunes with a dune climbing stairway to the top overlook. Winter hosts cross country skiing, sledding, and snowshoeing. Campsites on shaded dunes. Fishing, boating, and swimming.

The Gillette Sand Dune Visitor's Center has exhibits and hands-on displays. See a multi media presentation that illustrates and explains both dormant and living dunes. Nature trails to observation decks (one is handicap and stroller accessible). The Center has lots of live turtles and frogs, similar to ones that live in dune environments. The favorite for our kids was the giant crystal of sand and the samples of different types and color of sand found around America. Do you know what 3 things are needed to form dunes?

PORT CITY PRINCESS

Muskegon - 1133 West Western Ave (off US-31 - Downtown), 49441. **www.muskegon.org/tourist.htm**. *Activity:* Tours. (231) 728-8387. *Admission:* General $8.00. *Tours:* Daily at 3:30 pm. 90 minutes. (Memorial Day - Labor Day). A sightseeing tour of Muskegon Lake and if the weather is good a brief look at Lake Michigan.

USS SILVERSIDES

1346 Bluff at Pere Marquette Park (Southside of Channel Way)

Muskegon 49443

❑   Activity: Tours
❑   Telephone: (231) 755-1230
❑   Hours: Daily, 10:00 am - 5:30 pm. (June - August). Monday - Friday, 1:00 - 5:30 pm., Saturday & Sunday, 10:00 am - 5:30 pm. (May & September). Saturday & Sunday, 10:00 am - 5:30 pm (April & October)
❑   Admission: Adults $4.00, Seniors $2.50 (62+), Teens $3.00 (12-18), Children $2.00 (5-11)
❑   Miscellaneous: Watch out if you're claustrophobic. Difficult to take pre-schoolers around on poor footing, cramped quarters.

A restored, famous WW II submarine that was once used for sinking ships. Go through the sub's compartments and see how sailors work and live in such cramped quarters (for up to 2 months). Explore decks, engine rooms, and battle stations. Also, a Camp Aboard program is available for a real fun time!

WEST MICHIGAN CHILDREN'S MUSEUM

280 Muskegon Mall (2nd floor above the Hallmark store)

Muskegon 49443

❑   Activity: Museums
❑   Telephone: (231) 722-1425

❑   Hours: Wednesday - Friday 10:00 am - 5:00 pm. Saturday, 10:00
     am - 6:00 pm. Sunday 1:00 - 6:00 pm.
❑   Admission: General $2.50

Targeted to kids ages 2-12, the museum is divided into five
     main areas. The Expressions Room is for arts and crafts while
Our Town provides role playing in a pretend grocery store,
newspaper, hospital and TV Studio. Science is highlighted in the
SPARKS Room which features electricity experiments and animal
games. The Global Child Theater is a dressing room and puppet
stage to perform in. Coming soon is the LEGO exhibit.

MICHIGAN'S ADVENTURE AMUSEMENT
PARK & WILDWATER ADVENTURE

4750 Whitehall Road (I-96 to US-31)

Muskegon 49445

❑   Activity: Amusements
❑   Telephone: (231) 766-3377, **www.miadventure.com**
❑   Hours: Daily, 11:00 am - 9:00 pm. (Memorial Day weekend -
     Labor Day weekend) Hours vary slightly throughout the season.
     Call or visit website for complete schedule.
❑   Admission: General $20.00. (under 2 Free). Admission is good
     for both parks.

Summer...thrill rides, waterparks and food...right? Michigan's
     largest amusement park awaits your family for a day (*or 2*) of
summer's best. With over 40 rides with names like Mad Moose,
Big Dipper, Wolverine Wildcat, and Shivering Timbers (the 3rd
largest wooden roller coaster in the country), you can be sure that
your day will be fun-filled! Don't worry there are also some
"calmer" rides (7 are made just for younger children) including the
Zachary Zoomer, a special scaled down coaster just for younger
children. A tree house and play areas are also included for younger
children. Wildwater Adventure admission is also included (the
state's largest waterpark) with the Lazy River water tube ride, a
wave pool, and Michigan's longest waterslide.

MUSKEGON WINTER SPORTS COMPLEX

(Inside Muskegon State Park)

Muskegon 49445

❑   Activity: Outdoors

❑   Telephone: (231) 744-9629, **www.msports.org**

❑   Hours: Friday night, Saturday, Sunday.

❑   Admission: Orientation $17.00, All day passes $20.00 - 25.00.

A re Mom and Dad ready to re-live their glory days of winter fun? Of course there is the normal winter fun of ice skating and cross-country skiing trails, but that's only where the fun begins. Two luge tracks (ice covered with banked turns) allow beginners and advanced sledders to grow at their own pace (starting at different ascents on the tracks). Speeds range from 25 - 45 MPH! Hang on!

LITTLE SWITZERLAND RESORT & CAMPGROUND

Newaygo - 254 Pickeral Lake Drive (off M-37), 49337. *Activity:* Outdoors. (231) 652-7939. This resort offers 7 cottages and 80 campsites. (Open May - October)

NEWAYGO STATE PARK

Newaygo - 2793 Beech Street (US-131, exit 125 West), 49337. *Activity:* Outdoors. (231) 745-2888. Wooded rustic campsites, boating, and swimming access to Hardy Dam Pond.

DUCK LAKE STATE PARK

North Muskegon   - 3560 Memorial Drive, 49445. *Activity:* Outdoors. **www.dnr.state.mi.us/www/parks/ducklk.htm**. (231) 744-3480.(Day use park only). *Admission:* $4.00 per vehicle. A public beach with swimming and boating; fishing and hiking.

MUSKEGON STATE PARK

North Muskegon - 3560 Memorial Drive (US-31 to M-120 exit), 49445. **www.dnr.state.mi.us/www/parks/Muskegon.html**. (231) 744-3480. *Activity:* Outdoors. *Admission:* $4.00 per vehicle. Features over 2 miles of shoreline on Lake Michigan and over 1 mile on Muskegon Lake. Check out their four luge runs. Camping, hiking trails, boating, fishing, swimming, and winter sports.

MEARS STATE PARK

Pentwater - West Lowell Street, 49449. *Activity:* Outdoors. (231) 869-2051. **www.dnr.state.mi.us/www/parks/mears.htm**. *Admission:* $4.00 per vehicle. Located on Lake Michigan with several hundred yards of white sandy beach. Camping, hiking, fishing and swimming.

DREAMFIELD FARM

5100 Pierce Road (south off M-20)

Remus 49340

❑ Activity: Animals & Farms
❑ Telephone: (517) 967-8422
❑ Hours: Tuesday - Saturday, & Holiday Weekends, 10:00 am - 5:00 pm.
❑ Admission: General $5.00
❑ Miscellaneous: Seasonal hayrides. Nature trails and picnic areas.

A great 100 plus Centennial Farm offers hands-on educational farming. A agriculture display museum is here but most come for assisting in hand-feeding sheep, pigs, calves, rabbits and lambs. Farm Fun activities include swinging on ropes into haystacks and driving mini-tractors.

AAA CANOE RENTALS

Rockford - 12 East Bridge Street, 49341. *Activity:* Outdoors. (616) 866-9264. *Hours:* Daily, 9:00 am (mid-April to late October). *Admission:* General, $12.50 (age 6+). Prices are for a 2 hour trip.

4 hour trips are also available. A family friendly canoe trip on the Rogue River offering only calm water with no rapids. Life preservers are available for young children.

ROSIE'S DINERLAND
4500 Fourteen Mile Road (M-57) (off US-131, exit 101 east)
Rockford 49341

❑   Activity: Theme Restaurants
❑   Telephone: (616) 866-FOOD, **www.rosiesdiner.com**
❑   Hours: Sunday, 7:00 am - 8:00 pm, Monday & Tuesday, 6:00 am - 8:00 pm, Wednesday & Thursday, 6:00 am - 9:00 pm, Friday & Saturday, 6:00 am - 10:00 pm.
❑   Miscellaneous: Behind diner is Dinerland Mini-Golf. Each hole is a piece of diner food - pie, endless cup of coffee, hamburgers, meatloaf and mashed potatoes, eggs and sausage, etc. Very casual. Cruise Inn on Wednesday night - all summer long.

An American Roadside attraction with three vintage diners in a row! Rosie's Diner, The Diner Store, and The Delux Diner. The waitresses are dressed in diner dresses (remember the TV show "Alice") and it's the best place to get a burger and malt. These are authentic original 1940's and 50's streamlined diner cars and Rosie's Diner is the famous place where the commercial (starring Nancy Walker) for "the quicker picker upper", Bounty paper towels was filmed! (Remember Rosie, the waitress, never fretting about spills by the customers). If your kids have a tendency to spill while eating, you may get to experience Rosie's cleanup yourself!

DOUBLE JJ RESORT
5900 South Water Road (US-31 to Exit 136 - east)
Rothbury 49452

❑   Activity: Outdoors
❑   Telephone: (800) DOUBLEJJ or (231) 894-4444
     www.doublejj.com

❑   Admission: Prices are all inclusive for a week stay and are subject to change. Adults $565.00, Youth $490.00 (7-16), Children $390.00 (5-6), 4 and under Free. Meals are included in rates. Call or visit website for weekend and 3-day rates.

Did you know that Michigan has "Dude Ranches"? In fact this is one of three in the state. Well...Double JJ is actually more than a dude ranch. Daily rides are offered and staffed by experienced "cowpokes" who will teach you all the skills along the way. There is even a rodeo at the end of the week where you can test your newly acquired talent. There is something for all ages. Adults and children (with supervision) can learn separately at there own pace. Some of the attractions and fun include a swimming hole with waterslide, a petting farm, riding center, Wild West Shows for the adults in the dance hall (kids have their own shows), fishing, hot tubs, pools, and an award-winning golf 18 hole golf course "Thoroughbred". Aaahhh...the life of a cowboy!

SHELBY MAN-MADE GEMSTONES

1330 Industrial Drive (off US-31)

Shelby 49455

❑   Activity: Tours
❑   Telephone: (231) 861-2165
❑   Hours: Showroom, Monday - Friday, 9:00 am - 5:30 pm. Saturday, Noon - 4:00 pm.
❑   Admission: Free

In a 50 seat theatre you can learn the fascinating manufacturing process of how man can actually create gemstones such as diamonds, rubies, and sapphires. They are the largest manufacturer in the world of simulated and synthetic gemstones in the world. See how they can process smaller gems into larger ones at a much lesser cost. If your kids are into rock (especially pretty colored ones, like our daughter) they'll love this place!

SANDY BEACH CAMPGROUND

White Cloud - 6929 30th Street (M-37, East on 30th Street), 49349. *Activity:* Outdoors. (231) 689-7383. 150 sites with swimming beach. (mid-May to mid-September).

WHITE RIVER LIGHT STATION MUSEUM

6199 Murray Road

Whitehall 49461

- ❑ Activity: Museums
- ❑ Telephone: (231) 894-8265

  www.whitelake.org/attractions/whiteriver
- ❑ Hours: Tuesday - Friday, 11:00 pm - 5:00 pm. Saturday - Sunday, Noon - 6:00 pm. (Summer) Weekends only in September.
- ❑ Small admission fee.

This historic lighthouse was built in 1875 and your family can still climb the old spiral stairs to the top for a view of White Lake and Lake Michigan. Made of Michigan limestone and brick, it features photographs, paintings, artifacts and maritime stories.

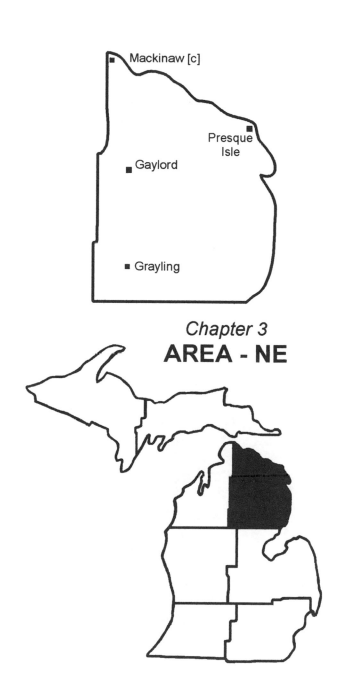

Mackinaw [c]

Presque
Isle

Gaylord

Grayling

Chapter 3
AREA - NE

Our Favorites...

- Hartwick Pines State Park
- Mackinac Bridge & Museum
- Fort Mackinac State Park
- Mackinac Island Carriage Tour
- Presque Isle Lighthouses

JESSE BESSER MUSEUM

491 Johnson Street (Off US-23 near Alpena General Hospital)

Alpena 49707

- ❑ Activity: Museums
- ❑ Telephone: (517) 356-2202, **www.oweb.com/upnorth/museum**
- ❑ Hours: Tuesday - Saturday, 10:00 am - 5:00 pm, Sunday, Noon - 5:00 pm.
- ❑ Admission: Adults $2.00, Seniors $1.00, Children $1.00 (5-17), Family $5.00. Kids age 5 and under are Free.
- ❑ Miscellaneous: Planetarium $1.00 extra. Planetarium programs are Sunday, 1:00 pm & 3:00 pm - year round. Programs are also shown in July and August at 7:30 p.m. on Thursdays. (Under age 5 not admitted to Planetarium)

Mostly local history with a re-created 1800's street of shops and cabins. If you come during a festival or special event weekend, make sure you see the display on the role of concrete in the area. The concrete block-making machine was perfected here in a land rich with limestone. Other permanent exhibits include: Gallery of Man, Lumbering and Farming, a Focult Pendulum, Area Fossils and Restored Historic Buildings.

CLEAR LAKE STATE PARK

Atlanta - 20500 M-33, 49709. *Activity:* Outdoors. (517) 785-4388. **www.dnr.state.mi.us/www/parks/clearlk.htm**. *Admission:* $4.00 per vehicle. Camping, hiking, boating, fishing, swimming, and winter sports.

WILDERNESS STATE PARK

Carp Lake - 898 Wilderness Park Drive (west of Mackinaw City by CR-81), 49718. *Activity:* Outdoors. *Admission:* $4.00 per vehicle. **www.dnr.state.mi.us/www/parks/wilderne.htm**. (231) 436-5381. Rough campsites and cabins. Hiking, boating, fishing, swimming, and bicycle trails.

ALOHA STATE PARK

Cheboygan - 4347 Third Street, (M-33 South), 49721. *Activity:* Outdoors. **www.dnr.state.mi.us/www/parks/aloha.htm**. (231) 625-2522. *Admission:* $4.00 per vehicle. The largest freshwater lake in Michigan is here along with activities such as camping/cabins, boating, fishing, and swimming.

CHEBOYGAN COUNTY HISTORICAL MUSEUM

Cheboygan - 404 South Huron Street, 49721. *Activity:* Museums. (231) 627-9597. *Admission:* Adults $2.00 (18+). High school age and under are admitted free. The county sheriff used to call this place home from 1882 - 1969 - it even was the area jail complete with 8 cells. Today, these cells have become exhibit areas featuring local history including: lumbering, farming, and lifestyle. See a recreated late 1800's "parlor room", bedrooms, and even a schoolroom.

CHEBOYGAN STATE PARK

Cheboygan - 4490 Beach Road, 49721. Activity: Outdoors. (231) 627-2811. **www.dnr.state.mi.us/www/parks/cheyboy.htm**. *Admission:* $4.00 per vehicle. One of the main highlights of the park is the Cheboygan Point Light. Camping/cabins, fishing, hiking, swimming and winter sports.

COAST GUARD "MACKINAW" TOURS

Cheboygan - Coast Guard Drive (M-27 to US-23 South, across bridge), 49721. *Activity:* Tours. (231) 627-7183. **www.continuouswave.com/boats/mackinaw**. Home port of Mackinaw along the Cheboygan River. The boat is not always in port (it visits around the Great Lakes). If in port, hop aboard and take a look around. Free admission.

LEGS INN

Cross Village - M-119 (US-31 to Carp Lake Village to Gill Road west through Bliss Township to Cross Village), 49723. *Activity:* Theme Restaurants. (231) 526-2281. *Hours:* Daily, Lunch and Dinner. (Mid-May to Mid-October). Included on the State Historic Register, this restaurant's roof line is ornamented with inverted cast-iron stove legs. The original Polish owner, Stanley Smolak, was also inducted into the Ottawa Indians tribe locally. His sculptures and whimsy decorating using tree trunks will intrigue you. Indoor/Outdoor dining plus no A/C. Casual dress. Moderate prices. Children's Menu.

CORSAIR SKI AREA

East Tawas - 218 West Bay Street, 48730. *Activity:* Outdoors. **www.skinordic.org/corsairski**.. (517) 362-2001 or (800) 55-TAWAS. *Admission:* Donation to pay for trail grooming. A cross country ski area with over 35 miles of groomed trails. All skill levels. Rentals are available in town. Great picnic area and hiking in summer and fall. Help your kids try their luck at trout fishing in the Silver Creek.

TAWAS POINT STATE PARK

East Tawas - 686 Tawas Beach Road (3 miles east of town off US- 23), 48730. **www.dnr.state.mi.us/www/parks/tawaspt1.htm**. *Activity:* Outdoors. (517) 362-5041. *Admission:* $4.00 per vehicle. Check out the 1876, 70 foot lighthouse open weekends and still working. Cabins and campsites, beach, birding (best in May), nature trails, boating and fishing are there too.

MICHIGAN AUSABLE VALLEY RAILROAD

230 South Abbe Road (off M-33, 3.5 miles south of the blinker light in town), **Fairview** 48621

❑   Activity: Tours
❑   Telephone: (517) 848-2229
   www.oscodacounty.com/train_ride.htm

❑   Hours: Weekends and Holidays 10:00 am - 5:00 pm. (Memorial
     Day - Labor Day)
❑   Admission: $3.00 (ages over 2).
❑   Tour: 1 and ½ mile trip is approximately 18 minutes long. Perfect
     for smaller kids.
❑   Miscellaneous: Quaint depot and gift shop where you can
     purchase tickets and fresh, hot popcorn.

This ¼ scale train offers visitors a calm, scenic tour which
travels through a jackpine forest (Huron National Forest) and
overlooks the Comins Creek Valley. You'll get to pass through a
115 foot wooden tunnel and over two wooden trestles (one of them
is 220 feet long). Some passengers get a glimpse of wildlife such
as deer, hawks, heron, beaver and maybe even elk or bear!

CALL OF THE WILD MUSEUM
850 South Wisconsin Avenue (east on Main Street, then south on
Wisconsin), **Gaylord** 49735

❑   Activity: Museums
❑   Telephone: (517) 732-4336 or (800) 835-4347
❑   Hours: 8:30 am - 9:00 pm. (mid-June - Labor Day), 9:30 am -
     6:00 pm. (Rest of year)
❑   Admission: Adults $5.00, Seniors $4.50, Children $3.00
❑   Miscellaneous: Also at location are Bavarian Falls Adventure
     Golf, Go Carts, Krazy Kars Tot Ride, and Gift Shop.

The museum is full of dioramas of over 60 North American
Animals in natural settings. As you look over displays of elk,
moose, black bear, timber wolves, etc., you'll learn about their
behavior and habitat and sounds. The Michigan History area has
stories recounted by an early fur trapper named Joseph. The Four
Seasons Display of Michigan changes as you watch. They've got
an observation beehive there too.

OSTEGO LAKE STATE PARK

Gaylord - 7136 Old 27 South (off I-75 south), 49735. *Activity:* Outdoors. **www.dnr.state.mi.us/www/parks/otsegolk.htm**. (517) 732-5485. *Admission:* $4.00 per vehicle. Camping/cabins, boating, fishing, swimming.

THE BOTTLE CAP MUSEUM

Gaylord - 4977 Sparr Road (5 miles east of Gaylord on F-44, next to Sparr Mall), 49735. *Activity:* Museums. (517) 732-1931. *Hours:* Wednesday - Saturday, 11:00 am - 5:00 pm. *Admission:* Adults $2.50, Seniors $2.00, Children $1.50 (ages 6-12). Plus you receive a free Coke and a season pass to the Museum. Bill Hicks personal huge collection of Coca-Cola memorabilia including hundreds of novelty items, 1930-1970 dispensers and coolers, signs and posters and vintage bottles. Be sure to peek in the Coca-Cola Christmas Room and Bathroom.

CRAWFORD COUNTY HISTORIC MUSEUM

Grayling - 97 Michigan Avenue (west end), 49738. *Activity:* Michigan History. (517) 348-4461. *Hours:* Monday - Saturday, 10:00 am - 4:00 pm. (Summer). *Admission:* $2.00 (ages 12 and up). Located in the former Michigan Central Depot, the museum details local history from Camp Grayling military history to lumbering and fire fighting. The museum also has a railroad caboose, a farm shed, a trapper's cabin and a display dedicated to the greatest archer of all time - Fred Bear. Audio visual tapes of some of the area's old-timers telling family histories and stories of the early days.

GRAYLING FISH HATCHERY

North Down River Road (I-75 to exit 254)

Grayling 49738

❑   Activity: Animals & Farms
❑   Telephone: (517) 348-9266, **www.hansonhills.org/hhfish.html**

❑   Hours: Daily, 10:00 am - 6:00 pm (Memorial Day - Labor Day)
❑   Admission: Adults $1.50, Children $1.00 (6-17), Family $6.00

It's always fun to watch kid's eyes light up at a "fish farm". See
11 ponds that contain more than 40,000 trout. See fish ranging
from tiny aquarium size (2 inches long) to several pounds (28
inches long), and yes, you can even buy some to take home (priced
by the inch). Fish food is available from dispensers for a nominal
fee and is a great way to really bring the fish to life.

HARTWICK PINES STATE PARK
4216 Ranger Road (I-75 exit 259 - on M-93)

Grayling 49738

❑   Activity: Outdoors
❑   Telephone: (800) 44-PARKS or (517) 348-7068
     www.dnr.state.mi.us/www/parks/hartp.htm
❑   Hours: 8:00 am - 10:00 pm. Museum buildings 9:00 am - 7:00
     pm (Summer). Open until only 4:00 pm and closed Mondays the
     rest of the year. Logging Museum is closed November - April.
❑   Admission: $4.00 per vehicle
❑   Miscellaneous: Bike trails, Braille trails, hiking, camping,
     fishing, picnic areas, winter sports, small gift shop. Summers-
     living history programs along the Forest Trail.

Some call it an "outdoor cathedral of nature", walking along the
Old Growth Forest Foot Trail as it winds through the forest
behind the Visitor Center. Along the 1 and ¼ mile long trail, you
can stop (1/4 mile from Visitor Center) at the Logging Museum
(open May-October only). Depending on the event, you'll see
logging wheels, and other logging equipment, and a steam sawmill
plus logger's quarters in place or in use. Be sure to stop in the
Michigan Forest Visitor Center before your walk out into the
pines. The history of logging- both past cut and run phases - and
the modern conservation forestry. The nine slide projector
audiovisual show gives you a great overview and details recent
statistics, such as : there is more paper recycled than trees cut
down presently. Find hands-on exhibits on computer (Forest

Management Simulation), dioramas (Reading the Rings, Sounds of Birds), and the talking "Living Tree" or talking Loggers and Rivermen displays.

SKYLINE SKI AREA

Grayling - 4020 Skyline Road (I-75 to exit 251), 49738. *Activity:* Outdoors. (517) 275-5445. *Hours:* Thursday, 4:30 - 9:00 pm. Friday - Monday, 10:00 am - 9:00 pm. 14 runs. Rentals, lessons and ski shop.

STEVENS FAMILY CIRCLE

Grayling - 231 North Michigan Avenue, 49738. *Activity:* Theme Restaurants. (517) 348-2111. *Hours:* Monday - Saturday, 8:00 am - 11:00 pm. Crank up the '50's tunes and step into a wonderful (both food and prices) family dining experience. Introduce your kids to the old-fashioned soda fountain that dispenses "phosphates" as they were called. Friendly folks make you feel like a "local". Lots of '50's and '60's stuff to entertain you while you wait for your meal.

HARRISVILLE STATE PARK

Harrisville - 248 State Park Road (US-23 South of M-72), 48740. *Activity:* Outdoors. (517) 724-5126. *Admission:* $4.00 per vehicle. **www.dnr.state.mi.us/www/parks/harrisvi.htm**. Over ½ mile of Lake Huron frontage with Camping/cabins, hiking, boating, fishing, swimming, bicycle trails, and winter sports.

NEGWEGON STATE PARK

Harrisville - 248 State Park Road, 48740. *Activity:* Outdoors. (517) 739-9730. A rustic, undeveloped area for hiking. No camping. No services.

BURT LAKE STATE PARK

Indian River - 6635 State Park Drive (I-75 exit 310 west to M-68 to Old US-27), 49749. Activity: Outdoors. (231) 238-9392. **www.dnr.state.mi.us/www/parks/burtlake.htm**. Admission: $4.00 per vehicle. Great beaches on the state's third largest lake, the park has numerous campsites and cabins, boating and rentals, fishing, swimming, and winter sports.

BUTTERFLY HOUSE

Mackinac Island - 1308 McGulpin Street (Huron Street north to Church Street west to McGulpin), 49757. *Activity:* Animals & Farms. (906) 847-3972. **www.mackinac.com/butterflyhouse**. *Hours:* 10:00 am - 7:00 pm, (Summers), Daily, 10:00 am - 6:00 pm (Labor Day - October). *Admission:* Adults $4.00, Children $2.00 (ages 6-12). See several hundred live butterflies from Asia, Central and South America and the United States in free flight. A great setting of tropical gardens. One of America's first butterfly houses featured in popular magazines.

FORT MACKINAC STATE PARK

(on the bluff above downtown Mackinac Island)

Mackinac Island 49757

❑   Activity: Michigan History

❑   Telephone: (906) 847-3328, **www.mackinacisland.com**

❑   Hours: Daily, 9:30 am - 6:30 pm (Mid-June to Mid August). Hours vary mid-April to mid-June and mid-August to early October but usually at least 10:00 am - 4:00 pm.

❑   Miscellaneous: Food available at Tea Room (lunch). Combo admission with Colonial Mackinac and Mill Creek sites available for discount. Summers- costumed interpreters. Beaumont Memorial (dedicated to the studies of human digestion), Blacksmith, Biddle House (crafts), McGulpin House, Indian Dorm are off premises but part of package fee in the summer.

Your carriage is greeted by a period dressed soldier inviting strangers to visit. Children and families will want to see the short audio visual presentation in the Post Commissary Theater. It's quick and simple but enough to "pull you in". Next, if it's close to the top of the hour, be sure to check out the kid-friendly, wonderfully amusing, cannon firing and rifle firing demonstrations. Maybe volunteer to help the soldiers (check out the funny, pointed hats). The Post Hospital and Officer's Quarters and Blockhouses will intrigue the kids. On your way in or out of the complex, be sure to visit the Soldier's Barracks exhibits featuring Mackinac: An Island Famous in These Regions". The Children's Discovery areas include: Mackinac island history from Furs (touch some) to Fish (step on a dock and listen to the fishermen come into port) to No Cars (1898 law) to Fudge! Oh yea, check and see if your ancestor was a Victorian soldier at Fort Mackinac.

MACKINAC ISLAND HORSE-DRAWN CARRIAGE TOURS

(Across from Arnold Ferry Dock - Downtown)

Mackinac Island 49757

- ❑ Activity: Tours
- ❑ Telephone: (906) 847-3307, **www.mict.com**
- ❑ Hours: Daily, 8:30 am - 5:00 pm (Mid - June - Labor Day).
  Daily, 8:30 am - 4:00 pm (Mid-May to Mid-June and Labor Day to Mid-October)
- ❑ Admission: Adults $13.50, children $6.50 (4-11).
- ❑ Tours: 1 hour & 45 minutes. You also have on/off privileges at several "hot spots".
- ❑ Miscellaneous: Since Motor vehicles aren't permitted on the Island, this is one fun way to leisurely see the sites. It keeps the island quaint to have the clip-clop sound of carriages - we think you'll agree!

It's guaranteed you'll hear amusing stories of the history (past & present) of the island. The multi-seated carriages stop at all of these highlights: Arch Rock (which story of formation do you believe?), Skull Cave, the Governor's Mansion, Grand Hotel (majestic, regal inn. Admission is $10.00/person just to walk around in the afternoon. Maybe stay for Lunch or High Tea), Fort Mackinac, Surrey Hill shops and snacks, and the horse's stable area. Look for several "parking lots" full of bikes and carriages! We recommend this tour on your first trip to the Island.

COLONIAL MICHILIMACKINAC STATE HISTORIC PARK

102 Straits Avenue (Downtown under the south side of Mackinac Bridge - Exit 339 off I-75), **Mackinaw City** 49701

❑   Activity: Michigan History
❑   Telephone: (231) 436-5563
     www.mackinacisland.com/historicparks/Michilimackinac/ index.html
❑   Hours: Daily, 9:00 am - 6:00 pm (Mid-June to Mid August).
     Hours vary Mid-April to Mid-June and Mid-August to Early
     October but usually at least 10:00 am - 4:00 pm.
❑   Admission: Adults $7.50, Children $4.50 (6-12), Family $22.00
❑   Miscellaneous: Combo tickets for Fort Mac, Colonial Michi and
     Mill Creek are available at great discounts. Many festivals are
     held here including encampments and Colonial weddings.

In the Summer, costumed docents (in character) demonstrate musket /cannon firing, cooking, blacksmithing, barracks living, church life, and trading. Originally occupied by the French, then the British - an audiovisual program will explain the details. Archeological digs are held in the summer to find ongoing significant finds. Be sure to check out the updated "Treasure From the Sand" exhibit as it takes you to a unique underground tunnel display of subterranean artifacts recovered. Meet Rebecca de Peyster (community's first lady) or Major Robert Rogers (leader of famed Roger's Rangers).

HISTORIC MILL CREEK

South US-23

Mackinaw City 49701

- ❏ Activity: Michigan History
- ❏ Telephone: (231) 436-7301
  www.mackinac.com/historicparks/MillCreek/index.html
- ❏ Hours: Daily, 9.00 am - 6.00 pm (Mid-June to Mid-August). (Mid-May to Mid-June) & (Labor Day to Mid-October) hours vary.
- ❏ Admission: Adults $6.50, Children $3.75 (6-12), Family $18.00
- ❏ Miscellaneous: Cook house Snack Pavilion. Museum Store.

As you walk along wooden planked paths, notice the different tree names - Thistleberry, Ironwood, etc. You'll have an opportunity to see a replica 18th century industrial complex - the oldest sawmill yard to provide finished lumber - in the Great Lakes Region. Water-powered sawmill demos are given daily (Summers -lumberjack demos). There's also a reconstructed millwrights house on site along with a museum. The audiovisual orientation is only 12 minutes long and is a great way to understand Michigan lumber history. Did you know a local teacher discovered this site, accidentally, in 1972? Learn the Mystery of the Mill!

MACKINAC BRIDGE MUSEUM AND "MIGHTY MAC" BRIDGE

231 East Central Avenue (Downtown within view of bridge)

Mackinaw City 49701

- ❏ Activity: Museums
- ❏ Telephone: (231) 436-5534, **www.mackinacbridge.org**
- ❏ Hours: Daily, 10:00 am - 9:00 pm (May - October)
- ❏ Admission: Free
- ❏ Miscellaneous: Located at Mama Mia's Pizza (museum is upstairs).

W atch the all new digitally re-mastered movie covering the history and construction of the Mackinac Bridge back in the mid-1950's. Why build the longest bridge ever - the "bridge that couldn't be built"? When you see the black & white photos of the long lines, staging cars to get on ferry boats to cross over the lake to the Upper Peninsula, you'll see the reason. On display are the original spinning wheels that spun and ran cable (41,000 miles of it!) across the bridge; the original wrench (9-10 feet long) used to tighten anchor bolts on the towers; and most interesting, the hard hats of the numerous iron workers hanging from the ceiling. Now, pay the $1.50 toll and cross the 5 mile long steel super-structure! P.S. On a windy day the bridge bows or swings out to the east or west as much as 20 feet!

MACKINAW CITY TRANSPORTATION TOURS

(Stops/Dock Pickups are clearly marked)

Mackinaw City 49701

❑   Activity: Tours
❑   **www.mackinawcity.com**

Call for season schedules. Rain or shine. Admissions vary. (early May - mid to late October)

❑   MACKINAW TROLLEY COMPANY. (231) 436-7812. Age 5+ $3.50 all day/ $1 boarding. Historic tours once or twice, daily.
❑   ARNOLD LINE FERRY. (800) 542-8528. Smooth trips, large ships, comfortable seats and cabins. Restrooms. *
❑   SHEPLER'S FERRY. (800) 828-6157. Fast 16 minute trips. Restrooms. *
❑   STAR LINE FERRY. (800) 638-9892. Newest fleet. Most scheduled daily departures. Restrooms. *
•   * Budget $7+ for kids (age 5-12). $14+ for adults. (RT)

ONAWAY STATE PARK

Onaway - 3622 North M-211, 49765. *Activity:* Outdoors. (517) 733-8279. **www.dnr.state.mi.us/www/parks/onaway.htm**. *Admission:* $4.00 per vehicle. Known for game fishing, they also have camping, hiking trails, boating, fishing and swimming.

AU SABLE RIVER QUEEN

West River Road (6 Miles West Of Oscoda)

Oscoda 48750

- ❑ Activity: Tours
- ❑ (517) 739-7351 or (517) 728-3775, **www.oscoda.net/arq**
- ❑ Hours: Departs once or twice daily. Call ahead or visit website for times. (Memorial Day weekend - 3rd weekend in October)
- ❑ Admission: Adults $9.50 (13+). Seniors $7.65 (60+), Children $4.50 (5-12). Prices can be slightly higher for fall color tours.
- ❑ Miscellaneous: Snack Bar on boat.

An authentic paddle wheel boat that has been touring this section of the river for over 40 years hosts you for a relaxing and narrated 19 mile trip. "Captain Bill" teaches about the area's history and wildlife along the journey. Glass enclosed decks are also available.

IARGO SPRINGS

Oscoda - (Au Sable River Road Scenic Byway), 48750. *Activity:* Outdoors. (800) 235-4625. *Hours:* Daily, year-round. Free admission. What once was a spot for tribal ceremonies (the Chippewas believed that the spring had medicinal qualities), today is a great place to take the family into nature. Be sure to tell your kids not use up too much energy as you descend the 294 steps down the banks to the spring (don't worry, there are benches to rest on the way back up!). A new nature boardwalk (with a 30' tall observation deck) and interpretive center were added recently.

DINOSAUR GARDENS PREHISTORIC ZOO

11160 US 23 South

Ossineke 49766

❑   Activity: Amusements
❑   Telephone: (517) 471-5477
❑   Hours: Daily, 10:00 am - 6:00 pm (mid-May to mid-October)
❑   Admission: Adults $5.00 (13+), Youth $4.00 (6-12), $3.00 (age 5 and under)
❑   Miscellaneous: Miniature golf. Snack bar.

An 80 foot long, 60,000 pound Brontosaurus is one of the many thrills that awaits your kids at this unique family tradition. Original owner Paul Domke spent some 38 years creating and sculpting 26 full scale dinosaurs that are "exploring" the forest of trees inside this attraction. A monstrous T-Rex in one exhibit is battling a Triceratops. Storyboards and sound effects accompany each exhibit to help bring them to life. This is a great way to see the size and scale of the creatures that once walked the earth. Neat gift shop full of dinosaur souvenirs.

PRESQUE ISLE LIGHTHOUSE MUSEUMS

East Grand Lake Road (US 23 to CR638)

Presque Isle 49777

❑   Activity: Museums
❑   Telephone: (517) 595-2787
     http://nautical.rogerscity.com/presque.html
❑   Hours: Daily, 9:00 am - 5:00 pm. (mid-May to mid-October)
❑   Admission: Adults $2.00, Children $1.00 (6-12)
❑   Gifts shops at both locations.

OLD LIGHTHOUSE: Supposedly haunted old lighthouse and keepers' house full of artifacts. Built in 1840, you can visit with the "lightkeeper lady" inside the keeper's cottage (so-o cute!). Kids can make noise blowing a foghorn or ringing a giant bell (*or as George called it when he visited with his family when he was 2* *years old... the Bongy Bell!).* Any age can climb the minimal 33 stairs to the top of the lighthouse for a great view.

NEW LIGHTHOUSE: A lightkeepers' quarters and a larger, more classical lighthouse. It's a challenge to climb the some odd 193 steps - but what a rush!

HOEFT STATE PARK

Rogers City - US-23 North, 49779. *Activity:* Outdoors. (517) 734-2543. **www.dnr.state.mi.us/www/parks/hoeft.htm**. *Admission:* $4.00 per vehicle. Huron dunes. Camping/cabins, hiking trails, fishing, swimming, boating and winter sports.

PRESQUE ISLE COUNTY HISTORICAL MUSEUM

Rogers City - 176 Michigan Street, 49779. *Activity:* Michigan History. (517) 734-4121 or (517) 734-2038. *Hours:* Weekdays, Noon - 4:00 pm. (June - October). Also Saturdays, (July - August). *Admission:* Donations. The restored Bradley House contains exhibits based on local history. In various theme rooms on three floors, see a re-created general store or Victorian parlor. Displays include marine, lumbering and American Indian artifacts.

THOMPSON'S HARBOR STATE PARK

Rogers City - US-23 North, 49779. *Activity:* Outdoors. (517) 734-2543. For the rugged outdoorsman in the family, explore over 6 miles of trails in an area that is located on the Lake Huron shoreline. Adjacent to the Presque Isle harbor. Park roads are undeveloped; call ahead for driving conditions. No camping. No service.

NORTH HIGGINS LAKE STATE PARK

11252 North Higgins Lake Drive (I-75 or US-27 exits - 7 miles west of town via US-27 and Military Road), **Roscommon** 48653

❑   Activity: Outdoors
❑   Telephone: (517) 821-6125 or (517) 373-3559 (CCC Museum)
     www.dnr.state.mi.us/www/parks/nhiggs.htm
❑   Hours: Park open dawn to dusk. Museum open 11:00 am - 4:00 pm. (Summer)
❑   Admission: $4.00 per vehicle

Over 400 acres available for camping/cabins, picnicking, hiking, boating, fishing, swimming, and winter sports. Most people find the Civilian Conservation Corps Museum is the reason for their trip here. During the Great Depression, many men without work were enrolled to perform conservation and reforestation projects throughout Michigan. CCC planted trees, taught and practiced fire fighting, constructed trails, built bridges and even built buildings (some are still standing). Housed in replica barracks, the museum has displays of highlights and techniques of their work. Interpretive, outside walks are available too.

SOUTH HIGGINS LAKE STATE PARK

Roscommon - 106 State Park Drive (I-75 at Roscommon Road south), 48653. *Activity:* Outdoors. (517) 821-6374. **www.dnr.state.mi.us/www/parks/plnm.htm#shiggins**. *Admission:* $4.00 per vehicle. Voted some of the most beautiful lakes in the world, this park caters to families. The beaches are family-friendly and there's plenty of camping sites. Boating and rentals, hiking trails, fishing, and winter sports are there too. For information on Canoe trip rentals call (517) 275-8760.

RIFLE RIVER RECREATION AREA

Rose City - (off M-33 southeast), 48654. *Activity:* Outdoors. (517) 473-2258. **www.dnr.state.mi.us/www/parks/rifle-ri.htm**. *Admission:* $4.00 per vehicle. Camping/cabins, hiking trails, boating, fishing, swimming and winter sports.

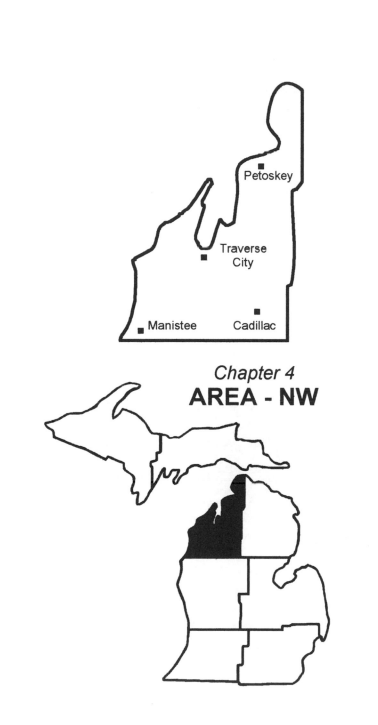

Petoskey

Traverse
City

Manistee   Cadillac

Chapter 4
AREA - NW

Our Favorites...

- Kilwin's Candy Kitchens
- Huron-Manistee National Forest
- Petosky State Park
- Sleeping Bear Dunes
- Beaver Island

SHANTY CREEK RESORT

Bellaire - One Shanty Creek Road (off M-88), 49615. *Activity:* Outdoors. **www.shantycreek.com**. (800) 678-4111 or (231) 533-8621. *Hours:* Resort is open year-round. Summer is golf, Winter is skiing. Great children's ski school. Babysitting is available. A resort that features 41 runs, ski lessons, and equipment rentals. Accommodations include a new slopeside hotel. An Arnold Palmer designed golf course awaits your golfing skills in the summer.

PLATTE RIVER STATE FISH HATCHERY

Beulah - 15120 US-31, 49617. *Activity:* Outdoors. (231) 325-4611. **www.dnr.state.mi.us/www/fish/html/platte_river.html**. *Hours:* Daily, 8:00 am - 4:00 pm. (year-round). Free self-guided tours. Fish hatcheries are always a family favorite. Best time to visit is in the fall when thousands of salmon can be seen.

BOYNE MOUNTAIN

Boyne Falls - (off US-131), 49713. *Activity:* Outdoors. (800) 462-6963 or (231) 549-2441. **www.boynecountry.com**. *Hours:* Resort is open year-round. Summer is golf, Winter is skiing. One of the Lower Peninsula's finest resorts, Boyne Mountain 40+ runs, many new trails, rentals, ski lessons, outdoor pool and slopeside lodging. A children's ski program and baby sitting are also available.

HURON-MANISTEE NATIONAL FORESTS

1755 South Mitchell Street (over 960,000 acres in the northern part of the Lower Peninsula), **Cadillac** 49601

- ❑ Activity: Outdoors
- ❑ Telephone: (800) 821-6263
  www.fs.fed.us/r9/hmnf/hmindex.htm
- ❑ Hours: Open 24 hours daily.
- ❑ Admission: $3.00 per carload per day.

Popular activities here are swimming in lakes Huron and
Michigan, cross-country skiing, snowmobiling, trout fishing,
modern and rough camping, boating and bicycle trails. Popular
spots within the forests are:

- ❑ THE NORDHOUSE DUNES - one mile of undeveloped
  shoreline along Lake Michigan.
- ❑ THE LODA LAKE WILDFLOWER SANCTUARY - one mile
  trail through marsh, forest and orchards. Over 40 miles of trails
  for hiking along the Manistee River.
- ❑ THE RIVER ROAD SCENIC BYWAY - runs 22 miles along
  the south bank of the Au Sable River. View reservoirs, bald
  eagles, salmon, the Canoeists Memorial and the Lumberman's
  Memorial and Visitors Center of logging.
- ❑ TUTTLE MARSH WILDLIFE AREA - Managed 5000 acres of
  fox, deer, coyote, muskrat, beaver, otter and weasel.

MITCHELL STATE PARK

6093 East M-115

Cadillac 49601

- ❑ Activity: Outdoors
- ❑ Telephone: (231) 775-7911
  www.dnr.state.mi.us/www/parks/plnm.htm#mitchell
- ❑ Admission: $4.00 per vehicle
- ❑ Miscellaneous: Camping and cabins, boating and rentals, fishing,
  swimming, and winter sports.

The Visitor's Center is also called the Carl T. Johnson Hunting
& Fishing Center & Heritage & Fisheries & Wildlife. Exhibits
include stuffed wildlife, a wall-length aquarium, and trapping and
conservation efforts. Many come here for the birding too. You may
see great blue heron, yellow finches and mallards. Center open
summers Tuesday - Sunday, 10:00 am - 8:00 pm. Weekends only
the rest of the year.

WEXFORD COUNTY HISTORICAL MUSEUM

Cadillac - 127 Beech Street (Carnegie Library), 49601. *Activity:* Michigan History. (231) 775-1717. Donations accepted. Exhibits include an early home interior, a post office, a general store, early fire equipment, railroad memorabilia, and items from the lumbering era. The building was originally the Cadillac Library.

SUGAR LOAF RESORT

Cedar - 4500 Sugar Loaf Mountain Road (off M-72), 49621. *Activity:* Outdoors. **www.theloaf.com**. (800) 952-6390 or (231) 228-1553. *Hours:* Resort is open year-round, but skiing is usually from December - March. Golf in summer. 20 runs, an excellent kids' ski schools (toddlers and up), rentals, lessons, outdoor and indoor pools, and a restaurant.

BEAVER ISLAND BOAT COMPANY

Charlevoix - 103 Bridge Park Drive, 49720. *Activity:* Tours. (231) 547-2311 or (888) 446-4095. *Admission:* Adults $31.00, Children $15.50 (5-12). Rates are roundtrip. Vehicle transport also available. Passenger and Car Ferry service from Charlevoix to Beaver Island, the Great Lakes' most remote inhabited island. Packages include round trip cruises and possible escorted island tours of museums and island lunches. Call for schedule and information.

FISHERMAN'S ISLAND STATE PARK

Charlevoix - Bells Bay Road (off US-31 southwest), 49720. *Activity:* Outdoors. **www.dnr.state.mi.us/www/parks/fish-is.htm** (231) 547-6641. *Admission:* $4.00 per vehicle. Camping, hiking, fishing, swimming and bicycle trails.

YOUNG STATE PARK

Charlevoix - 2280 Boyne City Road (US-131, west on M-75), 49720. **www.dnr.state.mi.us/www/parks/young.htm**. *Activity:* Outdoors. (231) 547-6641. *Admission:* $4.00 per vehicle. Camping, hiking, boating and rentals, fishing, swimming and winter sports.

SLEEPING BEAR DUNES NATIONAL LAKESHORE

9922 Front Street (M-72) (35 miles along northwest Lower Peninsula shores), **Empire** 49630

❑   Activity: Outdoors
❑   Telephone: (231) 326-5134, **www.nps.gov/slbe**
❑   Hours: (Visitor's Center) Daily, 9:00 am - 6:00 pm (Summer). Daily, 9:00 am - 4:00 pm (rest of year)
❑   Admission: $7.00 per week.
❑   Miscellaneous: Visitor's Center in Empire has nice slide show to understand area better.

The name of the shore comes from Chippewa Indian stories of a mom and her two bear cubs separated by a forest fire. The cubs now stand for the North and South Manitou Islands - still stranded. Among the dunes are rugged bluffs, ghost forests, and exposed bleached trees. Mid-May to Mid-October take the Pierce Stocking Scenic Drive route to view the dunes. On South Manitou Island climb the 100 foot lighthouse or view the wreck of a freighter or the Valley of Giants (white cedar trees). The islands are accessible by ferry from Leland. The Maritime Museum at the Coast Guard Station in Glen Haven displays maritime area history and is open summers only. Fishing, canoeing, hiking and cross-country skiing are favorite activities here.

BOYNE HIGHLANDS

Harbor Springs - 600 Highlands Drive, 49740. *Activity:* Outdoors **www.boynehighlands.com**. (800) GO-BOYNE or (231) 526-3000. Besides great family skiing (on your choice of 44 slopes), this resort offer a large heated outdoor pool that is warm even when the outside temperature is below zero! (*how... do they do that?*). Babysitting, rentals, slopeside lodging, children's activities and lessons are also available.

NUB'S NOB

Harbor Springs - 500 Nub's Nob Road, 49740. *Activity:* Outdoors (800) SKI-NUBS or (231) 526-2131. Across the street from Boyne Highlands (see listing), Nub's Nob offers 41 runs, rentals, instructions, and children's activities. Also, for the beginners, be sure to check out the Midwest's only Free LEARN-TO-SKI AREA (all ages) complete with its own chairlift.

FUN COUNTRY WATER PARK

Interlochen - 9320 US-31 South (US-31 & M-137), 49643. *Activity:* Amusements. (231) 276-6360. *Hours:* Daily, 11:00 am - 11:00 pm. Water slide closes at 6:30 pm. (Memorial Day - Labor Day). *Admission:* General $12.00 (4+), $6.00 (ages 3 and under). Two water slides over 300 feet long assures a day of summer fun. Also bumper boats, a carrousel, go-carts, and miniature golf.

INTERLOCHEN STATE PARK

Interlochen - M-137 (South of US-31), 49643. *Activity:* Outdoors. (231) 276-9511. **www.dnr.state.mi.us/www/parks/interloc.htm**. *Admission:* $4.00 per vehicle. Camping on the beach of the lake with bathhouses and boat rentals is popular especially in the summer. Summer Music Camp Shows. Hiking trails, fishing, boating, bicycle trails, and winter sports are available.

LAKE MICHIGAN RECREATION AREA

Manistee - (West of US-31 - South of M-55), 49660. *Activity:* Outdoors. (231) 723-2211. *Hours:* Daylight, (April - October 1). Free admission. $10.00 per night to camp. Bordering the Nordhouse Dunes Wilderness Area, this recreation area offers 90 campsites, great hiking and bike trails, a playground with picnic area, and a beach on Lake Michigan.

MANISTEE COUNTY MUSEUM

Manistee - 425 River Street (Lyman Building), 49660. *Activity:* Michigan History. **www.manistee.com/~edo/historicalsites.htm** (231) 723-5531. Open year-round. The museum features the Lyman Drugstore, period rooms, and is mostly Victorian in furnishings. Other buildings in town connected historically are: The Babcock House Museum, Our Savior Church, and The Waterworks Museum (logging, marine exhibits).

ORCHARD BEACH STATE PARK

Manistee - 2064 Lakeshore Road, 49660. *Activity:* Outdoors. (231) 723-7422. **www.dnr.state.mi.us/www/parks/orchard.htm**. *Admission:* $4.00 per vehicle. Lots of reasonable camp site rentals on the dunes, great beaches with swimming, hiking trails.

SCHOOLHOUSE CAFÉ

Maple City - 172 West Burkickville Road, 49664. *Activity:* Theme Restaurants. (231) 228-4688. *Hours:* Lunch and Dinner Daily, Tuesday - Sunday. An actual schoolhouse restored serving American food. Pictures from the actual classrooms adorn the walls. Moderate pricing. Children's menu.

LEELANAU STATE PARK

Northport - 15310 North Lighthouse Point Road (off M-201), 49670. **www.dnr.state.mi.us/www/parks/leelanau.htm**. *Activity:* Outdoors. (231) 386-5422 . *Admission:* $4.00 per vehicle. Grand

Traverse Lighthouse tours along coastal dunes are a big draw. Camping/cabins, hiking trails, fishing, swimming and winter sports.

KILWIN'S CANDY KITCHENS

355 North Division Street

Petoskey 49770

- ❑ Activity: Tours
- ❑ Telephone: (231) 347-3800, **www.kilwins.com**
- ❑ Hours: Monday - Friday, 9:00 am - 4:30 pm.
- ❑ Admission: Free
- ❑ Tours: Monday - Thursday, 10:30, 11:00 am, 2:00, 2:30 pm. 20 minutes (June - August)
- ❑ Miscellaneous: Retail store sells over 300 types of mouth-watering candy.

When first arriving, you'll probably park your car where the sign reads, "Chocolate Lovers Parking - All Others Will Be Towed". This is just the right kind of invitation to let you (and the kids) know that you are in for a real treat. Northern Michigan seems to have a real taste for fudge and candy and Kilwan's is one of the area's most respected candy-makers. Get "close to the action" on this tour and see all of the various production processes. The kids will love watching 2 workers stretching 3 foot slabs of peanut brittle!

LITTLE TRAVERSE HISTORICAL MUSEUM

Petoskey - 100 Depot Court (Waterfront at Bayfront Park), 49770. *Activity:* Museums. (231) 347-2620. *Hours:* Monday - Saturday, & Holidays, 10:00 am - 4:00 pm. (Summer). Tuesday - Saturday & Holidays, 10:00 am - 5:00 pm, Sunday 1:00 - 4:00 pm. (Day after Labor Day - December). *Admission:* Adults $1.00 (over 18). Housed in an old railroad depot, you'll find information about the area's Okawa Indians and pioneer times. Exhibits about Ernest Hemingway and Civil War author Bruce Catton.

PETOSKEY STATE PARK

Petoskey - 2475 M-119 (north of US-31), 49770. *Activity:* Outdoors. **www.dnr.state.mi.us/www/parks/petoskey.htm**. (231) 347-2311. *Admission:* $4.00 per vehicle. Campsites along Little Traverse Bay with a great beach and trails in and out of wooded dunes. There's well developed nature trails and in Spring, sort through Winter's debris for Petoskey stones (designated Michigan state stone). Look for the coral fossils in the stones and you've probably found one. Boating and winter sports are also available.

PIRATE'S COVE ADVENTURE GOLF

Petoskey - 1230 US-31 North (US-31 near M-119), 49770. *Activity:* Amusements. (231) 347-1123. **www.piratescove.net**. *Hours:* Daily, 9:30 am - 11:00 pm (May to mid-October). *Admission:* Adults $6.00, Children $5.50. Adventure Miniature golf in a fun-filled setting of lavish landscaping and delightful pirate themes. Putt your way over footbridges, under waterfalls, and through mountain caves.

CRYSTAL MOUNTAIN SKI AREA

Thompsonville - 12500 Crystal Mountain Drive (off M-115), 49683. *Activity:* Outdoors. (231) 378-2000 or (800) 968-4676. **www.crystalmtn.com**. *Hours:* Resort is open year-round. Skiing usually December - March. Golf in summer. Does your family want to discover the joys of skiing? Crystal Mountain is a "family-friendly" resort that offers 34 runs with a children's "learn to ski" program, indoor and outdoor pools, restaurant, and slopeside rooms.

TALL SHIPS "MALABAR" & "MANITOU"

Traverse City - 13390 SW Bay Shore Drive (Grand Traverse Bay - West arm), 46984. *Activity:* Tours. (231) 941-2000 or (800) 678-0383. **www.tallshipsailing.com**. *Admission:* Varies by length of "get-away". Call or visit website for sailing schedules and rates. (Summer). The Malabar (109') and Manitou (114') ships offer tours (90 minutes & up) and accommodations during the summer months. The sunset cruises can be breath-taking.

CLINCH PARK ZOO

Traverse City - Union & Grandview Parkway (Next to the beach), 49684. *Activity:* Outdoors. (231) 922-4904 **www.ci.traverse-city.mi.us/services/zoo.htm**. *Hours:* Daily, 9:30 am - 5:30 pm (Memorial Day - Labor Day). Daily, 10:00 am - 4:00 pm (Mid-April - Memorial Day & day after Labor Day - October). *Admission:* Adults $2.00, Children $1.50 (5-12), $0.50 (under 5). A smaller zoo that features wildlife that is native to Michigan. Picnic area and small train rides (Memorial Day - Labor Day).

PIRATE'S COVE ADVENTURE GOLF

1710 US-31 North

Traverse City 49684

❑ Activity: Amusements
❑ Telephone: (231) 938-9599, **www.piratescove.net**
❑ Hours: Daily, 11:00 am - 11:00 pm. (Memorial Day - Labor Day). Miniature golf is open until the season's first snowfall.
❑ Admission: Adults $6.00-9.50, Children $5.50-8.00. Rides use tokens which can be purchased 5/$5.00 - 25/$18.00

Adventure Miniature golf in a fun-filled setting of lavish landscaping and delightful pirate themes. Putt your way over footbridges, under waterfalls, and through mountain caves. Sharpen your putting skills on Blackbeard's Challenge Course, Captain Kidd's Adventure or The Original Course. A fun park for kids of all ages. Electric cars entertain the youngest kids while go-carts and waterslides (must be 42" tall to use) help keep the older kids entertained.

DENNOS MUSEUM CENTER

Traverse City - 1701 East Front Street (On campus of Northwest Michigan College), 49686. *Activity:* Museums. (231) 922-1055. **http://dmc.nmc.edu**. *Hours:* Monday - Saturday, 10:00 am - 5:00 pm, Sunday, 1:00 - 5:00 pm. *Admission:* Adults $4.00, Children $2.00 (under 18), Family $10.00. Exploring oriented art exhibits with themes like Discovery (hands-on art, science and high tech) and Inuit Eskimo Art.

OLD MISSION PENINSULA LIGHTHOUSE

Traverse City - (along M-37), 49686. *Activity:* Outdoors. View this 19th Century lighthouse and step back in time as your kids stand at the geographical point that is exactly halfway between the Equator and the North Pole.

SAND LAKES QUIET AREA

Traverse City - (M-72 to Broomhead Road - South), 49686. *Activity:* Outdoors. (231) 922-5280. *Hours:* Always open (year-round). Free admission. This adventurous place is so "quiet" (as the name implies) because all motor vehicles are banned from the 10 miles of trails that feature fishing and camping. Make your plans to hike in and camp and see how Michigan must have looked to the early pioneers and Native Americans. (Note: Trails are not stroller accessible).

TRAVERSE CITY STATE PARK

Traverse City - 1132 US-31 east, 49686. *Activity:* Outdoors. (231) 922-5270. **www.dnr.state.mi.us/www/parks/traverse.htm**. *Admission:* $4.00 per vehicle. Almost 350 campsites opposite Grand Traverse Bay with bridge to beach and close to attractions. Hiking trails, boating, fishing, swimming, and winter sports too.

YOGI BEAR'S JELLYSTONE PARK

Traverse City - 4050 Hammond Road, 49686. *Activity:* Outdoors. **www.michcampgrounds.com/yogibear**. (231) 947-2770 or (800) 909-BEAR. Family camping fun with 200+ campsites, pool with wading pool, children's activities, miniature golf.

Chapter 5
AREA - SE

Our Favorites...

- **Jiffy Mix Tour**
- **Henry Ford Museum, Greenfield Village & "Spirit of Ford"**
- **Diamond Jack's River Tours**
- **MSU's Children's Garden**
- **Marvin's Marvelous Mechanical Museum**
- **Michigan Historical Center**
- **Impression 5 Science Center**
- **Stagecoach Stop USA**

WILD SWAN THEATER

Ann Arbor - 416 West Huron Street, 48103. *Activity:* The Arts. (734) 995-0530. **http://comnet.org/wildswan**. A professional theater company that performs for family audiences using dance, masks, puppets and music.

ANN ARBOR HANDS-ON MUSEUM

220 East Ann Street (between 4th & 5th Avenue - Downtown)

Ann Arbor 48104

- ❑ Activity: Museums
- ❑ Telephone Number: (743) 995-5439, **www.aahom.org**
- ❑ Hours: Tuesday - Saturday, 10:00 am - 5:00 pm. Sunday, Noon - 5:00 pm.
- ❑ Admission: Adults $6.00, Children, Seniors, Students $4.00, Age 2 and under Free.
- ❑ Miscellaneous: Explore Store. Pre-school Gallery. "At Home" science projects featured each month on website.

Your kid's eyes will light up with amazement as you explore over 250 exhibits on 4 floors. Travelling exhibits (see website for complete details) feature such exhibits as "Clothing: Science from Head to Toe" that teaches kids about the clothes we wear and the materials they are made from. Watch your skeleton ride a bicycle as you explore human movement, play a song on a walk-on piano, see a working bee hive, watch a hot air balloon rise (with heat from a toaster), and whisper across the room to a friend (and they can hear you) are just a few of our favorites. (Remember Mom & Dad...you came for the children...but learning sure is fun!). Very well done boasting a great family educational and entertainment value.

ANN ARBOR YOUTH CHORALE

Ann Arbor - 1110 North Main Street, Suite 117, 48104. *Activity:* The Arts. (734) 996-4404. A children's (ages 9-16) choir comprised of 80 members from around the area. The kids come from different racial, economic, and religious backgrounds and perform various culturally diverse music. Local concerts are in the winter and spring. Admission.

YOUNG PEOPLE'S THEATER

Ann Arbor - 2301 Packard, 48104. *Activity:* The Arts. (734) 996-3888. Offers plays and musical productions for kids ages 5-18.

DOMINO'S FARMS
24 Frank Lloyd Wright / Earhart Road (East of US-22, exit 41)

Ann Arbor 48106

- ❑   Activity: Animals & Farms
- ❑   Telephone: (734) 930-5032
     www.dominos.com/jot/DominosFarms.cfm
- ❑   Hours: Monday - Friday, 9:30 am - 4:00 pm., Saturday & Sunday, 10:30 am - 5:00 pm. (April - October)
- ❑   Admission: Adults $3.00, Children $2.50 (2-12)
- ❑   Miscellaneous: Picnic area. Domino's Pizza available.

First pass a herd of buffalo of cows grazing on the grounds of the Domino's Pizza World Headquarters. Across the street is Domino Farms, an early 1900's depiction of Michigan farm life. The Petting Farm has 100+ chickens, goats, sheep, peacocks, pot-bellied pigs, and miniature horses. Take a hayride to buffalo fields and stop and get a close look at their shy, huge faces! Many animal demonstrations throughout the day. One of the cleanest farms you'll ever see. Nice outdoor activity to enjoy with a picnic.

UNIVERSITY OF MICHIGAN COLLEGE SPORTS

Ann Arbor – 48109. *Activity:* Sports (734) 647-2583 info or (734) 764-0247 tickets. **www.umich.edu.**

UNIVERSITY OF MICHIGAN MUSEUMS

(I-94 to State Street Exit)

Ann Arbor 48109

❑ Activity: Museums

❑ **www.umich.edu**

❑ Admission: Free (some ask for donations)

❑ Tours: Many of these facilities are included in a group tour- by appointment.

SPORTS MUSEUM - 1000 South State Street - (734) 647-2583. Captures the spirit of 100+ years of athletic competition with emphasis on the Rose Bowl, Big Ten and U.S. Olympics. Located in the nation's largest college stadium.

MUSEUM OF NATURAL HISTORY - 1109 Geddes Avenue - (734) 764-0478. Michigan birds and animals. Face to face with prehistoric allosaurus conquering a stegosaurus or a mastodon from Michigan. Evolution of whale's skeletons. Daily until 5:00 pm.

MUSEUM OF ARCHEOLOGY - 434 South State Street - (734) 764-9304. 100,000+ artifacts from ancient Egypt, Greece and Rome. See a mummy child! Open Daily until 4:00 pm, except Mondays.

STEARNS MUSICAL COLLECTION - 1100 Baits Drive - North Campus - (734) 763-4389. 2000+ musical instruments on display from around the world.

BOTANICAL GARDENS - 1800 North Dixboro Road - (734) 998-7061. Tropical, warm-tempered or desert plants. Nature trail. Prairie. Daily, 10:00 am - 4:30 pm.

RAINFOREST CAFÉ

4310 Baldwin Road (I-75, exit 84 - Great Lakes Crossing)

Auburn Hills 48326

- ❑ Activity: Theme Restaurants
- ❑ Telephone: (248) 333-0280, **www.rainforestcafe.com**
- ❑ Hours: Daily, Lunch and Dinner

A theme restaurant and wildlife preserve filled with live and mechanical animals; ongoing rainstorms (even thunder and lightning); a talking rainforest tree; giant "walk-through" aquarium (really cool!); hand-sculpted "cave like" rock everywhere. After awhile, you'll feel like you've been transported into a tropical South American island. The cute jungle names of food will wet your appetite for the American fare food to follow, (ex. Gorilla Grilled Cheese, Volcanic Salad, and Wild Waffle Fries). Their gift shop is almost as large as the restaurant - look out for the snake! Preschoolers and younger love the fish tank but are a little uneasy with the motorized large gorillas and elephants (request seating on the other side of the dining room). Although your food bill will be above moderate - it's the epitome of a theme restaurant that you are also paying for. "Your adventure safari begins now…" is the call of your hostess (safari leader) as you are seated…you won't be bored for a minute - believe us!

DETROIT NEON SOCCER

Auburn Hills (Detroit) - 2 Championship Drive (Palace of Auburn Hills), 48326. *Activity:* Sports. (248) 377-0100. A Continental Indoor Soccer League team.

DETROIT PISTONS BASKETBALL

Auburn Hills (Detroit) - 2 Championship Drive (The Palace of Auburn Hills), 48326. *Activity:* Sports. **www.nba.com/pistons**. (248) 377-0100. *Admission:* $15.00-65.00. NBA team with all star players.

DETROIT ROCKERS SOCCER

Auburn Hills (Detroit) - 2 Championship Drive (The Palace of Auburn Hills), 48326. *Activity:* Sports. **www.detroitrockers.net**. (248) 366-6254. *Admission:* $11.00-16.00. Soccer team plays October - March.

DETROIT SHOCK WOMEN'S BASKETBALL

Auburn Hills (Detroit) - 2 Championship Drive (Palace of Auburn Hills), 48326. *Activity:* Sports. **www.wnba.com/shock**. (248) 377-0100. *Admission:* $8.00-75.00. WNBA team.

DETROIT VIPERS HOCKEY

Auburn Hills (Detroit) - 2 Championship Drive (Palace of Auburn Hills), 48326. *Activity:* Sports. (248) 377-0100. **www.detroitvipers.com**. *Admission:* $5.00-35.00. IHL Hockey team plays September - April.

YANKEE AIR FORCE MUSEUM

2041 Willow Run Airport

Belleville 48111

- ❑ Activity: Museums
- ❑ Telephone: (734) 483-4030
- ❑ Hours: Tuesday - Saturday, 10:00 am - 4:00 pm. Sunday, Noon - 4:00 pm. Closed Mondays & Holidays. Call for Winter Hours - January & February
- ❑ Admission: Adults $5.00, Seniors $4.00, Children $3.00 (5-12)

During WW II, B-24 bombers mechanics were schooled here marking one of Michigan's many roles in the war and aviation history. This museum which was started as a way to commemorate this has actually grown to one of the most unique in the country (in our opinion) for several reasons. The first is that some of the "relic" museum aircraft (21 aircraft in all) are actually some of the only "still flyable" examples left today. The flyable B-25 Mitchell and B-17 (a large 4 engine bomber) are a couple examples of these planes and are a wonderful way to bring this "conflict in history" to life. Outside, children can see a large B52D jet-propelled bomber and can even get the chance to climb inside (with a prior appointment). Be sure to see the tribute to Amelia Earhart and other female aircraft pioneers in the "Women in Aviation" room. Very well done!

ADRIAN & BLISSFIELD RAILROAD

(US-23 - Downtown - leaves from depot)

Blissfield 49228

❑   Activity: Tours
❑   Telephone: (888) GO-RAIL-1 or (517) 486-5979
   www.tc3net.com/railroad
❑   Hours: Wednesdays and Weekends (Summer), Saturdays & Sundays (rest of year)
❑   Admission: Adults $8.00, Seniors $7.00, Children $5.00 (3-12)

As the powerful "larger than life" diesel engine rumbles into the station, your kids will be standing in awe! Enjoy a 90-minute scenic train ride though the countryside that includes two old bridges (or trestles as they're called in railroader lingo) across the Raisin River.

MOUNT BRIGHTON SKI AREA

Brighton - (I-96 - Exit 145), 48114. *Activity:* Outdoors. (810) 229-9581. **www.michigan.org**. A "family-friendly" attraction that offers 26 runs of various skill levels. Snowboarding, lessons and rentals are available.

ISLAND LAKE RECREATION AREA

Brighton - 12950 East Grand River (I-96, exit 151), 48116. **www.dnr.state.mi.us/www/parks/plse.htm#islandlake**. *Activity:* Outdoors. (810) 229-7067. *Admission:* $4.00 per vehicle. A canoe livery offers relaxing trips down the scenic Huron River. Hiking trails, beaches, boating, fishing, swimming, bicycle trails, winter sports and cabins available.

BRIGHTON STATE PARK

Brighton - 6360 Chilson Road (I-96 exit 145 south), 48843. **www.dnr.state.mi.us/www/parks/brighton.htm**. *Activity:* Outdoors. (810) 229-6566. *Admission:* $4.00 per vehicle. Beaches, swimming, and trout fishing are most popular here. Other features include hiking, winter sports, modern and rough camping, boating and bicycle trails.

WALKER TAVERN STATE HISTORIC COMPLEX

13220 M-50 (US-12 & M-50)

Brooklyn 48230

- ❑   Activity: Tours
- ❑   Telephone: (517) 467-4401
     www.sos.state.mi.us/history/museum/musewalk/index.html
- ❑   Hours: Wednesday - Sunday, 11:30 am - 4:00 pm (Memorial Day - Labor Day). By appointment - rest of the year.
- ❑   Admission: Free
- ❑   Tours: Approximately 1 hour

In the mid-1800's, the journey between Detroit and Chicago (by stagecoach) was a 5-8 day event (one-way, can you imagine?). This farmhouse tavern was the original stopping point (along what is now known as US 12) where travelers could have a meal, relax, or spend the night. Discover how life was in the 1840's with realistic exhibits that show a barroom, dining room, parlor and kitchen. The Visitor's Center also features a movie about a young boy's travels from New York to Chicago in the 1840's.

MICHIGAN SPEEDWAY

12626 US-12 (1 mile west of M-50)

Brooklyn 49230

- ❑   Activity: Sports
- ❑   Telephone: (800) 354-1010 or (517) 592-6666
  www.penskemotorsports.com
- ❑   Hours: Call or visit website for current schedule. (Summer)
- ❑   Admission: $30.00 - $95.00 per person.

Gentlemen (and ladies) start your engines! The thrill of world class professional motorsports is alive and well in Michigan. This speedway is a D-shaped, 2-mile oval that offers high-banked (18 degree) turns to a variety of racing vehicles including NASCAR, CART, and the NASCAR Craftsman Truck Series. Also see the fastest 500 mile race in history, the annual Marlboro 500.

CALDER DAIRY FARM

9334 Finzel Road (I-275 - Telegraph Road Exit (south), to Stoney Creek Road - West to Finzel Road South - follow signs),

Carleton 48117

- ❑   Activity: Animals & Farms
- ❑   Telephone: (734) 654-2622
- ❑   Hours: Monday - Thursday, 10:00 am - 8:30 pm., Friday - Sunday (until 9:00 pm). Winter hours vary.
- ❑   Admission: Free
- ❑   Miscellaneous: Farm Store and Ice Cream Shop. Main Store - watch milk arriving and fed through series of pipes for processing.

See how luscious ice cream is made - right from the Brown Swiss Cow's milk! Pet the Holstein and Swiss Cows plus numerous other animals that you're likely to see on a farm (pigs, ducks, sheep). They make creamy ice cream, chocolate milk, eggnog, plus milk right from the cows - fresh in glass bottles. Check out the milking machines behind the store to see cows milked by the dozen. Take a tour in a hay wagon (horse driven) and you'll see fields of llamas, deer and bright peacocks. At the end of your visit to the land of "Babe", be sure to get a generous souvenir cup of fresh ice cream!

CHELSEA MILLING - "JIFFY MIX"

201 West North Street (I-94 west to Chelsea exit - north - follow signs), **Chelsea** 48118I

- ❑ Activity: Tours
- ❑ Telephone: (734) 475-1361, **www.jiffymix.com**
- ❑ Hours: Monday - Friday, 9:00 am - 1:30 pm. Closed Holidays.
- ❑ Admission: Free
- ❑ Tour: By appointment only. (45 minutes to 1 hour)
- ❑ Miscellaneous: Souvenir box of Jiffy Mix given with recipe booklets & little sticky "Jiffy Guy" souvenirs.

In a time when manufacturing tours are minimal or eliminated, this is a good, old-fashioned tour! Inside the world headquarters of the internationally known Jiffy Mix Baking Products, you'll begin in the auditorium with a slide show narrated by your tour guide. Because they're veteran associates, they talk about each operator by name. Learn some history about the company including how they got the name "Jiffy". In 1930, Grandma Mabel Holmes named the famous, low-priced, blue and white baking mix boxes "Jiffy" after hearing cooks exclaim, "The muffins will be ready in a jiffy!". Their flour is from Michigan and is milled using silk material similar to your kid's blanket edging. You'll see the packaging process, first in the slide show, then actually out in the factory. After you have a snack of Jiffy Mix cookies and juice, everyone adorns a hair net and takes a 20 minute walking tour of the packaging process. It's neat to see waxed paper formed in a block, filled, boxed and then sealed. The sealing machine is a cute 8 legged machine. Did you know their #1 selling product is "Corn Muffin" mix? At the end of the tour you can choose from muffin or another mix box to take home...yummies there...yummies at home!

WATERLOO STATE PARK

16345 McClure Road (7 miles west off I-94)

Chelsea 48118

❏   Activity: Outdoors
❏   Telephone: (734) 475-8307
     www.dnr.state.mi.us/www/parks/waterloo.htm
❏   Admission: $4.00 per vehicle

The lower peninsula's largest state park, it features cross-country skiing, horse rental and trails, modern and rough camping and cabins, beaches and boating, fishing, bicycle trails, and winter sports. For an additional small charge, you can tour the Farm Museum buildings. There's also long hiking trails and an Audubon Society preserve adjacent. Many visit often to the Eddy Geology center where you can view changing samples of geos from the Great Lakes, Michigan and the Midwest. There's also a slide show, hands-on activities and professional demonstrations.

LIONEL TRAINS VISITOR'S CENTER

26750 Russell Smith Drive (23 Mile Road) (I-94 to Exit 243)

Chesterfield 48051

❏   Activity: Tours
❏   Telephone: (810) 949-4100, **www.lionel.com**
❏   Hours: Gift Shop is open during all tours. It is also open Tuesday
     through Friday, 1:30 pm - 4:30 pm, and on Saturday, from 10:00
     am - 12:30 pm.
❏   Admission: Free
❏   Tours: (For reservation call: (810) 949-4100 ext. 1211)
     Wednesday & Thursday, 10:00 am, 3:00 and 4:00 pm. Friday,
     10:00 am, 1:30, 2:30 pm. Saturday, 9:00, 10:00, 11:00 am &
     Noon. Closed Sunday, Monday, Tuesday and Holidays
❏   Miscellaneous: Gift shop.

Since 1900, Lionel has been delighting hearts (both young and old) with the illusionary world of model train villages. Not only will you have fun watching and learning each step of the manufacturing process, but this tour allows plenty of time to "play" with the creations that make Lionel so special. See 10 trains running (on a 14 X 40 layout) simultaneously from village to village, over bridges and through tunnels just like a miniature movie set. Kids can interact with the display by pushing several buttons that create a movement or reaction in the display. There is also a smaller children's layout where kids get to operate the trains. If you're a collector (or about to become one), be sure to buy one of the Visitor's Center boxcars that are available only in the gift shop.

MORLEY CANDY MAKERS

23770 Hall Road (I-94 to Hall Road M-59 Exit)

Clinton Township 48036

- ❑ Activity: Tours
- ❑ Telephone: (810) 468-4300 or (800) 682-2760
  www.morleycandy.com
- ❑ Admission: Free
- ❑ Tours: Self-guided, Monday - Friday, 7:00 am - 3:30 pm. Guided group tours with video are available Monday - Friday between 10:00 am & 1:00 pm. Call to schedule appointment.

One of Michigan's largest candy makers, this tour is sure to delight chocolate lovers of all ages. Both educational and fun, see Morley's cooking chocolate in huge copper kettles (gallons at a time). The aroma of sugar and chocolate is simply delicious. The nearly 200 foot long observation hallway is a great way to see all the candy making in action. Don't leave without your edible souvenirs!

AUTOMOBILE HALL OF FAME

21400 Oakwood Blvd. (Next to Greenfield Village)

Dearborn 48121

❑   Activity: Museums

❑   Telephone: (888) 29-VISIT or (313) 240-4000

❑   Hours: Daily, 10:00 am -5:00 pm. (Memorial Day -October).
     Closed Mondays the rest of the year. Closed major winter
     holidays.

❑   Admission: Adults $6.00, Seniors $5.50 (62+), Children $3.00
     (5-12).

B egin by picking out a souvenir card that steers you to the
people who are most like you. "The Driving Spirit" is a big
screen theater and along with the dramatic 65 foot mural, most kids
think these are neat. Before you leave, be sure to start up a replica
of the first gasoline-powered car, listen in on a meeting that led to
forming the world's largest corporation, emboss a souvenir car, or
apply for a job at GM in 1910.

HENRY FORD MUSEUM & GREENFIELD VILLAGE

20900 Oakwood Blvd. (I-94 to M-39 north to Oakwood Blvd.)

Dearborn 48124

❑   Activity: Michigan History

❑   Telephone: (313) 271-1620, **www.hfmgv.org**

❑   Hours: Daily 9:00 am - 5:00 pm. Greenfield Village is closed in
     winter, (January - March)

❑   Admission: Adults $12.50, Seniors $11.50 (62+), Children $7.50
     (5-12) for each museum. (Combo prices and additional
     attractions are available)

❑   Miscellaneous: Horse-drawn carriage or sleigh rides. IMAX
     Theatre where you'll learn of fascinating innovations. Steam train
     and steamboat rides. We recommend children be at least 5 years
     old to visit and gain from the learning experience.

A merica's largest indoor-outdoor museum examines our country from rural to industrial societies. A special focus is places on accomplishments and inventions of famous Americans. Greenfield Village highlights:

- ❑ HENRY FORD BIRTHPLACE - he certainly loved and cherished his mother. See what he played with as a boy.
- ❑ FORD COMPANY - the hostess recommends you don't buy the model A, but wait for the Model C (better radiator).
- ❑ COHEN MILLINERY - try on hats of olden days.
- ❑ GEORGE WASHINGTON CARVER - PEANUTS! A great look at the possibilities of products made with peanuts. Carver helped find industrial uses for peanuts to help poor Southerners find new crops to grow and new uses for the crops they had.
- ❑ WRIGHT BROTHERS CYCLE SHOP & HOME
- ❑ MATTOX HOUSE - Recycling before the work existed! Newspaper wallpaper, license plate shingles, and layered cardboard ceilings.
- ❑ EDISON'S MENLO PARK LAB - Learn about Edison's brilliant and showy sides. Using a loud child as a volunteer, they demonstrate a real Edison phonograph (it really worked) and souvenir piece of tin foil used as the secret to the phonograph's success.
- ❑ TASTE OF HISTORY RESTAURANT - try a Railroaders Lunch made with hobo bread just like 19th century railroad workers ate - round raisin nut bread filled with turkey and cheese. Sounds funny but it's really good! In the foyer of the casual restaurant is a machine that, for $1, your child can make plastic model T souvenir cars.

Henry Ford Museum highlights:

- ❑ HOME ARTS - evolution of home appliances
- ❑ MADE IN AMERICA - production of goods in the USA. What's My Assembly Line Game Show.
- ❑ INNOVATION STATION - interactively be an innovator or team project player. Really hands-on!. Furniture Fun Packs.

Henry Ford Museum highlights: (cont.)

❑   <u>YOUR PLACE IN TIME</u> - explore the 1900's from your own
      life history experiences. Kids find it silly to see what was
      considered "technology" years ago.

Compared to our visits as children years ago, we noticed a
much more interactive, kid-friendly environment. The guides
and actors really are skilled at engaging the kid's curiosity and use
kids, not adults, as part of their demos.

SPIRIT OF FORD

1151 Village Road

Dearborn 48124

❑   Activity: Museums
❑   Telephone: (313) 31-SPIRIT, **www.spiritofford.com**
❑   Hours: Daily, 9:00 am - 5:00 pm. (Open all holidays except
      Thanksgiving Day, Christmas Eve, Christmas Day and New
      Year's Day) Closed Mondays during January & February.
❑   Admission: Adults $6.00 (13+), Seniors $5.00 (62+), Children
      $4.00 (5-12). Age 4 and under Free.
❑   Miscellaneous: Exit Ramp Gift Shop.

A complete museum dedicated to the automobile.   A fantastic
hands-on exhibit that teaches the principles of aerodynamics,
metal tolerances and weight characteristics, braking systems, etc.
in an extremely fun and educational way. The "concept cars" that
you may have seen in popular car magazines make you and the
kids say…WOW!   If you show up 15 minutes early for the
NASCAR pit crew demonstration, you may be selected to be part
of the crew!   The final thrill of this outstanding tribute to the
automobile is the "Turbo Tour".   A thrill ride that allows you to sit
it roller coaster type seats (with seatbelts) that actually move in
ALL directions on command with the large screen presentation.
YOU are actually the car being built and raced through the

assembly line (as your seat jerks up and down, side to side to the conveyor). Bright red strobe lights are timed with the robotic welding sequences that actually make you feel a part of the action. At the conclusion, you, *THE RED CONVERTIBLE SPORTS CAR* are raced at speeds that cause the audience to scream with exhilaration. By the way, non-moving seats are available (and are required for kids under 42" tall).

FAIR LANE

4901 Evergreen Road (On the campus of University of Michigan)

Dearborn 48128

❑   Activity: Museums
❑   Telephone: (313) 593-5590. "The Pool" - (313) 436-9196
    www.umd.umich.edu/fairlane
❑   Hours: Monday - Saturday, 10:00 am - 3:00 pm, Sunday, 1:00 - 4:30 pm. (April - December). Monday - Friday tour available only at 1:30 pm (January - March). (Closed winter holidays plus Easter)
❑   Admission: (Guided Tours- 90 minutes) Adults $8.00, Seniors $7.00, Children $5.00 (5-12).

Much more than just another mansion tour...this was the home of visionary, Henry Ford. In many ways, our lives have been shaped and changed by decisions and visions that Henry Ford saw and created. A 90 minute tour takes you into the fascinating 6-level mansion which had many innovations. The on-site electric generating power plant (the Rouge River was the energy source) produced enough electricity to power the mansion and part of the university campus! See many of Ford's personal vehicles in the garage that include the famous Model A and Model T, an early 1900's innovative "camper" (some people say that he started the RV industry), a "Fordson" tractor, and even an electric car that he was going to partner into production with Thomas Edison. Complete your tour with lunch at "The Pool" restaurant (named because it was built over the estate's swimming pool).

DETROIT SYMPHONY ORCHESTRA

Detroit - 3663 Woodward Avenue #100, 48201. *Activity:* The Arts. Tickets: (313) 576-5111 or Office: (313) 576-5100. **www.detroitsymphony.com**. Be sure to ask about "Young People Series".

MUSEUM OF AFRICAN-AMERICAN HISTORY

315 East Warren Avenue (off I-94 or I-75)

Detroit 48201

❑   Activity: Museums

❑   Telephone: (313) 494-5800, **www.detnews.com/maah/**

❑   Hours: Tuesday - Sunday, 9:30 am - 5:00 pm.

❑   Admission: Adults $5.00 (18+), $3.00 (17 and under)

A tribute to the history and culture of Detroit's African-American community. Visitors will be greeted with the haunting vision of an almost full-scale replica slave ship that was used to transport Africans to America. The exhibit, "Of the People: The African-American Experience" traces the history and operations of the slave trade. Learn also that Detroit was one of the most active stops in the "Underground Railroad" (a network of safe stops that helped slaves escape from the south before the Civil War). Once reaching Detroit they could cross the Detroit River into Canada. See the space suit worn by Mae Jemision, the first African-American women to travel in space in 1992. Other fun and educational exhibits trace the history of African music and how it transformed present American music including the famous Detroit "Motown Sound".

DETROIT CHILDREN'S MUSEUM

67 East Kirby

Detroit 48202

❑ Activity: Museums
❑ Telephone: (313) 873-8100
   www.detpub.k12.mi.us/museum/docs/index.htm
❑ Hours: Monday - Friday, 1:00 - 4:00 pm, Saturday, 9:00 am -
   4:00 pm (October - May). Weekdays, Noon - 4:00 pm (late June -
   early August)
❑ Admission: Free

A 900 lb. chrome horse (the museum's mascot - made from recycled bumpers) on the front lawn awaits your energetic youngsters. Your kids (target age 4-9) will be encouraged at this museum to test their imagination and creativity at its various interactive attractions. Be sure to ask for the "Treasure Hunt Game" that gets kids involved in a discovery adventure throughout the building. There is a 32-seat planetarium that teaches what to see in the night sky and even a full-size Bengal tiger to teach children about wild animals. Younger children will find lots to do in the Discovery Room where they can test their skills with many interactive teaching toys. Parents hang on tight to those little ones!

DETROIT HISTORICAL MUSEUM

5401 Woodward Avenue (Woodward and Kirby)

Detroit 48202

❑ Activity: Michigan History
❑ Telephone: (313) 833-1805, **www.detroithistorical.org**
❑ Hours: Wednesday - Friday, 9:30 am -5:00 pm. Saturday &
   Sunday, 10:00 am -5:00 pm.
❑ Admission: Adults $3.00, Seniors $1.50 (62+), Children $1.50
   (12-18).

❑   Miscellaneous: Free admission on Wednesdays. Train-cam mini-
        train setup is new feature where camera displays the view from
        the little train goin' around the town.

After you've wondered through Frontiers to Factories:
Detroiters at Work before the Motor City and the Streets of
Old Detroit, be sure to plan most of your time in the Motor City
exhibits. See the first car in Detroit - a horseless carriage that was
driven down Woodward Avenue. Then, around the corner, you can
crank up a Model T and then sit in it (*great photo op!*). The best
part of this exhibit has to be the Body Drop! First, watch it happen
on video (actual footage from a Ford Assembly plant). Then see
the 70 foot section of actual assembly plant and the performance of
the final steps of production. Some mannequins are in the pits
below, some workers are above one floor as they "drop" the car
body onto the chassis below. Did you know that Mr. Cadillac's full
name is Antoine de la Mothe Cadillac?   No wonder they're so
fancy!

DETROIT INSTITUTE OF ARTS
5200 Woodward Avenue (off I-94 or I-75)

Detroit 48202

❑   Activity: The Arts
❑   Telephone: (313) 833-7900, **www.dia.org**
❑   Hours: Wednesday - Friday, 11:00 am - 4:00 pm, Saturday and
        Sunday, 11:00 am - 5:00 pm.
❑   Admission: Donations. Suggested - Adults $4.00, Children $1.00
        (14 and under)
❑   Tours: 1:00 pm, Wednesday - Saturday. 1:00 & 2:30 pm, Sunday.

Shhhh...we won't tell your kids that this cool place is really an
"art museum" if you don't! A great place for kids of all ages
to interact and explore (and the museum even likes it when kids
come to visit!). Most exhibits are very "kid-friendly" and
interactive and there is even a treasure hunt game called "The
Mystery of the Five Fragments" that encourages kids to "want to
discover" the museum and its treasures. See exhibits such as "The

American House", "The Spiral Staircase" and even "The Donkey" (which invites kids to hang, climb, and burn up excess energy) while at the museum. Fun, interactive computer programs also entertain and teach. The Great Hall features many suits of armor from the 13th to 18th century. But, above all, the masked mummy (kept safely in a display case) in the Egyptian art and artifacts exhibit is always a way to get the kids to say "wow" or "wooooo".

DETROIT SCIENCE CENTER

5020 John R Street (I-75 - Warren Exit)

Detroit 48202

❑ Activity: Museums
❑ Telephone: (313) SCIENCE, **www.sciencedetroit.org**
❑ Hours: Monday - Thursday, 9:30 am - 2:00 pm. Friday, 9:30 am - 2:00 pm & 6:30 pm - 8:00 pm. Saturday, 10:30 - 5:00 pm & 6:30 pm - 8:00 pm. Sunday, 12:30 - 5:00 pm. (extended summer hours)
❑ Admission: Adults $3-7.00, Seniors $2-6.00 (60+), Children $2-6.00 (3-17)

Just a block away from the Detroit Institute of Arts is another wonderful example of what learning "outside of the books" is all about. Toddlers and up can appreciate and learn from exhibits that encourage learning and make it fun. See a laser display and other science experiments in the Discovery Theater (the upper floor allows kid's hair to "stand straight up" with the static electricity generator) and "The Magic Schoolbus Corner" has touch screen computers designed to create an interest in the science world. But...the main highlight of this museum is the chance to ride in an Indy racing car, fly aboard the space shuttle, or whitewater raft in the 16 speaker, 3-story IMAX theater. It's O.K...you can have fun too Mom and Dad!

BELLE ISLE

(I-75 to East Grand Blvd. Take MacArthur Bridge over to the Isle
on the Detroit River), **Detroit** 48207

❑   Activity: Outdoors
❑   Telephone: (313) 852-4075
❑   Hours: Dawn to Dusk. See specific hours for special parks
      within the Isle.
❑   Admission: Free. Separate admission for facilities found on the Isle.
❑   Miscellaneous: Trails, Picnic areas, beach, Nature Center.
      Common to see many deer. There's also a wild animal hospital
      and playgrounds.

The well-used 1000 acre park and playground, still in site of the
skyscrapers of Detroit offers:

❑   **ZOO** -(313) 852-4083. **http://detroitzoo.org/belle_isle_zoo.htm**.
      Hours: Daily, 10:00 am - 5:00 pm. (May - October). *Admission:*
      $1-3.00. Elevated boardwalk along overview of 100+ animals in
      un-caged natural settings. Farm petting zoo. World of spiders.
❑   **AQUARIUM AND CONSERVATORY** - (313) 852-4141.
      http://detroitzoo.org/belle_isle_aquarium.htm. *Hours:* Daily,
      10:00 am - 5:00 pm. *Admission:* $1-3.00. Old aquarium focuses
      on freshwater species found in Michigan and the tropics (ex.
      Electric eel and a stingray). The adjacent conservatory explores
      plants and flowers mostly in desert and tropical settings (ex.
      Cacti, ferns, palm trees, banana trees and orchids).
❑   **DOSSIN GREAT LAKES MUSEUM** - 100 Strand Drive
      (South Shore of Belle Isle). (313) 852-4051. *Hours:* Wednesday -
      Sunday, 10:00 am - 5:00 pm. *Admission:* Adults $2.00, Seniors
      $1.00 (62+). Children $1.00 (12-18). **www.detroithistorical.org/
      html/Information/dossin.html.** You're greeted by two Battle of
      Lake Erie cannons and the actual anchor recovered from the
      Edmund Fitzgerald shipwreck. Stand in the pilot house of an ore
      carrier. As the marine radio sends out requests, turn the ship
      wheel to steer it on course or use the periscope. The 1912 Great
      Lakes Luxury Steamer Lounge Room is handsome (all oak

carvings) - reminiscent of scenes in the movie "Titanic". The speedboat hydroplane, "The Miss Pepsi" on display, is the first to break the 100 mph barrier on a closed course.

MOTOWN HISTORICAL MUSEUM

2648 West Grand Blvd. (M-10 to West Grand Blvd. Exit)

Detroit 48208

❑   Activity: Museums
❑   Telephone: (313) 875-2264
   www.recordingeq.com/motown.htm
❑   Hours: Sunday & Monday, Noon - 5:00 pm, Tuesday - Saturday, 10:00 am - 5:00 pm. (Closed holidays)
❑   Admission: Adults $6.00, Seniors $5.00 (60+), Students $4.00 (12-17), Children $3.00 (age 11 and under)

In two homes that are next to each other, the music world was changed forever by Berry Gordy, composer and producer. The original recording studio "A" not only helped to build the "Motown" sound, but discovered and built the careers of Stevie Wonder, the Temptations, the Four Tops, Diana Ross and Marvin Gaye, just to name a few. A great stop in musical history!

DETROIT TIGERS BASEBALL

Detroit - Corner of Brush & Adams Streets (Comerica Park), 48216. *Activity:* Sports. **www.detroittigers.com**. Tickets: (313) 471-BALL. *Admission:* General $8.00-30.00. Major league baseball played April-September.

DETROIT RED WINGS HOCKEY

Detroit - 600 Civic Center Drive (Joe Lewis Arena), 48226. *Activity:* Sports. (313) 396-7444. **www.detroitredwings.com**. NHL top five teams in the League play September-April. Call or visit website for ticket availability.

LAFAYETTE CONEY ISLAND

118 West Lafayette

Detroit 48226

❑ Activity: Theme Restaurants
❑ Telephone: (313) 964-8198
❑ Hours: Daily, 24 hours

Ever since 1918, the crowds have loved these famous "Coney Island Dogs" (real hot dogs smothered with chili, mustard, and onions). Take your kids "a step back to the past" and listen as the diner comes to life with its own language as orders are called out by the servers. Also features chili and hamburgers that have also become a Detroit tradition. The American Coney Island, 115 Michigan Avenue, (313) 961-7758 is just 3 blocks away.

MUSIC HALL CENTER - DETROIT YOUTHEATER

350 Madison Avenue (I-75, exit at Madison Avenue)

Detroit 48226

❑ Activity: The Arts
❑ Telephone: (313) 963-7622 or (313) 963-2366
❑ Admission: $8.00 at door, $7.00 in advance

This fun and interactive (in over half of the productions the performers answer questions from the audience after the shows) theater features two series of shows to best reach the age levels of the children. The "Wiggle Club" features shows that are geared for children ages 3-6. The "Movin' Up" Club is for children that are age 7 and older. A wonderful way to introduce your children to the performing arts. More than 12 different productions are featured each season. Performing arts workshops are available to help teach your children the basics of dance and acting. (October - May)

DIAMOND JACK'S RIVER TOURS

25088 Old Depot Court (Hart Plaza, foot of Woodward, downtown)

Detroit (Grosse Ile) 48138

- ❑ Activity: Tours
- ❑ Telephone: (313) 843-7676, **www.diamondjack.com**
- ❑ Hours: Daily, (Memorial Day - Labor Day). Weekends only in September.
- ❑ Admission: Adults $12.00, Seniors $11.00, Children $9.00 (6-16).
- ❑ Tours: 2-hour leisurely narrated cruise departs at 2:00, 4:00 and 6:00 pm.
- ❑ Miscellaneous: Snacks and beverages available on board. Safest parking available at the Renaissance Center.

The 65-foot "mini-ship" cruises down the Detroit River around Belle Isle and back to Ambassador Bridge. This is the world's busiest international waterway along the U.S. and Canadian shorelines. There's a good chance that large freighters and ocean ships will pass by. You'll see a great view of both the Detroit and downtown Windsor, Canada skylines and pass by the historic Warehouse District, Mayor's Residence (if he's out back, he'll wave), Yacht Clubs, Islands, Bridges and a Fireboat. See the world's only marble Art Deco lighthouse or one of only two International Marine Mailboats in the world. They told us the boat has its own zip code and delivers mail to the freighters by a pail on a pulley.

CRANBROOK ART AND SCIENCE MUSEUMS

1221 North Woodward Avenue (I-75 exit to Square Lake Road (West) to Woodward, I-696 exit - Woodward)

Detroit Vicinity (Bloomfield Hills) 48303

❑ Activity: Museums

❑ Telephone: (877) GO-CRANB, **www.cranbrook.edu**

❑ Hours: Art: Tuesday - Sunday, 11:00 am - 5:00 pm. Thursday until 8:00 pm. Science: Daily, 10:00 am - 5:00 pm. Friday until 10:00 pm. Sunday, 12:00 - 5:00 pm

❑ Admission: Adults $5-7.00, Seniors $3-4.00 (65+), Children $3-4.00 (3-17)

❑ Miscellaneous: Picnic areas. Planetarium and Laser Shows. $1-2.00 extra. Café. Gift shop.

Different areas to check out are:

❑ Our Dynamic Earth (15 foot T-Rex, wooly mastodon), Gem & Mineral Hall, Nature Place (live reptiles, turtles, and bugs - native to Michigan), Art (metalwork, realism sculpture "Body Builder", outdoor sculpture), Physics Hall (hands-on experiments about lasers and light, movement, and air).

DELHI METROPARK

Dexter - Huron River Drive (on the banks of the Huron River), 48130. *Activity:* Outdoors. (800) 477-3191 or (734) 426-8211. **www.metroparks.com**. *Hours:* Daily, 6:00 am - 10:00 pm. *Admission:* $3.00 per vehicle (weekends), $2.00 per vehicle (weekdays). Free on Wednesdays. Fishing, Picnic Facilities, Canoe Rentals.

SPRING VALLEY TROUT FARM

Dexter - 12190 Island Lake Road, 48130. *Activity:* Animals & Farms. (734) 426-4772. Natural, organic (non-polluted water) fed trout in spring-fed ponds are waiting to be caught. They'll clean the fish and pack them in ice to take home. Fees charged. Picnic/grilling areas.

GREATER LANSING SYMPHONY ORCHESTRA

East Lansing - Bogue Street & Wilson (MSU Campus - Wharton Center for Performing Arts), 48824. *Activity:* The Arts. (517) 487-5001 or (800) WHARTON. **http://lansing.com/symphony**. Free Young People's Concerts and music for Broadway shows like "Beauty & the Beast".

MICHIGAN STATE UNIVERSITY
West Circle Drive (Off M-43)

East Lansing 48825

- ☐ Activity: Tours
- ☐ Telephone: (517) 355-7474, **www.museum.cl.msu.edu**
- ☐ Hours: Monday - Friday, 9:00 am - 5:00 pm. Saturday, 10:00 am - 5:00 pm. Sunday, 1- 5:00 pm. Closed all state holidays.
- ☐ Admission: Free
- ☐ Miscellaneous: Of all the offerings here, our favorite garden for kids (in the state and Midwest) is the Children's Garden. So colorful and artistically done (on a kid's level).

MUSEUM: Natural wonders of the Great Lakes, world cultures, animal diversity. 3 stories of special exhibits. Museum store.

KRESGE ART MUSEUM: Culturally diverse art. Free. (517) 355-7631.

BEAUMONT TOWER: Site of Old College Hall - the 1st building erected for instruction in scientific agriculture. Recently renovated. Weekly carillon concerts.

FARMS: Observe milking cows mid-afternoon. Also sheep, horse and swine areas. Weekdays only. (517) 355-8383. South Campus.

HORTICULTURE GARDENS AND GREEN HOUSE: Bogue & Wilson Road. (517) 355-0348. American Trial Garden test site. Children's Garden - 63 theme gardens - Secret Garden (just like movie), Pizza Garden (wheat for dough, toppings and spices, tomatoes), Peter Rabbit Garden (bunny food favorites), Sensation Garden (guess which plant it is by smell), 2 Treehouses, and a Butterfly Garden. (517) 353-4800. Small Admission donation. Weekdays only. June-September.

BUG HOUSE: Natural Science Building. Farm Lane & East Circle Drive. (517) 355-4662. Noisy cockroaches, millipedes and giant grasshoppers.

ABRAMS PLANETARIUM: Shaw Lane & Science Road. (517) 355-STAR. Small Admission. Weekend matinees are suggested for younger ones.

MARVIN'S MARVELOUS MECHANICAL MUSEUM

31005 Orchard Lake Road (I-696 exit Orchard Lake Road North)

Farmington Hills 48334

❑   Activity: Amusements
❑   Telephone: (248) 626-5020, **www.marvin3m.com**
❑   Hours: Monday-Thursday, 10:00 am -9:00 pm, Friday - Saturday, 10:00 am - 11:00 pm, Sunday 11:00 am - 9:00 pm.
❑   Admission: Free. Each device takes a quarter to operate.
❑   Miscellaneous: Concessions. Modern pinball and interactive games are there too.

Pass back in time to an old-fashioned carnival full of antique slot and pinball machines, mechanical memorabilia and games. It's a very busy place with lights flashing and marionette music playing all around you. Here are some games that were really unique: a bulldozer mechanical game, Old Time Photos,

Marionette and Clown Dancing Shows, and miniature carrousel and Ferris wheel. Once you're inside, it's hard to know what game to play first! *P.S. Grandparents get real sentimental here.*

SEVEN LAKES STATE PARK

Fenton - 2220 Tinsman Road (I-75, exit 101), 48430. *Activity:* Outdoors. (248) 634-7271. **www.dnr.state.mi.us/www/parks/ plse.htm#sevenlakes**. *Admission:* $4.00 per vehicle. Camping, hiking trails, boating and rentals, fishing, swimming, bicycle trails, and winter sports.

CHILDS' PLACE BUFFALO RANCH

12770 Roundtree Road

Hanover 49241

- ❑ Activity: Animals & Farms
- ❑ Telephone: (517) 563-8249
- ❑ Hours: Tuesday - Sunday, 9:00 am - 4:00 pm (Memorial Day - Labor Day).
- ❑ Admission: Buffalo herd visit $4.00 per person. Horseback riding $16.00 per hour. Rodeo: Adults $8.00, Children $5.00 (6-12).

Here's a visit that your kids are sure to tell their friends about! Take a hay wagon ride out into Gary Childs' pastures to see some of his more than 100 buffalo. Brave kids will usually get the opportunity to reach out and actually touch a live buffalo (if the herd is cooperating that day). This ranch was also fortunate enough (1/40 million chance) to have given birth to a white buffalo (which is a powerful Native American spiritual symbol). For story and photograph of the white buffalo visit: www.freep.com/news/ mich/qbuffalo2.htm.

W.C. WETZEL STATE PARK

Harrison Township - 28681 Old North River (3 miles Northwest from New Haven), 48045. *Activity:* Outdoors. (810) 465-2160. An undeveloped park providing areas for cross-country skiing, snowmobiling and hiking. No camping. No services.

HOLLY RECREATION AREA

Holly - 8100 Grange Hall Road (off I-75 exit 101), 48442. *Activity:* Outdoors. (248) 634-8811. *Admission:* $4.00 per vehicle. **www.dnr.state.mi.us/www/parks/plse.htm#holly**. Camping, hiking, boating, fishing, swimming, bicycle trails and winter sports.

DAHLEM ENVIRONMENTAL EDUCATION CENTER

7117 South Jackson Road (I-94 to exit 138 - south)

Jackson 49201

- ❑ Activity: Outdoors
- ❑ (517) 782-3453, **www.jackson.cc.mi.us/DahlemCenter**
- ❑ Hours: Tuesday - Friday, 9:00 am - 4:30 pm. Saturday & Sunday, Noon - 5:00 pm. Trails open Daily, 8:00 am - sunset.
- ❑ Free admission.
- ❑ Miscellaneous: Gift shop. Cross-country skiing in winter.

Over 5 miles of hiking trails allow you to explore the fields, marshes, ponds, and forest of this "piece of nature" just a short drive from the city. All, regardless of age and physical abilities, can explore on the special needs (1/2 mile) trail. (All-terrain wheelchairs are available on request). Call or visit website for details on upcoming nature programs.

MICHIGAN SPACE CENTER

2111 Emmons Road (Jackson Community College) (I-94 to US-127 south to M-50)

Jackson 49201

- ❑ Activity: Museums
- ❑ Telephone: (517) 787-4425
  www.jackson.cc.mi.us/spacecenter
- ❑ Hours: (Year-round) Tuesday - Saturday, 10:00 am - 5:00 pm (Closed Sunday and Monday). Open Sundays, Noon - 5:00 pm (May - October)
- ❑ Admission: Adults $4.00, Seniors $2.75 (60+), Students $2.75, Family $11.00
- ❑ Miscellaneous: Picnic areas.

L ook for the gold dome and 85 foot Mercury rocket and you'll know you're close. Inside see an Apollo 9 Command module, memorial to the Challenger, satellites (something you don't see at many museums), spacesuits, a moon rock, a lunar surveyor, and black holes. Be sure to check out these too: The Astrotheatre - film of Apollo 9 flight or live broadcast of current space shuttle flight; Infinity Room; Hubble Space Telescope model; Space Capsule (climb in); and computer exhibit games. Open all year.

PHYLLIS HAEHNLE MEMORIAL SANCTUARY

Jackson - Seymour Road (I-94 to exit 147), 49201. *Activity:* Outdoors. (517) 769-6891. **http://mas.mi.audubon.org**. Free admission. In October each year, more than 2000 sandhill cranes gather at the woods, ponds, and wetlands of this site.

CASCADES

1992 Warren Avenue (I-94 exit 138, south on West Avenue)

Jackson 49203

- ❑ Activity: Outdoors
- ❑ Telephone: (517) 788-4320

❑   Hours: Park open 11:00 am - 11:000 pm. Cascades illuminated
      dusk - 11:00 pm in the Summer.
❑   Admission: General $2-3.00 (ages 6+).
❑   Miscellaneous: Snack Bar. Gift store and restrooms. Paddleboats,
      mini-golf.

It began in 1932 and you can still view the colorful and musical
waterfalls and fountains. Use seating provided or climb to the
top and be refreshed by spraying water. Continuously changing
patterns keep it lively. The Cascades Falls history museum is
within the park.

SLEEPY HOLLOW STATE PARK

Laingsburg - 7835 Price Road (off US-27 east on Price Road),
48848. *Activity:* Outdoors. (517) 651-6217. **www.dnr.state.mi.us/
www/parks/sleepyho.htm**. *Admission:* $4.00 per vehicle. A "no
wake" lake environment is great for fishing and rough camping
plus other features include a beach with snack bar, boating, hiking
and bike trails, and winter sports.

BALD MOUNTAIN STATE PARK

Lake Orion - 1330 Greenshield (I-75 exit M-24 north - 7 miles),
48360. *Activity:* Outdoors. (810) 693-6767. **www.dnr.state.mi.us/
www/parks/baldmtn.htm**. *Hours:* 8:00 am - Dusk. *Admission:*
$4.00 per vehicle. Beginning with a great kiddie beach at Lower
Trout Lake, the park also features hiking trails, fishing, boating,
horseback riding, winter sports, and cabins for camping.

FENNER NATURE CENTER

Lansing - 2020 East Mount Hope Avenue, 48910. *Activity:*
Outdoors. (517) 483-4224. **www.lansing.org**. *Hours:* Weekdays,
9:00 am - 4:00 pm. Weekends, 11:00 am - 4:00 pm (year-round).
Free admission. A visitor's center and gift shop plus self-guided
trails. Call or visit website for special seasonal children's
programs.

LANSING LUGNUTS

Lansing - 505 East Michigan Avenue (Oldsmobile Park), 48912. *Activity:* Sports. (517) 485-4500.   **www.lansinglugnuts.com**. *Admission:* Box $6.00, Reserved $5.50, General $4.50. Class "A" Midwest League - Chicago Cubs Affiliate. (Early April - Early September)

POTTER ZOO AND ZOOLOGICAL GARDENS

1301 South Pennsylvania Avenue

Lansing 48912

❑   Activity: Outdoors
❑   (517) 483-4222.   **http://ci.lansing.mi.us/depts/zoo/zoo.html**
❑   Hours: Daily, 9:00 am - 7:00 pm (Memorial Day - Labor Day). Daily, 9:00 am (10:00 am Winter) - 5:00 pm (rest of the year)
❑   Admission: Adults $5.00, Seniors $3.00 (60+), Children $1.00 (3-15)

More than 400 animals (get a virtual visit on the website) await your family at this great educational and family friendly zoo. Snow Leopards, Black Rhinos, Siberian Tigers, Reindeer, and Red Pandas are just a few of the exhibits featured.

MICHIGAN HISTORICAL CENTER

717 West Allegan (I-496 exit ML King, exit north follow signs to Capital Loop), **Lansing** 48918

❑   Activity: Michigan History
❑   Telephone: (517) 373-3559
www.sos.state.mi.us/history/history.html
❑   Hours: Monday - Friday, 9:00 am - 4:30 pm. Saturday, 10:00 am - 4:00 pm. Sunday 1 - 5:00 pm. Closed state holidays.
❑   Admission: Free
❑   Miscellaneous: Museum store. Snack Shop open weekdays.

A great way to understand Michigan society, land, and industry - and all in one building. If your travel plans around Michigan are limited, this would be a history time-saver. We really enjoy museum layouts with untraditional "real life" settings and odd turns and corners. We've found this keeps children's curiosity peaked! "Don't misses" include: the look and touch 3840 pound Float Copper that spans 4 feet by 8 feet and is hollow-sounding; rooms like the Mine Shaft or Lumber Barons parlor or old-time theater; learning words you may not know like Riverhog; and the Create-A-Car Touch Screen Computer. As you enter (or exit) you'll find the three-story relief map of Michigan - it's wonderful to gaze at from many angles.

IMPRESSION 5 SCIENCE CENTER

200 Museum Drive (Banks of Grand River, off Michigan Avenue, downtown), **Lansing** 48933

- ❏ Activity: Museums
- ❏ Telephone: (517) 485-8116, **www.impression5.org**
- ❏ Hours: Monday - Saturday, 10:00 am - 5:00 pm. Closed major holidays.
- ❏ Admission: Adults $4.50, Seniors $3.00 (62+), Children $3.00 (3-17).
- ❏ Miscellaneous: Impressions to Go Café.

150 displays challenge all five senses (i.e. the reason for Impression 5 name). Although it's smaller than many science centers, it's well worth the visit and includes many exhibits we haven't encountered before. Highlights include:

- ❏ THROWING THINGS - using different principles of physics, kids play with different forms of projectiles and balls. We've never seen this before - so many different ways to throw things!
- ❏ HEART WORKS - a walk through Heart Maze with sound effects, push button arteries (clear and clogged), try on a "fat vest" and find out what it feels like to carry an extra 20 pounds around, display of actual horse, cat, and mouse hearts.

❏   BUBBLES - create bubble walls, circles.

❏   SENSORY STREET - grab a can, close your eyes, walk around
     a sample house and neighborhood using all your senses except
     sight - it's really different and a little hard unless you concentrate.

❏   COMPUTER LAB AND REAL CHEMISTRY LAB - where
     techs help you make your own experiment -slime! $1.00 extra
     and you get to take home your experiment!

MICHIGAN STATE CAPITAL

Capital & Michigan Avenues (I-496 exit M.L. King Street. Follow
Capital Loop), **Lansing** 48933

❏   Activity: Michigan History
❏   Telephone: (517) 373-2353
     www.housedems.com/capitoltour.htm
❏   Hours: Monday - Friday, 9:00 am - 4:00 pm. Saturday, 10:00 am
     - 3:00 pm. Closed Sundays and Holiday weekends.
❏   Admission: Free
❏   Tours: Every half hour.

The House and Senate Galleries are situated inside a building
that looks like the US Capital. Recently restored, the building
was originally designed by foremost architect, Elijah E. Myers
during the Gilded Age. You'll start out under the dome which is a
view upward over 600 feet. This gets the kids' attention. Next, you
take a peek in the Governor's Office (if he's in, he'll wave or come
over to say "hi"). It's a very stately, very large office that was
cleaned during the restoration with cotton swabs (at least, the
ceiling was). The kids try to imagine doing their cleaning chores
with only cleaning solution and cotton swabs - sounds impossible!
Another highlight of this tour is the Senate Room. Magnificent to
view (from the public access balcony), it has so much detail, the
kids are mesmerized. They'll also learn about contemporary
legislative processes and how citizens get involved.

MICHIGAN WOMEN'S HISTORICAL CENTER AND HALL OF FAME

Lansing - 213 West Main Street, 48933. *Activity:* Museums. (517) 484-1880. **http://members.tripod.com/mwfame**. *Hours:* Wednesday - Saturday, Noon - 5:00 pm and Sunday 2:00 - 4:00 pm. Closed Saturdays during the Summer. Closed major holidays. *Admission:* Adults $2.50, Seniors $2.00 (60+), Children $1.00 (5-14). Rotating exhibits of Michigan Women's artworks and achievements on display.

PLANET WALK

Lansing - River Trail along Grand & Red Cedar River (Outside Science Center - 200 Museum Drive), 48933. *Activity:* Outdoors. (517) 371-6730. Travel 93 million miles from the Earth to the Sun, almost another 4 billion miles to the farthest planet, Pluto. Want to walk it? Begin at the scaled down version of the sun (it's about the size of a giant play ball). Each step further out covers 1 million scale miles. Pass earth, the size of a pea, and Jupiter, the size of an orange. The total walking distance from the Sun to Pluto is 2 miles.

R.E. OLDS TRANSPORTATION MUSEUM

Lansing - 240 Museum Drive (Downtown off Michigan Avenue), 48933. *Activity:* Museums. (517) 372-0529 or (888) ASK-OLDS. **www.reolds.com**. *Hours:* Monday-Saturday, 10:00 am - 5:00 pm. Sunday, Noon-5:00 pm. Closed major holidays. *Admission:* $2-4.00 (over age 5). See the first Oldsmobile (1897), REO's, Toronado (first 1966), Stars, Durants and Olds car advertising. The museum is a reflection of R.E. Olds life and contribution to the transport industry from 1883 to the present are featured, too.

RIVERWALK THEATRE SHOWS

Lansing - 228 Museum Drive, 48933. *Activity:* The Arts. (517) 482-5700 or (517) 372-0945. **http://riverwalk.thetheater.com**. *Hours:* Children's theatre shows are Friday at 7:30 pm, Saturday and Sunday at 2:00 pm and 4:30 pm. *Admission:* Adults $10.00-12.00, Seniors $9.00-11.00, Students $5.00, Children $4.00. (Children's shows are Adults $6.00, Children $4.00).

GREENMEAD HISTORICAL PARK

Livonia - 20501 Newburgh Road (junction of 8 Mile and Newburgh Roads), 48150. *Activity:* Museums. (248) 477-7375. **www.ci.livonia.mi.us/Community/Greenmead.htm**. *Hours:* Grounds open Daily, dawn to dusk. (May - October, and in December). Closed holidays. *Admission:* Adults $2.00, Youth (under 18) $1.00. *Tours:* Guided tours are offered only on Sundays between 1:00 - 4:00 pm. Eight historical outline regional history, especially during scheduled events or Sundays. The 95-acre farmsite has picnicking facilities.

JEEPERS! AT WONDERLAND MALL

29859 Plymouth Road (I-96 - exit Middlebelt Road)

Livonia 48150

❑ Activity: Amusements

❑ Telephone: (800) 533-7377 or (734) 762-5118
www.jeepers.com

❑ Hours: Monday - Thursday, 11:00 am - 9:00 pm, Friday, 11:00 am - 10:00 pm, Saturday, 10:00 am - 10:00 pm, Sunday, 11:00 am - 8:00 pm.

❑ Admission: Weekends, General $10.00 for rides, Children $3.99 (under 36 inches). School Days, General $6.99 - Free admission for parents - except for bumper cars and games.

A climbing area, bumper cars, video games and 6 rides all make for a great "year-round" way to help keep the kids entertained. Tickets that are awarded can be redeemed for prizes. O.K. Dad, this is your assignment so Mom can get some *real* shopping done!

ALGONAC STATE PARK

Marine City - 8732 River Road (2 miles north of the city on M-29), 48039. *Activity:* Outdoors. (810) 765-5605 (April 16 - Oct. 30) or (810) 465-2160 (November 1- April 16), **www.dnr.state. mi.us/www/parks/algonac.html**. *Admission:* $4.00 per vehicle. On the St. Clair River you can watch the large freighters pass by from this park. Other features include winter sports, hiking trails along a prairie area, fishing (walleye), rough camping, and boating.

HEATH BEACH
16339 Cone Road (US-23 to exit 22 - follow signs)

Milan 48160

❑   Activity: Outdoors
❑   Telephone: (734) 439-1818, **www.heathbeach.com**
❑   Hours: Daily, 10:30 am - 7:30 pm (Memorial Day Weekend - Labor Day Weekend)
❑   Admission: Adults $6.00 (weekends), $5.00 (weekdays), Children $3.00 (9-12), Under 8 Free (all the time).

Some people see a hole in the ground (in this case caused by the construction of US-23)...others see opportunity. In 1962, area resident Charles Heath gained a 6-acre lake (in his former cow pasture) along the new construction. For years they used this recreation area as a family swimming hole. With the persuading of friends, Charles decided to make some improvements and open it to the public. Today this family tradition can easily be spotted everywhere in the region with the help of the bumper sticker campaign promoting this family fun spot.

MILAN DRAGWAY

10860 Plank Road (US-23 to exit 25)

Milan 48160

- Activity: Sports
- Telephone: (734) 439-7368, **www.milandragway.com**
- Hours: Season is April-October. Auto races held in the day, Saturday & Sunday. Motorcycle races held Friday nights.
- Admission: Adults $8.00, Children $4.00 (7-12), Free (ages 6 and under) - Weekdays. Adults $10.00, other rates the same on weekends. During special events - rates can be higher. Call or visit website for details.
- Miscellaneous: Drag and bracket racing. Events include junior racing, nostalgia days, RAM chargers, Harlet drags and invitationals. There's even a new track for off-road truck races.

A race that lasts 6 seconds or less? Don't blink or you might just miss it! See Michigan's (and nationally known) racers compete to see who can travel the fastest on the ¼ mile drag "strip". Special events feature "dragsters" that can reach speeds of over 300 MPH (in a little over 4 seconds!) Be sure to bring earplugs for the kids (& parents) since these "open header" vehicles can be extremely loud! Hey Moms and Dads... Wednesday and Friday allow you (for an entry fee) to see just how fast the family "dragster" can go! Kids can also compete in special miniature drag cars...wow!

KENSINGTON METROPARK

2240 West Buno Road (I-96 - Next exit past Milford)

Milford 48380

- Activity: Outdoors
- (248) 685-1561 or (800) 477-3178
  www.metroparks.com/kensington.html
- Hours: Daily, 6:00 am - 10:00 pm
- Admission: Weekends $3.00 per vehicle, Weekdays $2.00 per vehicle.

S panning over 4,000 acres (including the 1200 acre Lake Kent), this park offers family fun year-round. Some of the educational attractions include the Farm Center (discover and touch numerous animals) and the Nature Center (with wildlife exhibits and nature trails). For a break from the action, step aboard the Island Queen paddlewheel boat for a scenic trip around the lake. Speaking of Lake Kent, it offers great fishing (you can even bring your own boat or use rentals including sailboats which are available) and 2 beaches in the summertime. Golfing is also available on the 18-hole course of the south side of the lake. Winter brings sled riding, tobogganing, cross-country skiing, and sleigh rides (minimum snow base of 4-6 inches required) to the park.

PROUD LAKE STATE PARK

Milford - 3500 Wixom Road (I-96 exit Wixom Road north), 48382. *Activity:* Outdoors. (810) 685-2433. **www.dnr.state.mi.us/ www/parks/proudlk.htm**. *Hours:* 8:00 am-Dusk. *Admission:* $4.00 per vehicle. Including part of the upper Huron River, features include hiking trails, beaches and swimming, boating and canoeing, camping, winter sports. It is also a great place to be (beginning the last weekend of April) when the site releases large batches of trout for fishing.

MONROE COUNTY HISTORICAL MUSEUM

Monroe - 126 South Monroe Street, 48161. *Activity:* Michigan History. (734) 243-7137. *Hours:* Daily, 10:00 am - 5:00 pm. Closed Monday and Tuesday, (October - April). Closed major holidays. *Admission:* Adults $2.00, Children (7-17) $1.00. Free to all, June - August. In the old post office building, you'll find exhibits on the family of General George A. Custer as well as area history. They're known for local maps, Victorian furnishings and displays about Indian and French pioneer history.

RIVER RAISIN BATTLEFIELD VISITOR'S CENTER

1403 East Elm Street (I-75, exit 14)

Monroe 48161

❑ Activity: Michigan History

❑ Telephone: (734) 243-7136 or (743) 243-7137
   http://monroe.lib.mi.us/cwis/mchc.htm#battlefield

❑ Hours: Daily, 10:00 am - 5:00 pm (Memorial Day - Labor Day),
   Weekends, 10:00 am - 5:00 pm (Rest of the Year)

❑ Admission: Free (donations accepted)

An important stop for interesting regional history, this visitor's center focuses on the battle (during the War of 1812) that was the worst defeat for the Americans. The British and Chief Tecumseh's Indians killed over 800 settlers during this battle. A 10 minute presentation (with maps, mannequins, and dioramas) summarizes the importance of who was in control of the Great Lakes.

STERLING STATE PARK

Monroe - 2800 State Park Road (off I-75), 48161. *Activity:* Outdoors.   **www.dnr.state.mi.us/www/parks/plse.htm#sterling**. (313) 289-2715. *Admission:* $4.00 per vehicle. Camping, hiking trails, boating, fishing and swimming.

METRO BEACH METROPARK

Mount Clemens - Metropolitan Parkway, 48043. *Activity:* Outdoors. **www.metroparks.com/metrobeach.html**. (810) 463-4581 or (800) 477-3172. *Hours:* Monday - Friday, 8:00 am - 8:00 pm. Weekends & Holidays, 8:00 am – Dusk. *Admission:* Weekdays $2.00 per vehicle, Weekends $3.00 per vehicle. A lakeside summer beach retreat (with a boardwalk over a mile long) that has several unique attractions including: The Tot Lot (a place for kids as young as 3 can ride their bikes without running over someone), Educational Nature Programs, and a heated pool.

MARQUIS THEATER

135 East Main Street

Northville 48167

- ❏ Activity: The Arts
- ❏ Telephone: (248) 349-8110
- ❏ Admission: $5.00 for all child-actor performances, $6.50 for performances with adult and child actors

Does your child like to perform like a "star" around the house? We could closely relate to that statement since our 6-year-old daughter Jenny, loves singing and performing. In fact, it is this personality that has promoted her to the title of "Marketing and Publicity Director" with Kids Love Publications. Owner and producer, Inge Zayti produces mostly plays with children actors between the ages of 8-18. There is even a 2 week day camp that teaches acting and singing who might want to give this career a try.

MAYBURY STATE PARK

Northville - 20145 Beck Road (I-96 to I-275 north, west on Eight Mile Road), 48167. *Activity:* Outdoors. (248) 349-8390. **www.dnr.state.mi.us/www/parks/maybury.htm**. *Hours:* 8:00 am – Dusk. *Admission:* $4.00 per vehicle. Mostly forest, features include horseback riding, cross-country skiing, hiking trails, bike trails, fishing, winter sports, and a visitors center and living farm featuring a petting area for kids.

MOTORSPORTS MUSEUM & HALL OF FAME OF AMERICA

43700 Expo Center Drive (I-96, exit 162)

Novi 48375

- ❏ Activity: Museums
- ❏ Telephone: (248) 349-7223, **www.mshf.com**
- ❏ Hours: Daily, 10:00 am - 5:00 pm. (Closed Easter & Christmas)
- ❏ Admission: Adults $5.00, Seniors $3.00, Children $3.00 (under 12)

If there is a racing fan in your family this is a "must stop". See over 100 vehicles including powerboats, motorcycles, "Indy style" racecars, NASCAR style racecars, dragsters, and even snowmobiles. Get their photo taken in the driver's seat of an actual Winston Cup racecar and then take the challenge of racing on the 4-lane scale slot car track or video simulation race car.

MERIDIAN TOWNSHIP'S CENTRAL PARK

5150 Marsh Road

Okemos 48864

❑ Activity: Museums

❑ Telephone: (517) 347-7300 or (517) 349-5777 Nokomis
   www.nokomis.org

❑ Hours: (Nokomis Learning Center), Tuesday -Friday, 10:00 am - 5:00 pm, Saturday Noon - 5:00 pm. (Meridian Historical Village), Saturday 2:00 -5:00 pm (November & April 1 - June) and 10:00 am - 1:00 pm (July-October).

❑ Gift shop at Nokomis.

NOKOMIS LEARNING CENTER - center for focus of woodland Indians of the Great Lakes; specifically the Ojibwa, Ottawa, and Potawatomi tribes known as the People of the Three Fires.

MERIDIAN HISTORICAL VILLAGE - the only known Plank Road Tollhouse still around in the state is part of this small village. It includes a furnished farmhouse and one-room schoolhouse with a school bell ringing the beginning of class.

HAYES STATE PARK

Onstead - 1220 Wampler's Lake Road (US-12 west to M-124), 49265. **www.dnr.state.mi.us/www/parks/hayes.htm**. *Activity:* Outdoors. (517) 467-7401. *Admission:* $4.00 per vehicle. Camping, boating, fishing, swimming and winter sports are offered.

LAKE HUDSON STATE PARK

Onstead - 1220 Wampler's Lake Road (M-156 SE), 49265. *Activity:* Outdoors. (517) 445-2265. *Admission:* $4.00 per vehicle. **www.dnr.state.mi.us/www/parks/hudson.htm.** Camping, hiking, boating, fishing, swimming and winter sports.

MYSTERY HILL

7611 US Highway 12 - (opposite Hayes State Park)

Onsted (Irish Hills) 49265

- ❑ Activity: Amusements
- ❑ Telephone: (517) 467-2517
- ❑ Hours: Daily, 11:00 am - 6:00 pm. (Summer) Weekends only, (May, September, October)
- ❑ Admission: Adults $5.00, Children $4.00 (4-16)
- ❑ Tours: 30 minute guided.
- ❑ Miscellaneous: Gift shop. Miniature Golf Course.

E xhibits seem to defy gravity and your sense of balance goes. Water runs uphill and people stand sideways without falling over. The principles demonstrated are studied and applied by psychology departments of universities everywhere. It's an illusion experiment (or is it real?...) and you're the assistant!

PREHISTORIC FOREST

8203 US Highway 12 (Across from Hayes State Park. Near M-124)

Onsted (Irish Hills) 49265

- ❑ Activity: Amusements
- ❑ Telephone: (517) 467-2514
- ❑ Hours: Daily 10:30 am - 7:00 pm (Summer). Weekends Only, (Rest of year)
- ❑ Admission: Adults $6.00, Seniors $4.00 (60+), Children $4.00 (4-16).

❑   Miscellaneous: Food available. Waterslide arcade, trampolines, maze, Sinking Ship Slide - all for additional fee. Combo discount prices available.

G uided train tours that transport visitors back to the prehistoric age. Go through a tunnel under a giant waterfall (serves as a time tunnel) to a forest maze of 60 life-size dinosaurs. Some even move and growl. You'll meet Professor Otto in his lab and see his museum of fossils. Learn how dinos slept and ate (ate things whole and then ate rocks to crush and "digest" food).

STAGECOACH STOP USA
7203 US-12
Onsted (Irish Hills) 49265

❑   Activity: Amusements
❑   Telephone: (517) 467-2300, **www.stagecoachstop.com**
❑   Hours: Tuesday - Friday, 10:30 am - 5:30 pm (Summer). Weekends, 10:30 am - 6:30 pm. Weekends only (May)
❑   Admission: Adults $10.00, Seniors $6.00 (65+), Children $6.00 (4-11)
❑   Miscellaneous: Petting zoo, Fort Wilderness playground, picnic area, and kiddie rides. Food. Closed Tuesdays following a Monday holiday. Jamboree Theatre with country music entertainment.

T ravel back to the Old West made to look like an authentic 19th century western village with wooden plank sidewalks and dirt streets. Listen closely to the Marshall when he makes announcements every few minutes about the activity about to begin. Maybe start out slow by watching a craftsman blacksmith, glass-blower, or worker in the sawmill. Stop by the petting zoo and then pan for gold with an old prospector (watch out, they're greedy!). Parents can sip on a Sarsaparilla (old-fashioned non-alcohol beverage) as kids play on rides like Runaway Mine Cars, the Incredible Flying Machine, or White Water Rapids Indian Canoe Ride. Silly, staged gunfights challenge the Marshall against thieves. Remember, the bad guy always gets it in the end! Wander through the shops of a barber, bank, carriage house, etc. and stop in a saloon (café) for a chuckwagon meal or treat. Be sure to take a Wild Country Train ride before leaving.

ORTONVILLE RECREATION AREA

Ortonville - 5779 Hadley Road, 48462. *Activity:* Outdoors. (248) 627-3828. **www.dnr.state.mi.us/www/parks/ortonvil.htm**. *Admission:* $4.00 per vehicle. Camping/cabins, hiking trails, boating, fishing, swimming and winter sports.

LAKELANDS TRAIL STATE PARK

Pinckney - 8555 Silver Hill, Rt. 1, 48169. *Activity:* Outdoors. (313) 426-4913. A 13-mile gravel trail that connects Pinckney and Stockbridge. Along the way you'll pass through rolling farmland and wooded areas that offer spectacular views. The Pinckney trailhead is a quarter mile north of M-36 on D-19 in Pinckney. The Stockbridge trailhead is on M-52 in Stockbridge.

PINCKNEY RECREATION AREA

Pinckney - 8555 Silver Hill, Rt. 1 (I-94 exit 159, North), 48169. *Activity:* Outdoors. (734) 426-4913. *Admission:* $4.00 per vehicle. **www.dnr.state.mi.us/www/parks/pinckney.htm#top**. Camping, hiking (Lakelands trail is popular - see separate listing above), boating, fishing, swimming, bicycle trails and winter sports.

PLYMOUTH HISTORICAL MUSEUM

Plymouth - 155 South Main Street (one block north of Kellogg Park), 48170. **www.plymouth.lib.mi.us/%7Ehistory**. *Activity:* Museums. (734) 455-8940. *Hours:* Wednesday, Thursday, Saturday 1:00 -4:00 pm. Sunday, 2:00 - 5:00 pm. *Admission:* Adults $2.00, Youth $0.50 (ages 5-17), Family Rate $5.00. GALLERY - Main Street Shops and offices of 19th century professions, Victorian Room, Then and Now Hands-on Center, Automobiles - 1st Alter Car & many autos built in early 1900's.

DETROIT LIONS FOOTBALL

Pontiac - 1200 Featherstone Road (Pontiac Silverdome), 48342. *Activity:* Sports. **www.detroitlions.com**. (800) 616-ROAR. *Admission:* $20.00-35.00. Be sure to ask about "Family Fun Zone". NFL football (over 65 seasons) season runs September-December.

PAINT CREEK CIDER MILL RESTAURANT

Rochester (Detroit) - 4480 Orion Road (2 miles Northwest of town), 48306. *Activity:* Theme Restaurants. (248) 651-8361. Serving Lunch and Dinner. Children's Menu. Moderate + dining prices. Since 1959 they've pressed cider on the pretty banks of Paint Creek. Their mill is open and operating in the Fall but food is served year-round.

WOLCOTT MILL METROPARK
(between 29 and 30 Mile Road)
Romeo 48065

- ❑ Activity: Outdoors
- ❑ Telephone: (810) 749-5997 or (800) 477-3175
  www.metroparks.com/wolcottmill.html
- ❑ Hours: Weekdays, 9:00 am - 5:00 pm, Weekends, 9:00 am - 7:00 pm (May - October). Closes at 5:00 pm (November - April)
- ❑ Admission: Weekends, $3.00 per vehicle. Free weekdays.

A gristmill is always a fun experience (really, explain it to the kids like it is a giant "mousetrap" game inside - full of large gears and rubberbands, etc.). See the mid-1800's era gristmill grind wheat into flour on the huge millstones. (*It's interesting to note that in a hundred years, most mills would only wear out maybe one set of millstones*). Also featured is the Farm Learning Center (on Wolcott Road) that teaches the methods and importance of farming today. See cow milking, sheep demonstrations, and experimental vegetable plots.

DETROIT ZOO

8450 West Ten Mile Road (I-75 to I-696 West - Woodward Avenue Exit), **Royal Oak** 48068

❑   Activity: Animals & Farms

❑   Telephone: (248) 398-0900, **http://detroitzoo.org**

❑   Hours: Daily, 10:00 am - 5:00 pm - open later Wednesdays. (April - October). Daily, 10:00 am - 4:00 pm. (November - March)

❑   Admission: Adults $7.50 (18+), Seniors $5.50 (62+), Student $5.50 (13-18), Children $4.50 (2-12)

❑   Miscellaneous: Picnic areas and playground. Strollers and Adult roller chairs available for rent.

Simply put...your family is in for a real day of adventure and fun when visiting the Detroit Zoo. Innovational in many ways, this zoo was the first in the county to use what is now know as "barless cages". This effect brings you very close to the animals (safely) by using elevations and natural habitat barriers (such as moats). Your benefit is that you see the animals in a more natural environment...less like a zoo (cool!). Here's a few of the many (and constantly changing) exhibits that you'll see: The Mandrill Exhibit (a very colorful baboon), The Wilson Aviary Wing (30 species of birds in a large free-flying building - much like an indoor jungle - there is even a waterfall), The Penguinarium (love that name! - see underwater views of these birds that cannot fly), The Chimps of Harambee (a forest setting with rock habitats...what a show!), and The Wildlife Interpretive Gallery (huge aquarium, theater, hummingbird and butterfly garden). And if all this wasn't enough...take an excursion on the famous Detroit Zoo Miniature Railroad (*it transports over 500,000 passengers a year!*).

FOUR BEARS WATERPARK

3000 Auburn Road (I-75 - Rochester Road Exit)

Shelby Township 48317

❑ Activity: Outdoors

❑ Telephone: (810) 739-5860, **www.fourbearswaterpark.com**

❑ Hours: Monday - Friday, 10:00 am - 3:00 pm. Saturday &
Sunday, 11:00 am - 7:00 pm. (Memorial Day - June 15). Daily,
11:00 am - 7:00 pm. (June 16 - Labor Day)

❑ Admission: General $12.95 (over 48" tall), $6.95 (48 inches tall
and under). Children 2 and Seniors (65 ↑) are Free.

❑ Miscellaneous: Large picnic grounds. Food service is also
available.

A summer paradise for kids of all ages, this waterpark boasts
the state's largest collection of water slides. Some of the
additional attractions include: A sand-filled beach on a 50 acre
lake, paddle and bumper boats and special slides for non-
swimmers. Land attractions include: (some have a slight additional
charge) go-carts, carnival rides, batting cages, petting zoo, and bird
and animal shows.

MCCOURTIE PARK

Somerset Center - (US-12 and US-127 – 1 ½ miles west - enter
from South Jackson Road), 49282. *Activity:* Outdoors. Open dawn
to dusk. Picnic facilities, ballfields. Walk over 17 concrete bridges
(each a different style), visit the underground apartments and
garages, see the giant birdhouse and their tree chimneys. All of
this concrete! Until you get up close, it will fool you - it looks like
wood! Herb McCourtie, a concrete baron, left the park grounds to
his hometown. It's unique enough to definitely write home about!

CROSSWINDS MARSH WETLAND INTERPRETIVE PRESERVE

Sumpter Township - (I-94 to exit 8 - go west), 48111. *Activity:* Outdoors. **http://imc.lisd.k12.mi.us/marsh/crosswinds.html**. (734) 261-1990. Free admission. Over 100 species of birds (binocular rentals available for $1.00) can be viewed at this 1000 acre artificially created wetland - one of the largest in the country. Learn more about the plants and wildlife that were moved to this area by taking a 2 mile canoe trip that has interpretive markers to describe what you are seeing. (Canoe rentals are available for $5.00 per hour).

COE RAIL SCENIC TRAIN

Walled Lake - 840 North Pontiac Trail (I-96 - Wixom Road Exit - North), 48390. *Activity:* Tours. **www.michiganstarclipper.com**. (248) 960-9440. *Admission:* Averages $8.00 per person. *Tours:* Train departs Sundays at 1:00 and 2:30 pm, One hour long. (late April - October). Train rides through scenic countryside of Walled Lake and West Bloomfield in old-fashioned cars.

PONTIAC LAKE RECREATION AREA

Waterford - 7800 Gale Road (off M-59), 48327. *Activity:* Outdoors. **www.dnr.state.mi.us/www/parks/pontiac.htm**. (248) 666-1020. *Admission:* $4.00 per vehicle. Archery ranges and horse trails/rentals make this park unique. Camping, hiking trails, boating, fishing, swimming, bicycle trails and winter sports.

DODGE NO. 4 STATE PARK

Waterford - 4250 Parkway Drive (off M-59 west to Cass Elizabeth Road), 48328. *Activity:* Outdoors. (248) 666-1020. **www.dnr.state.mi.us/www/parks/dodge4.htm**. *Admission:* $4.00 per vehicle. Camping, fishing, boating, swimming and winter sports.

THE FRIDGE

Scott Lake Road (I-75 to Dixie Highway Exit - South)

Waterford 48328

- ❏ Activity: Outdoors
- ❏ Telephone: In season: (248) 975-4440. Off season: (248) 858-0906, **www.co.oakland.mi.us/c_serv/parks/fridge.html**
- ❏ Hours: Wednesday - Friday, 4:00 - 9:30 pm. Saturday, 10:00 am - 10:00 pm. Sunday, Noon - 8:00 pm. (All times are weather permitting). Closed Christmas Eve and Day. (Mid-December to Mid-March)
- ❏ Admission: General $8.00. Youth $4.00 (Under 43" tall). No riders under 43" tall permitted, and riders under age 10 must be accompanied by an adult.

Drop 55 feet (rather quickly) and then travel over 1000 feet as you and 3 close friends discover the thrill of tobogganing. The park has 2 runs, over 200 toboggans, and even a place to warm up with a fireplace and food. In the summer you'll find tennis courts, a 5-story raft ride, wave pool, and BMX bicycle course.

DRAYTON PLAINS NATURE CENTER

Waterford - 2125 Denby Drive (junction of US-24 and Hatchery Road, following signs), 48329. *Activity:* Outdoors. (248) 674-2119. *Hours:* Grounds open 8:00 am - 9:00 pm, (April -October). Only open until 6:00 pm rest of year. Interpretive Center open Tuesday - Friday, 11:00 am - 2:00 pm and Weekends, Noon - 4:00 pm. Free admission. 137 acres of trails along the Clinton River plus a nice Interpretive Center. In the center there are displays of mounted animals in recreated scenes of their natural habitats.

HIGHLAND RECREATION AREA

White Lake - 5200 East Highland Road (off M-59 East), 48363. *Activity:* Outdoors. (248) 889-3750. **www.dnr.state.mi.us/www/parks/highland.htm**. *Admission:* $4.00/vehicle. Camping, hiking, boating, fishing, swimming & winter sports. Horse rentals & trails.

ALPINE VALLEY SKI AREA

White Lake - 6775 East Highland Road (I-96 - Milford Road exit to M-59 West), 48383. *Activity:* Outdoors. (248) 887-4183. **www.skialpinevalley.com**. You'll have a real "Alpine" feeling since this resort offers 25 runs (some of which have many trees and are steep). Rental equipment: Skis (also shaped skis to learn easier) and snowboards.

ROOFTOP LANDING REINDEER FARM RESTAURANT

2980 North Williamston Road (South of downtown, I-96 Williamston Exit north), **Williamston** 48895

❑　Activity: Theme Restaurants

❑　Telephone: (517) 655-5234

❑　Hours: Monday - Saturday, 11:000 am - 10:00 pm. Sunday, 8:00 am - 8:00 pm.

❑　Miscellaneous: Gift shop. Children's Menu. Moderate prices.

Tame reindeer live on site as pets. On 80+ degree F. days, they will probably be indoors and not visible. See the Heliport where Santa's sleigh and helicopter might want to land. Stop for lunch/dinner from the children's menu selections of Dancer (burger), Blitzen (chicken tenders), Donner (hot dog), etc. and you'll have to order Rudolph's Red Nose Sundae (with a red cherry on top). Great spot for a holiday, winter family meal in a lodge setting.

ROLLING HILLS COUNTY PARK

Ypsilanti - 7660 Stoney Creek Road, 48197. *Activity:* Outdoors. (734) 482-3866. Summers: Wave pool, water slide, zero-depth pool, waterfall, picnic area, sports fields, fishing pond, grassy sunbathing area, sandy beach, 9-hole Frisbee golf course, tube rentals. Winter: Dual toboggan chutes, ice skating, and cross-county skiing.

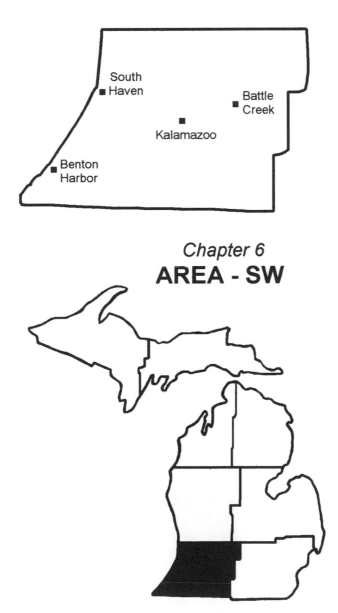

Chapter 6
AREA - SW

Our Favorites...

- Kellogg's Cereal City
- Deer Forest
- S/S Keewatin
- Kalamazoo Valley Museum
- Dune Rides

WHITEHOUSE NATURE CENTER

Albion - 1381 East Erie Street (Albion College), 49224. *Activity:* Outdoors. (517) 629-0582. *Hours:* Monday - Friday, 9:30 am - 4:30pm. Weekends, 10:30 am - 4:30pm. Closed major and college holidays. Free Admission. A 135 acre outdoor facility for education that features 6 nature trails and 175 species of birds. Includes an observation room with live exhibits.

FORT CUSTER RECREATION AREA

Augusta - 5163 West Fort Custer Drive (M-96 West), 49012. *Activity:* Outdoors. (616) 731-4200. **www.dnr.state.mi.us/www/ parks/plmm.htm#fc**. *Admission:* $4.00 per vehicle. Camping, hiking, boating, fishing, swimming, bicycle trails, winter sports.

KELLOGG BIRD SANCTUARY

12685 East C Avenue (13 miles northwest on M-89, between 40th and East Gull Lake Drive), **Augusta** 49012

- ❑ Activity: Outdoors
- ❑ Telephone: (616) 671-2510
  http://kbs.msu.edu/www/sanctuary
- ❑ Hours: Daily, 9:00 am - 8:00 pm. (May-October). Daily, 9:00 am - 5:00 pm. (rest of year)
- ❑ Admission: Adults $2.50, Seniors $2.00, Children $1.00 (2-12)

An MSU experimental facility of birds of prey, wild geese, ducks, swans, pheasants and peacocks. There are displays and observation decks.

BINDER PARK ZOO

7400 Division Drive (I-94 to exit 100 - go south)

Battle Creek 49014

- ❑ Activity: Animals & Farms
- ❑ Telephone: (616) 979-1351, **www.binderparkzoo.org**

- ❑ Hours: Monday - Friday, 9:00 am - 5:00 pm (until 8:00 pm on Wednesday & Thursdays - Summers). Saturday & Holidays, 9:00 am - 6:00 pm. Sunday, 11:00 am - 6:00 pm. (mid-April to mid-October)
- ❑ Admission: Adults $4.95 (13+), Seniors $3.95, Children $2.75 (3-12)
- ❑ Miscellaneous: Gift shop with unique animal items.

Natural settings offer over 250 animals in 80 exhibits that you can see while strolling along wooden boardwalks. See exhibits like a Chinese Red Panda and a Mexican Grey Wolf. Interact with insects, and have fun learning at the Conservation Stations (a hands-on exhibit). The hands-on playground at the children's zoo is said to have the world's largest and most accurate dinosaur replicas, a petting zoo, and miniature railroad.

BATTLE CREEK BATTLECATS

Battle Creek - 1392 Capital Avenue NE (I-94 to exit 98B - go north), 49017. *Activity:* Sports. (616) 660-CATS (2287), **www.michiganbattlecats.com**. *Admission:* Field Box $8.00, Box $6.00, Reserved $5.00, Bleachers $4.00. Seniors (60+) and Children (14 and under) $3.00. This class "A" Midwest League Affiliate for the Houston Astros offers plenty of family entertainment value. Be sure to call about special family "free-bee" nights that include free fireworks, balls, hats, etc. Can't you just smell the hot dogs?

FULL BLAST & BATTLE CREEK YOUTH CENTER

35 Hamblin Avenue (I-94 to I-194/M-66 - north)

Battle Creek 49017

- ❑ Activity: Amusements
- ❑ Telephone: (616) 966-3667, **www.fullblast.org**

❑ Hours: Monday - Friday, 6:00 am - 9:00 pm. Saturday, 8:00 am - 9:00 pm. Sunday, 11:00 am - 8:00 pm. "Gully Washer" (indoor), Monday - Saturday, 10:00 am - 7:00 pm. (Winter hours opens weekdays at 3:30 pm) Sunday, 11:00 am - 7:00 pm. (Same hours for "Flash Flood" - Outdoor - waterpark in summer).

❑ Admission: $5.00 per person with waterpark entry. $3.00 per person without waterpark entry.

A family fun attraction with something for everyone. Attractions include a skateboard park, indoor and outdoor waterparks (with 200 foot waterslides), an indoor playground, a river float, 3 basketball courts, full-service health club, café and food court, and teen nightclub.

KELLOGG'S CEREAL CITY USA

171 West Michigan Avenue (I-94 exit 98B to I-194/M 66 north. On the riverfront.)

Battle Creek 49017

❑ Activity: Tours

❑ Telephone: (616) 962-6230, **www.kelloggscerealcityusa.com**

❑ Hours: Monday - Friday, 9:30 am - 5:00 pm. Saturday, 9:30 am - 6:00 pm. Sunday, 11:00 am - 5:00 pm (Summer). Tuesday - Friday, 10:00 am - 4:00 pm. Saturday, 10:00 am - 5:00 pm. Sunday, 12:00 pm - 5:00 pm (September - May)

❑ Admission: Adults $6.50, Seniors $5.50, Children $4.50 (3-12)

❑ Miscellaneous: Red Onion Grill - a 1930's style diner serves sandwiches. The Factory Store. Half of the facility is for older kids (in all of us) and another half is for younger kids. You may want to separate for a little while.

F lakes started as an experiment for a new healthy breakfast food by Dr. Kellogg in the late 1800's. Within a couple of years, almost 40 different cereal companies had started in the Battle Creek area - including POST (one of the only surviving still). You'll learn this and more in the theater presentation on the first floor. Adults will find some of their marketing strategies unique - like asking people to stop eating their flakes because they were in short supply. As you go upstairs, don't be surprised to " bump" into Tony the Tiger or Snap, Crackle & Pop (we have video tape of big hugs from our kids to these characters)! The simulated working production line tour is where you can see, smell and taste a warm sample of freshly made flakes. This is narrated by a kernel of corn hoping he becomes a cereal flake. Cereal City has hands-on interactives in a cobblestone lane setting. The "Tony" and "Tony Jr." is a soft play area where younger sets can climb up inside a cereal box and slide down as you're poured out of the box! There's a ball pit with gym too. Before you leave, buy a box of special Corn Flakes with your photo on the front - a must souvenir for cereal lovers!

LEILA ARBORETUM & KINGMAN MUSEUM OF NATURAL HISTORY

928 West Michigan Avenue

Battle Creek 49017

❑   Activity: Museums

❑   Telephone: Museum (616) 965-5117, Arboretum (616) 969-0270

❑   Hours: (Museum) Tuesday - Friday, 9:00 am - 5:00 pm. Saturday & Sunday, 1:00 - 5:00 pm. Open Monday during July & August. (Arboretum) Daily, Dawn to Dusk.

❑   Admission: (Museum) Adults $2.00, Students $1.00. The arboretum admission is Free.

Originally built in 1922, this attraction was closed during the Great Depression of 1929.   Re-opened in 1982, it now features a sunken garden, a visitor's center, a children's adventure garden, and large floral displays (depending on season). The Kingman Museum of Natural History (West Michigan at 20th) has 3 floors of exhibits including dinosaurs and a planetarium.

1839 HISTORIC COURTHOUSE MUSEUM

Berrien Springs - 313 North Cass Street, 49103. *Activity:* Michigan History. (616) 471-1202. *Hours:* Tuesday - Friday, 9:00 am - 4:00 pm. Saturday & Sunday, 1:00 - 4:00 pm. (May to mid-

January).   Closed Monday - Wednesday (mid-February to April).
Admission: Adults $2.50, Students $1.00 (ages 6-17). The restored
courtroom and courthouse are surrounded by an 1870 sheriff's
residence and jail, 1830's log house, and a mid-1800's county
office. All focus on local history.

COOK ENERGY INFO CENTER AND DUNES

1 Cook Place (I-94 exit 16 or 23, follow signs - off Red Arrow
Highway), **Bridgman** 49106

❑   Activity: Outdoors
❑   Telephone: (800) 548-2555, **www.cookinfo.com**
❑   Hours: Tuesday - Sunday, 10:00 am - 5 :00 pm. (mid-January to
     mid-December) Closed all holidays.
❑   Admission: Free
❑   Tours: 45 minute guided.
❑   Miscellaneous: Picnic areas.

Technology and nature together - sounds impossible. Nuclear
power, electricity and future energy sources are explained. A
model of the plant explains its functions, then view the wide-
screen tour film. Hike dune trails along Lake Michigan shoreline
including forests and wetlands. There are also energy video games
and hands-on displays.

BEAR CAVE

Buchanan - (4 miles north on Red Bud Trail), 49107. *Activity:*
Outdoors. (616) 695-3050. *Hours:* Daily, 10:00 am - 4:00 pm
(Memorial Day - Labor Day). *Admission:* Adults $3.00, Children
$1.50 (6-12). One of the few caves in Michigan that is accessible
to the public, Bear Cave (150-feet long) is accessed by a narrow,
winding stairway. The temperature is a constant 58 degrees F. so
be sure to dress appropriately. A taped narration explains the sights
of stalactites, flowstone, and petrified leaves.   A warning
though…the cave does contain bats. However, if you don't bother
them, they usually won't bother you!

TIBBITS OPERA HOUSE

Coldwater - 14 Hanchett Street (South of US-12), 49036. *Activity:* The Arts. (517) 278-6029. *Admission:* "Popcorn Theater", Adults $5.00, Children $3.00 (12 and under). Tickets for other shows vary but begin at around $9.00. *Tours:* Free, Monday - Friday, 9:00 am - 6:00 pm (advance reservation required). An opera and theater since 1882, you can still see community plays year-round and professional summer stock productions in June through August. A family favorite is the "Popcorn Theater" that is specially produced for children ages 5 and older and is scheduled for Friday and Saturday mornings.

DEER FOREST

Paw Paw Lake Road (I-94 exit 39 north, follow signs)

Coloma 49038

- ❑   Activity: Animals & Farms
- ❑   Telephone: (616) 468-4961, **www.deerforest.com**
- ❑   Hours: Daily, 10:00 am - 6:00 pm (Memorial Weekend - Labor Day)
- ❑   Admission: Adults $12.00, Children $10.00 (3-11)
- ❑   Miscellaneous: Gift shop. Picnic areas. "Wild Child Play Habitat". Santa's Summer Home. Kid's entertainment like magicians. Mostly in the woods and shaded.

Their slogan, "More fun than a zoo" is true, mostly because it's designed as an Animal and an Amusement Park. Different animals to pet are baby zebras and mini-horses (the size of dogs) or sit between the humps of a camel. Most every animal here is tame enough to pet (making it different than a zoo). You can also ride ponies and camels, a treetop Ferris wheel, a carrousel or mini-train. Our favorite part had to be Storybook Lane, a large park within the park, where you meander around the lane. Each setting illustrates a different Nursery Rhyme scene like "3 Men in a Tub" (in a pond with real frogs and small fish) or "Baa Baa Black Sheep" (with what else but, black sheep). To get your money's worth, be sure to spend several hours here and plan a picnic or buy at the snack bar. Also, lots of photo ops everywhere.

CITY OF DOUGLAS

Douglas - Highway A-2 (Near Saugatuck-Douglas Bridge - Harbor Village), 49406. *Activity:* Tours. (616) 857-2107. *Hours:* Afternoons, Call for schedule. *Admission:* Adults $8.00, Children $5.00 (3-12). A sightseeing boat that offers scenic trips onto the river and Lake Michigan (as long as the weather cooperates).

S/S KEEWATIN

CR-A2 (Blue Star Highway & Union Street) (Kalamazoo River near bridge at Harbour Village), **Douglas** 49406

- ❑ Activity: Tours
- ❑ Telephone: (616) 857 2464
- ❑ Hours: Daily, 10:00 am - 4:30 pm. (Summers only)
- ❑ Admission: Adults $5.00, Children $2.50 (6-12)
- ❑ Miscellaneous: Extensive nautical gift shop and museum. To keep the kids curious, tell them to look for the captain's boots he left on the ship (Note: you'll find them towards the very end of the tour!)

This visit sure was nostalgic. As we approached the large vessel (350 feet long), I *(Michele)* remembered the same eerie feeling it gave me as a child. It went out of service in 1965 and was brought here as a museum in 1967. I was about 10-12 years old when I first visited. Now, with my children and husband in tow, we escaped back to the time of luxury liners, elegant dining rooms, handsome staterooms, and the grand ballroom. Occasionally, pictures from the movie "Titanic" appeared on the walls and with good reason. If you liked the movie, or just the romance of the grandiose "floating hotel" - Keewatin (Key-way-tin) will fill your dreams. However, the ship is not fully restored, and is a mix of pristine wood and etched Italian glass mixed with the smell and look of old upholstery and worn paint. Well, back to reality - your kids will love that they get to go inside the "really huge boat" and even get to climb up to the top deck and turn the ship's wheel.

SOUTHWESTERN MICHIGAN COLLEGE AND CASS COUNTY MUSEUM

Dowagiac - 58900 Cherry Grove Road (east on M-62 from M-51), 49047. *Activity:* Michigan History. (616) 782-1374. *Hours:* Tuesday - Saturday, 10:00 am - 5:00 pm. Closed holidays. Free admission. Cass County history is explored through displays on science, agriculture, industry, American Indians, the Underground Railroad. Most areas have hands-on activities for kids.

J & K STEAMBOAT LINE

Grand Ledge - (various departure spots on the Grand River), 48837. *Activity:* Tours. (517) 627-2154. *Admission:* $8.00 - $49.00 depending on the type of cruise. Children (3-12) are at 50% Adult rate. This cruise line features 3 riverboats and a variety of cruising options. "Spirit of Lansing", "Princess Laura" and the largest, the "Michigan Princess" (which has three levels and luxurious woodwork and crystal). Be sure to ask about the "Kids Spectacular" cruise.

VAN BUREN COUNTY HISTORICAL MUSEUM

Hartford - 58471 Red Arrow Highway (located between Hartford and Lawrence, next to county fairgrounds), 49057. *Activity:* Michigan History. (616) 621-2188. *Hours:* Wednesday - Saturday, 10:00 am - 4:00 pm. Sunday 1:00 - 4:00 pm. 30 rooms (former county poor house) including a one-room school, children's room, general store, music room, old-fashioned kitchen, parlor, doctor's operating room, blacksmith shop and dentist's office.

GILMORE CLASSIC CAR CLUB OF AMERICA MUSEUM

6865 Hickory Road

Hickory Corners 49060

❑ Activity: Museums
❑ Telephone: (616) 671-5089, **www.gilmorcarmuseum.org**

❑   Hours: Daily, 10:00 am - 5:00 pm (May 1 - October 31)
❑   Admission: Adults $6.00, Seniors $5.00 (62+), Children $3.00
    (7-15). Kids 6 and under are Free.
❑   Miscellaneous: Picnic and playground areas.

Have you ever had a dream about finding that "priceless" antique car in someone's barn? See more than 130 unique and rare cars all displayed in antique barns. A few cars that you will see include Cadillacs, Packards, and even a steam powered car. Also, you'll find a reproduction of the Wright Brother's plane and a narrow gauge train.

MICHIGAN K-WINGS HOCKEY

Kalamazoo - 3600 Vanrick Drive (I-94 - Sprinkle Road exit - Wings Stadium), 49001. *Activity:* Sports. (616) 345-5101. **www.kwings.com**. *Admission:* Adults $7.50-14.50 (13+), Seniors $7.50-9.00, Children $4.50 (12 and under). (Public Skating) $3.00. (Rental Skates) $1.00. An IHL affiliate team for the NHL's Dallas Stars, the Wings pack lots of excitement into 40+ home games each year. (October - April).

ECHO VALLEY
8495 East H Avenue
Kalamazoo 49004

❑   Activity: Outdoors
❑   Telephone: (616) 349-3291
❑   Hours: Friday, 6:00-10:00 pm. Saturday, 10:00 am - 10:00 pm.
    Sunday, Noon - 7:00 pm. (mid-December to mid-March)
❑   Admission: (Toboggans) Adults $8.00. All day passes $10.00.
    (Inner Tubing) $7.00. (Ice Skating) $5.00
❑   Miscellaneous: Lodge and snack bar. Outdoor ice skating rink.

Aaah...the feeling of that sled racing down a fresh snow covered hill...and the air getting colder on my face...is a childhood memory that I will never forget. Relive those memories and introduce your kids to the fun of tubing and tobogganing that makes winter a blast. Eight icy and fast tracks await you as you fly down a hill of over 120 feet, at speeds of up to 60 miles per hour. The best part of all is that at this resort (*instead of George's back yard as a child*), there is a <u>tow rope</u> to pull the toboggans back up the hill (*we won't have to put the neighbor's big dog to work!*).

KALAMAZOO NATURE CENTER

7000 North Westnedge Avenue (I-94 to US-131, exit 44 east)

Kalamazoo 49004

- ❑   Activity: Outdoors
- ❑   Telephone: (616) 381-1574, **www.naturecenter.org**
- ❑   Hours: Monday - Saturday, 9:00 am - 5:00 pm. Sunday, 1-5:00 pm. (Extended summer hours)
- ❑   Admission: Adults $4.50, Seniors $3.50 (55+), Children $2.50 (4-13)
- ❑   Miscellaneous: Nature trails (one is wheelchair and stroller accessible). Gift shop - large variety of "Insect Inside Candy".

When you enter, either walk over to the Tropical Rainforest (3 stories) that's home to parrots, iguanas, tropical plants and exotic fish or walk through Nature Up Close. You'll walk through giant tree trunks and discover nature 10 times the size of life. Imagine 8 foot tall flowers and watch out for that huge frog - it's Bugs Life! We especially liked the pollen exhibit where the kids can try to help bees pollinate flowers. It's a clever demo and we learned bees pollinate by accident. The Expedition Station is outstanding with a collection of stuffed birds and real bones - all hands-on. Outside, walk through 1000 acres of dense hardwood forest and check out the Butterfly House, Hummingbird Garden or Delano Pioneer Homestead - early life in Michigan.

KALAMAZOO CIVIC YOUTH THEATRE

Kalamazoo - 426 South Park Street (Carver Center), 49007. *Activity:* The Arts. (616) 343-1313.

KALAMAZOO SYMPHONY ORCHESTRA

Kalamazoo - 126 East South Street, 49007. *Activity:* The Arts. **www.kazoosymphony.com.** (616) 349-7759. Tickets: (800) 228-9858. *Admission:* Sunday Classics, Adults $14.00, Students $7.00. Family Discovery Series, Adults $10.00, Children $6.00. The season includes family concerts and free summer outdoor concerts.

KALAMAZOO VALLEY MUSEUM

230 North Rose Street (I-94 Westnedge Ave. exit 76 north to M-43 East), **Kalamazoo** 49007

❑ Activity: Museums

❑ Telephone: (616) 373-7990

❑ Hours: Monday - Saturday, 10:00 am - 6:00 pm. Sunday, 1-5:00 pm. Wednesday, 6-9:00 pm also. Closed all major holidays.

❑ Admission: Free general admission. $2-3 per pay activity.

❑ Miscellaneous: Digistar Planetarium. Challenger Mini-Mission. Interactive Learning Hall. Small admission charged.

What an unexpected surprise! The Kalamazoo Valley should be proud. It's interesting to learn that funds for the museum were raised by the community with the museum artifacts found mostly by locals in their attics and basements. Women and girls will freak out when they see the Home Perm Machine from the early 1900's - long cords attached to giant metal clamps. Our favorite hands-on displays were: create your own sand dunes; tornadoes - can you stop them?; and the Tower Sculpture that shows you it's easier to work together than alone. What impressed us was that most displays were actual hands-on, not just push buttons. It was also interesting to learn about all of the products manufactured in the area over the years. Don't forget to catch the display "What Happens When I Catch a Cold" and every young kid loves the Children's Landscape Play Area. Their special activities are inexpensive and very well done (I.e. Challenger & Planetarium, Interactive Hall). Oops, almost forgot - check out their 2500 year old woman (mummy)!

KALAMAZOO AVIATION HISTORY MUSEUM (AIR ZOO)

3101 East Milham Road (I-94 exit 78 to airport)

Kalamazoo (Portage) 49002

- ❑   Activity: Museums
- ❑   Telephone: (616) 382-6555, **www.airzoo.org**
- ❑   Hours: Monday - Saturday, 9:00 am - 6:00 pm (until 8:00 pm on Wednesdays). Sunday, Noon - 6:00 pm. (June - August) Monday - Saturday, 9:00 am -5:00 pm. Sunday, Noon - 5:00 pm (September - May)
- ❑   Admission: Adults $10.00, Seniors $8.00 (60+), Children $5.00 (6-15)
- ❑   Tours: Ride in an antique plane Ford Tri-Motor for $45.00 per person. Call or visit website for schedule.
- ❑   Miscellaneous: Gift shop. Theater (old war movies).

"It's a land of lions and tigers and bears" - its an Air Zoo! Enter the world of imaginative and colorful aircraft with names like Tin Goose...Gooney Bird...Flying Tiger and the "cats", Wildcat...Hellcat...Bearcat...Tigercat...and Tomcat. What a great way to intrigue those little guys who don't find aircraft museums amusing...until now. Let your kids try to count the number of different "species" represented. Would-be aviators can try a virtual reality ride as a family in a flight simulator (tilt, turns, even engine and wind noise) or cockpit cutaways where you can press, pull and push levers and buttons.

CORNWELL'S TURKEYVILLE USA

18935 15 ½ Mile Road (I-94 to I-69 exit 42)

Marshall 49068

❑ Activity: Theme Restaurants

❑ (800) 228-4315 or (616) 781-4293, **www.turkeyville.com**

❑ Hours: 11:00 am - 8:00 pm. (April - September) 11:00 am - 7:00 pm (October - March)

❑ Miscellaneous: Dinner Theatre. Call or visit website for schedule. Also, while on the website, be sure to hear the "turkey music" from around the world - hilarious!

You're invited to the County Fair by Grandma and Grandpa Cornwell where tradition starts with farm-raised, preservative-free turkey. Choose from fun menu items (all contain turkey!) like "Sloppy Tom" barbecue sandwich or "Buttered Tom" cold sandwich. Also Ice Cream Parlour, General Store and Country Junction bakery for dessert. If your kids need to use restrooms, make sure they know the difference between "Toms" and "Hens".

WOLF LAKE FISHERY INTERPRETIVE CENTER

34270 County Road 652 (US-131 exit 38 West)

Mattawan 49071

❑ Activity: Animals & Farms

❑ Telephone: (616) 668-2876
   www.dnr.state.mi.us/www/fish/html/wolf_lake.html

❑ Hours: Monday - Saturday, 9:00 am - 5:00 pm. Sunday, Noon - 5:00 pm. (Call for Winter hours)

❑ Admission: Free

❑ Miscellaneous: Picnic Area. Trails.

If you've never been to a "fish farm" it's worth a trip. This one has a museum center with a stuffed sturgeon - it's big - the largest fish caught in the state - 87 inches long and 193 pounds! Learn about fish life cycles and habitats, as well as why they even have fisheries. There's a slide show of hatchery operations and hourly hatchery tours. It looks like a giant scientific engineering lab with all the pipes, basins and valves. Outside, there are display ponds with steelhead, grayling, sturgeon and Chinook salmon - you can feed the fish and watch them jump for food. Kids will love the "Small Fry Fishing Frenzy" on Saturdays at 2:00 pm (June-August). If you want them to have a positive fishing experience, they're almost guaranteed to catch here.

YANKEE SPRINGS RECREATION AREA

Middleville - 2104 Gun Lake Road (US-131, exit 61. East on A-42), 49333. *Activity:* Outdoors. (616) 795-9081. **www.dnr.state. mi.us/www/parks/yankee.htm**. *Admission:* $4.00 per vehicle. Camping/cabins, hiking trails, boating, fishing, swimming, bicycle trails, and winter sports.

BITTERSWEET SKI AREA

Otsego - 600 River Road, 49078. *Activity:* Outdoors. (616) 694-2032. **www.skibittersweet.com**. *Hours:* Daily, (December - March). 16 runs. Night skiing, lessons, rentals. Food service available.

DUNE RIDES
Blue Star Highway (A2) (I-196, exit 41southwest)

Saugatuck 49453

❑   Activity: Tours
❑   Telephone: (616) 857-2253
❑   Hours: Daily, 10:00 am - 5:30pm. (May to mid-September), Open until 7:30 (July & August). Weekends only, (mid-September to mid-October)
❑   Admission: Adults $10.50, Children $6.50 (3-10)

❑   Tours last 35 minutes.

A calm, relaxing dune ride - *NOT!* An *amusement thrill ride* is more like it! The scenic ride on 20-passenger dune schooners (with airplane tires for "flying") goes over dunes between Lake Michigan and Goshorn Lake. On a clear day, you'll get a view of the coastline from a tall peak, speed through woodlands and maybe get a view of the lost city of Singapore - an old lumber town left as a ghost town. The trip is well worth the money and very entertaining. Our driver was hilarious and there were dozens of comical signs along the way like "Bridge Out" or "Men Working". Meet the family of beech trees and the tree shaped just like the number four. Ladies, be prepared for a new hairdo by the end of your trip. They only go 35 mph but it's enough to give you butterflies every now and then. It may frighten small pre-school children - unless they love kiddie roller coasters.

MOUNT BALDHEAD

Saugatuck - (by the river near Oval Beach), 49453. *Activity:* Outdoors. Climb the 279 steps and you'll be rewarded with a great view of this huge dune and Lake Michigan.

STAR OF SAUGATUCK

Saugatuck - 716 Water Street, 49453. *Activity:* Tours. (616) 857-4261. *Hours:* Leaves every 2 hours beginning at 11:00 am. Last trip departs at 8:00 pm. (Memorial Day - Labor Day). *Admission:* Adults $8.50, Children $5.00 (3-12). A 90 minute scenic cruise on the Kalamazoo River. The 67 foot paddlewheeler offers 2 decks, live narration, and can seat 82 passengers per trip.

GRAND MERE STATE PARK

Sawyer - 12032 Red Arrow Highway (I-94, exit 22 west), 49125. *Activity:* Outdoors. (616) 426-4013. **www.dnr.state.mi.us/www/parks/plwc.htm#grandmere**. *Admission:* $4.00 per vehicle. Great sand dunes and over a mile of shoreline on Lake Michigan. Natural area behind dunes with 3 lakes. No camping. Warren Dunes State Park is also here (see separate listing below).

WARREN DUNES STATE PARK

12032 Red Arrow Highway (I-94, exit 16 - South)

Sawyer 49125

❑ Activity: Outdoors

❑ Telephone: (616) 426-4013

www. dnr.state.mi.us/www/parks/warrendu.htm

❑ Admission: $4.00 per vehicle

The highlight is obvious - over 2 miles of Lake Michigan shoreline complete with sandy/grassy dunes. The dunes are always changing, so each visitor is greeted by a different formation on each visit. If it's a windy day you can almost hear the sand sing (or some say, squeak). Also featured are hundreds of modern campsites, cabins, hiking, swimming and winter sports. Grand Mere State Park is also here and administered by Warren Dunes.

CAPTAIN NICHOLS' & CAPTAIN CHUCK'S PERCH BOATS

South Haven – 49090. *Activity:* Outdoors. Captain Nichols' (616) 637-2507, Captain Chuck's (616) 637-8007. *Hours:* Leaves the dock at 8:00 am and in the afternoons. Call for departure times. *Admission:* Adults $30.00, Children $22.00 (12 and under). On Fridays kids go for ½ fare with paying adult. Fishing licenses are required (sold at dock) $7.00 for non-residents, $6.00 for residents. Perch fishing, fish cleaning available for a small charge. Capacity: 40 people per trip.

DR. LIBERTY HYDE BAILEY MUSEUM

South Haven - 903 Bailey Avenue (off Blue Star Highway & Aylworth Avenue on Bailey Avenue), 49090. *Activity:* Museums. (616) 637-3251 or (616) 637-3141. *Hours:* Tuesday, Friday and Sundays, 2:00 - 4:00 pm. Saturdays, 10:00 am - 4:00 pm. (May-

October). Donations accepted. The Museum marks the birthplace of world-famous botanist and horticulturist, Liberty Hyde Bailey. He designed the first horticultural laboratory building at Michigan Agricultural College (now Michigan State). You'll find lots of Bailey family artifacts.

KAL-HAVEN TRAIL STATE PARK

South Haven - 23960 Ruggles Road (I-96, exit 22 west), 49090. *Activity:* Outdoors. (616) 637-2788. Journey onto the 34-mile crushed limestone path connecting South Haven and Kalamazoo. The trail wanders past farm lands, through wooded areas, and over streams and rivers. Along the way see a camelback and covered bridge.

MICHIGAN MARITIME MUSEUM

260 Dyckman Avenue (I-196, exit 20 west)

South Haven 49090

❑   Activity: Museums
❑   Telephone: (800) 747-3810 or (616) 637-8078
❑   Hours: Wednesday-Saturday, 10:00 am - 5:00 pm. Sunday, Noon - 5:00 pm. Limited seasonal hours on Monday and Tuesday. Closed Christmas and Easter.
❑   Admission: Adults $2.50, Seniors $1.50 (62+), Children $1.50 (5-12)
❑   Miscellaneous: Boardwalk, museum shop.

Near South Pier Lighthouse - Great Lakes maritime history showcase tells stories of vessels that passed through these waters and the people who built them. They have displays featuring lumber ships, luxury steamboats, Native Americans, fur traders, and settlers. The kids' favorite part is the US Lifesaving Service and Coast Guard Exhibit. See actual full-size rescue boats and stations (May - October).

THE IDLER RIVERBOAT

South Haven - 515 Williams Street (Moored at Nichols Landing, part of Old Harbor Village), 49090. *Activity:* Theme Restaurants. (616) 637-8435. *Hours:* Daily, Lunch and Dinner. No dress code. Moderate prices. A historic paddlewheeler docked in the harbor. Grab a table on deck for lite food at the Bayou Beach Club including shrimp, 'gator wings, sandwiches and their famous South Haven iced tea. In the slightly more formal Magnolia Grille, you can even eat in a real stateroom used once for trips back and forth to New Orleans.

VAN BUREN STATE PARK

South Haven - 23960 Ruggels Road (south of town on Blue Star Highway to entrance), 49090. *Activity:* Outdoors. (616) 637-2788. *Admission:* $4.00 per vehicle. There main attraction is the large, duned beach and swimming. A couple hundred campsites and hiking trails too. www.dnr.state.mi.us/www/parks/plwc.htm#vanburen.

CURIOSITY KIDS' MUSEUM

415 Lake Blvd. (I-94, exit 27 north, downtown)

St. Joseph 49085

❑   Activity: Museums
❑   Telephone: (616) 983-CKID, **www.curiouskidsmuseum.org**
❑   Hours: Wednesday - Saturday, 10:00 am - 5:00 pm. Sunday, Noon - 5:00 pm. Also Wednesday evenings until 8:00 pm. (Extended summer hours)
❑   Admission: General $3.50 (age 1+)

This fun place has hands-on learning and curiosity building exhibits. Each exhibit has costumes to wear that match the type of activity. Serve customers in a diner or pick apples from trees, then process them and sell apple products at the market. Make a hot air balloon rise and then listen to a teddy bear's heartbeat as you play doctor or dance with Mr. Bones. An especially interesting exhibit is trying crutches on for size, going up the ramp on a wheelchair, or typing your name in bumpy Braille. Isn't that neat?

ROXY'S DEPOT RESTAURANT

St. Joseph - 410 Vine Street (St. Joseph Train Station below the bluff at the entrance to Silver Beach), 49085. *Activity:* Theme Restaurants. (616) 985-9000. *Hours:* Daily, Lunch and Dinner except Tuesdays. Moderate pricing. Very casual. In a historic, and still used, railroad station, you can try Rail Spikes (kabobs), Choo Choo Bread, Northwoods Chili (lumber campstyle) or a Silver Beach Chicken. The restaurant's motto: "A place in Time with People in Mind" - so relax...the next train isn't due for awhile."

CARNEGIE CENTER OF THE ARTS

Three Rivers - 107 North Main Street, 49093. *Activity:* The Arts. (616) 273-8882. *Hours:* Tuesday - Sunday, 10:00 am - 6:00 pm. Free or small admission charge. Art exhibits, traveling theme exhibits and the "Kids Work" Museum.

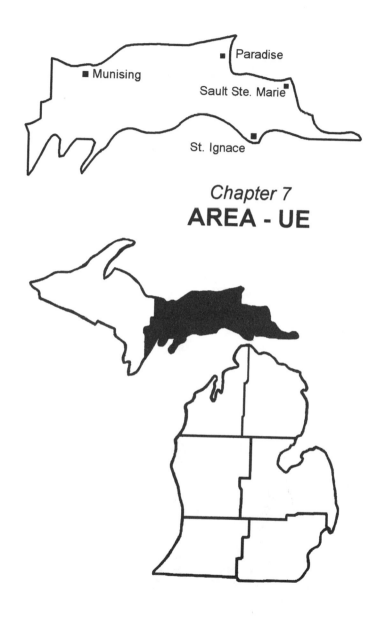

Chapter 7
AREA - UE

Our Favorites...

- Pictured Rocks
- Great Lakes Shipwreck Museum
- Tahquamenon Falls
- Soo Locks
- Father Marquette Museum

HIAWATHA NATIONAL FOREST

2727 North Lincoln Road (shorelines on lakes Huron, Michigan and
Superior), **Escanaba** 49829

❑   Activity: Outdoors

❑   Telephone: (906) 786-4062, **www.fs.fed.us/r9/hiawatha**

❑   Hours: Daily, open 24 hours

The forest manages two uninhabited islands, Round and
Government Islands. Both are accessible by boat and boating
and other outdoor activities are allowed on Government Island. On
the northern tip of the forest, is the Grand Island National
Recreation Area and Pictured Rocks National Lakeshore. Fishing
for bass, pike, trout and walleye are good. Cross-country skiing
and snowmobiling, camping, canoeing, hiking or bicycling trails,
and swimming are available. There is a visitor's center and cabin
rentals too. Near Munising are the Bay Furnace ruins, the remains
of an 1870's iron furnace.

FAYETTE STATE HISTORIC PARK

13700 13.25 Lane (US-2 to M-183 South)

Garden 49835

❑   Activity: Outdoors

❑   Phone: (906) 644-2603

www.dnr.state.mi.us/www/parks/fayette.htm

❑   Hours: Daily, 9:00 am - 7:00 pm (Summer) Daily, 9:00 am - 5:00
pm (Labor Day to mid-October)

❑   Admission: $4.00 per vehicle.

Travel back in time over 100 years as you walk around a
preserved industrial community. The Visitor's Center has a
scale model of the city when it was buzzing and info on hiking
trails around the complex. See docks where schooners tramped and
mostly reconstructed iron furnaces and kilns along with support
buildings for the then, booming, industry. Camping, boating,
fishing, swimming, and winter sports are also available.

MICHIHISTRIGAN MINI-GOLF

Gould City - US-2 (Halfway between M-77 and M-117), 49838.
Activity: Theme Restaurants. (800) 924-8873. *Hours:* (Late May -
late September). *Admission:* $4.00/round. Locals and visitors stay
at cabins and campgrounds on the premises plus eat at the
restaurant full of Michigan pride. By accident, the owners "threw"
clay creating forms looking like the Upper and Lower Peninsula of
Michigan. Using aerial photos of the state, they built a scale model
of Michigan covering many acres. Each hole is a different
important town. After 18 holes, fish the stocked "Great Lakes"
around the course. This is one-of-a-kind!

TOONERVILLE TROLLEY & RIVERBOAT RIDE TO TAHQUAMENON FALLS

Soo Junction (North off M-28 - Watch for signs to CR-38)

Hulbert 49748

❑   Activity: Tours
❑   Telephone: (888) 778-7246 or (906) 876-2311
   www.uptravel.com/uptravel/attractions/17.htm
❑   Hours: Times vary - call ahead for schedule. (mid-June - early
    October). Train only excursions, Tuesday - Saturday (July &
    August only)
❑   Admission: (Train & Riverboat - 6 ½ hours), Adults $20.00,
    Children $10.00 (6-15). (Train only - 1 ¾ hours), Adults $10.00,
    Children $5.00 (6-15). Kids 4 and under are Free.

Nearly a day (a 6 ½ tour) awaits you as you journey to see
Michigan's largest falls (100' high), The Tahquamenon Falls
(see separate listing). Start with a 5 mile, 35 minute narrow gauge
rail trip, and then connect with a narrated 21-mile riverboat cruise
with lots of chances to see area wildlife. Once the boat docks, take
a short walking trip to see the falls. What's really neat is that the
falls are undisturbed and really do look like Niagara Falls might
have looked to early settlers (smaller, but still very coool!).

INDIAN LAKE STATE PARK

Manistique - CR-442 West, 49854. *Activity:* Outdoors. (906) 341-2355. **www.dnr.state.mi.us/www/parks/indianlk.htm**. Located on Indian Lake, the 4th largest inland lake in the Upper Peninsula. Camping/cabins, hiking, boating, fishing, swimming, bicycle trails, and winter sports. *Admission:* $4.00 per vehicle.

PALMS BOOK STATE PARK (BIG SPRING)

Manistique - (US-2 to M-149), 49854. (906) 341-2355. *Activity:* Outdoors. **www.dnr.state.mi.us/www/parks/palmbo-1.htm**. Admission: $4.00 per vehicle. Beaching and boating are the only activities offered (no fishing or camping) but most come to board rafts and float across the wide spring. In the middle of the spring, look below at the huge trout being swished around by the hot springs flowing out from below - and yet the water is kept at 45 degrees constantly. The American Indians call this area "kitch-iti-kipi" or "Mirror of Heaven".

GRAND ISLAND SHIPWRECK TOURS

1204 Commercial Street (M-28 west of town - watch for signs)

Munising 49862

❑   Activity: Tours
❑   Telephone: (906) 387-4477, **www.shipwrecktours.com**
❑   Admission: Adults $20.00, Children $8.50 (6-12)
❑   Tours: (2 ½ hours) @ 10:00 am & 1:00 pm (June, September, October). 10:00 am, 1:00 & 4:00 pm (July & August). Weather permitting.

When you realize that there are over 5000 shipwrecks on the bottom of the Great Lakes…it makes you probably wonder…why are you about to get on a boat? Don't worry, today you can safely voyage (and see) the underwater world of Lake Superior. Board Michigan's only glass-bottomed boat for your chance to see 3 of these wrecks. The clarity of the water is amazing and you will actually see an intact 136', 1860's cargo ship…right under your boat! It's a great idea to visit their website for the complete story (and photographs) of each boat that you will see. Also pass by the South Lighthouse and an original settlement on Grand Island.

PICTURED ROCKS CRUISES

(Boats depart from Munising's harbor - downtown)

Munising 49862

- ❑ Activity: Tours
- ❑ Telephone: (906) 387-2033, **www.picturedrocks.com**
- ❑ Admission: Adults $22.00, Children $7.00 (5-12).
- ❑ Tours: Departure times can vary - generally there are 2-7 trips per day (weather permitting). Call or visit website for schedule. (Memorial Day weekend - mid-October)

A picturesque 37-mile (3-hour) tour that takes you as close to the rocks as you can safely get (you can almost touch them). See colorful and majestic formations along Lake Superior's shore, some are sharp pointed and rise over 200 ft. high.

PICTURED ROCKS NATIONAL LAKESHORE

M-28 and CR-H58

Munising 49862

- ❑ Activity: Outdoors
- ❑ Telephone: (906) 387-3700, **www.nps.gov/piro**
- ❑ Hours: (Visitor Center) Monday - Saturday, 9:00 am - 4:30 pm. (year-round). Daily with longer hours (mid-May through October)
- ❑ Miscellaneous: Camping, hiking trails, boating, fishing, swimming, winter sports.

Tens of thousands of acres of wilderness along over 40 miles of Lake Superior where ice-carved rocks resemble familiar shapes. Look for parts of ships or castle turrets. The rocks are also multi-colored from the minerals that seep into the soil. There are several awe-inspiring platform stops (some 200 foot cliffs) like Miners' Castle or Grand Sable Dunes. Rough camping and rugged backpack hiking is popular for those accustomed to it.

WAGNER FALLS SCENIC SITE

Munising - (a mile east of Munising on M-28), 49862. *Activity:* Outdoors. (906) 341-2355. A beautiful waterfall is nestled amongst hemlock and virgin pine trees. ½ mile trail. No camping. No services.

GARLYN FARM & ZOOLOGICAL PARK

US-2, **Naubinway** 49762

❑   Activity: Animals & Farms
❑   Telephone: (906) 477-1085
     www.angelfire.com/biz/garlynfarm
❑   Hours: Daily, 11:00 am - 7:00 pm. (April - October). Saturday & Sunday Only, 11:00 am - 5:00 pm (November & December)
❑   Admission: Adults $4.75, Children $3.75 (3-16)
❑   Miscellaneous: Gift shop.

The UP's biggest collection of animals (25+ species) that includes - black bears, white-tail deer, camels, wallabies, reindeer, llamas and more.

MUSKALLONGE LAKE STATE PARK

Newberry - (CR-407), 49868. *Activity:* Outdoors. (906) 658-3338. **www.dnr.state.mi.us/www/parks/plup.htm#muskallonge**. *Admission:* $4.00 per vehicle. Camping, hiking, boating, fishing and swimming.

GREAT LAKES SHIPWRECK MUSEUM

110 Whitefish Point Road (Museum located on Whitefish Point)

Paradise 49768

❑ Activity: Museums
❑ Telephone: (906) 635-1742 or (877) SHIPWRECK
   www.shipwreckmuseum.com
❑ Hours: Daily, 10:00 am - 6:00 pm, (Mid-May to Mid-October)
❑ Admission: Adults $7.00, Seniors $6.00, Children $4.00 (12 & under), Family $20.00

A working lighthouse and restored keeper's quarters are the oldest on Lake Superior since 1849 and a crucial point on the Lake. Gordon Lightfoot's ballad, "The Wreck of the Edmund Fitzgerald", plays as you view the actual bell recovered from the ship. Displays of ships claimed by Lake Superior's storms include the Invincible 1816, the Independence (story of sailor "The Man Who Never Smiled Again" survivor), and the Edmund Fitzgerald in the 1970's (29 sailors aboard, all perished). See the short film on the history of Edmund Fitzgerald and the raising of the bell honoring a request by surviving family members to establish a permanent memorial. To add to what is already an extremely emotional visit, take a reflective walk out on to the boardwalk and beach of Whitefish Point - the "Graveyard of the Great Lakes" as you watch large freighters fight the turbulent waters.

TAHQUAMENON FALLS STATE PARK

41382 West M-123 (Off M-123, then west 5-12 miles. Watch for entrance signs), **Paradise** 49768

❑ Activity: Outdoors
❑ Telephone: (906) 492-3415 or (800) 44-PARKS
   www.dnr.state.mi.us/www/parks/ta-falls.htm
❑ Hours: Daily, Dawn to Dusk.
❑ Admission: $4.00 per vehicle

❑ Miscellaneous: Modern camping near falls or on river. Picnicking. Hiking trails. Fishing. Canoeing. Snow-mobiling, snow-shoeing, cross-country skiing. Gift shop, snack bar & Camp 33 Restaurant at Upper Falls.

This is the land of Longfellow's Hiawatha - "by the rushing Tahquamenaw" Hiawatha built his canoe. On the hiking trails moose, balk eagles, black bear, coyotes, otter, deer, fox, porcupine, beaver and mink may be occasionally spotted. The short 4/10 of a mile walk out to the Upper Falls reveals one of the largest waterfalls east of the Mississippi. Nearly 50 feet tall and more than 200 feet across, it's amber color is a pleasing site. The amber color of the water is not from mud or rust - discover what causes it. The Lower Falls are four miles downstream. They are a series of five smaller falls and rapids cascading around an island. For the best photo-ops, we suggest wide angle lens (or purchase great postcards at the gift shop). May we suggest a stop for a bite to eat at Camp 33 Restaurant. The replica 1950 logging camp has two focal points - the beautifully displayed animal skins and the warm fireplace. This is a great place to try UP specialties like whitefish or pasties *(pronounced p.aaa.sties - so you'll sound like a local!)*.

SOO LOCKS PARK

Downtown. Portage Avenue (Within view of International Bridge. Follow signs off I-75), **Sault St. Marie** 49783

❑ Activity: Museums

❑ Telephone: (906) 632-2394
   www.lre.usace.army.mil/behind/excensoo.html

❑ Hours: Daily, 7:00 am – 11:00 pm. (Mid-May to Mid-October)

❑ Admission: Free

❑ Miscellaneous: Run by the US Army Corp of Engineers. To view live pictures of the Soo Locks, visit their website. Theater shows film on the history of operations.

(Soo Locks Park cont.)

The highlights here are:

❏   Observation Platform - 2nd level or Riverside view of the locks.
       It's unbelievable how actual freight ships move precisely into
       concrete locks and then are lowered or raised to the level of the
       next part of the lake. How do they do it? (*Learn how...and they
       do not use pumps*). Now the longest in the world, they are still the
       largest waterway traffic system on earth. A public address
       system lets visitors know which vessels are coming through the
       locks and what their size, cargo, nationality and destination are.
❏   Working Model of a Lock (with real water moving a model boat)
       is inside the museum building and best to watch before outdoor
       viewing.

Dress appropriately for weather outside because you'll want to
watch the large freighters rise up in the water before your eyes!

MUSEUM SHIP - VALLEY CAMP

501 East Water Street (east of the locks - waterfront)

Sault Ste. Marie 49783

❏   Activity: Museums
❏   Telephone: (888) 744-7867
       http://soohistoricinc.sault.com/valleycamp.htm
❏   Hours: Daily, 9:00 am - 9:00 pm (July-August). Daily, 10:00 am
       - 6:00 pm (mid-May - June). Daily, 10:00 am - 6:00 pm
       (September - mid- October).
❏   Admission: Adults $6.50, Children $3.50 (6-16). Kids 5 and
       under are Free.

Walk-in tours are offered of the 1917 steam powered freighter
containing the world's largest Great Lakes maritime
museum. Many come to see the Edmund Fitzgerald Exhibit - two
lifeboats from the actual boat along with multimedia shows of the
tragic event. Several mechanical (dormant) parts of the ship are
touchable. A long aquarium is along one wall with marine life

found in the area. After seeing the large freighters and their crew go through the locks, kids will love to see an actual ship's pilot house, dining rooms and crew's quarters.

RIVER OF HISTORY MUSEUM

209 East Portage Avenue (1st floor of restored Federal Building)

Sault Ste. Marie 49783

- ❑ Activity: Museums
- ❑ Telephone: (906) 632-1999
- ❑ Hours: Monday - Saturday, 10:00 am - 5:00 pm. Sunday, Noon - 5:00 pm. (mid-May to mid-October)
- ❑ Admission: Adults $3.00, Seniors $2.00, Children $1.50 (8-16)

St. Mary's River history through exhibit galleries of sight and sound. Follow Chippewa Indians to French fur traders to modern industry. The sound of locks and canals being built is one of the audio enhanced exhibits.

SOO LOCKS TOUR TRAIN

Sault Ste. Marie - 315 West Portage Street, 49783. *Activity:* Tours. (800) 387-6200 or (906) 635-5241. *Admission:* Adults $6.00, Children $4.00 (6-16). *Tours:* Every ½ hour - 1 hour ride. (Memorial Day - early October). See the city's historical sites and get a great view (from 135' feet up on the International Bridge) of the Soo Locks.

TOWER OF HISTORY

326 East Portage Avenue (east of the locks)

Sault Ste. Marie 49783

- ❑ Activity: Museums
- ❑ Telephone: (888) 744-7867
  http://soohistoricinc.sault.com/towerofhistory.htm
- ❑ Hours: Daily, 10:00 am - 6:00 pm. (mid-May to mid-October)
- ❑ Admission: Adults $3.25, Children $1.75 (6-16)

A 21-story tower offering a panoramic view of the Soo Locks, the St. Mary's River Rapids, and many historical homes. The tower museum has Native American artifacts and a video show depicting the history of the Great Lakes and Sault Ste. Marie. You ride to the top by elevator.

SENEY NATIONAL WILDLIFE REFUGE

Seney - (M-77, 5 miles south of Seney), 49883. *Activity:* Outdoors. (906) 586-9851. **www.fws.gov/r3pao/seney/index.htm**. *Hours:* Daily, 9:00am-5:00pm (mid-May to mid-October). Free admission. Take the family on a driving journey (7 miles, self-guided, starts at Visitor's Center parking lot) that allows the chance to see wildlife such as: nesting loons, cranes, swans, Canadian geese, bald eagles, deer, and others. Over 70 miles of trails are also available for your hiking adventures.

FATHER MARQUETTE NATIONAL MEMORIAL AND MUSEUM

Straits State Park (just over the Big Mac Bridge, Northwest on US-2)

St Ignace 49781

❑   Activity: Museums
❑   Telephone: (906) 643-9394
      www.sos.state.mi.us/history/museum/musemarq/index.html
❑   Hours: Daily, 9:30 am - 5:00 pm. (Memorial Day-mid June)
      Daily, 9:30 am - 8:00 pm. (mid-June to Late September)
❑   Admission: $4.00 per vehicle
❑   Miscellaneous: Picnic area.

K ids will really "get into the act" by pretending to be famous, early American explorers! You'll really appreciate this facility's wealth of hands-on tools that you can touch and gently play with. The museum's purpose is to depict the life's work of French Jesuit missionary and explorer Father Marquette. The audio visual presentation in the auditorium is a good place to start. You'll then have a good understanding of the journeys of people exploring early, undeveloped land in the mid-1600's, living amongst the Great Lakes and Mississippi Indians. French and Indians were cordial to each other then because fur trade was very profitable at this time. Speaking of Indians and trade, see the first "bar code" on skins or peek inside a Ojibwa longhouse and canoe. Also, see how animal furs were used by the elite to have hats made. The phrase "Mad as a hatter" comes from this time period when hatters used mercury to remove the rough guard hair off fur pelts. It was poisonous to their brains. You'll love to see the old-fashioned travel aids they had back then: metal tobacco pouches with burning lens built right in, a sundial/compass, or the traveling ink stand! Well done museum!

CASTLE ROCK

Castle Rock Road (I-75 to exit 348)

St. Ignace 49781

- ❑ Activity: Outdoors
- ❑ (906) 643-8268, **www.yoopcr.com/at_castlcrock.html**
- ❑ Hours: Daily, 9:00 am - 9:00 pm. (May 1 - October 15)
- ❑ Admission: Only 25 cents per person.
- ❑ Miscellaneous: Gift shop and campground.

See and climb (189 steps) the legendary Castle Rock (a limestone "sea stack" - nearly 200 feet tall) that Native Americans once used as a lookout. Be sure to check out Paul Bunyan and Babe! A great piece of history and what a view for a quarter!

DEER RANCH

St. Ignace - 1510 US Highway 2 west (US-2, 4 miles west of Big Mac Bridge), 49781. *Activity:* Animals & Farms. (906) 643-7760. **www.deerranch.com**. Gift Shop featuring Deer skin products including many sizes of moccasins. They have a nature trail where you can feed and photograph native Michigan Whitetail Deer and fawns.

MUSEUM OF OJIBWA CULTURE

500-566 North State Street (at the north end of the boardwalk, downtown), **St. Ignace** 49781

❑ Activity: Museums
❑ Telephone: (906) 643-9161
   www.stignace.com/attractions/ojibwa
❑ Hours: Monday - Saturday, 11:00 am - 5:00 pm. Sunday, 1:00 - 5:00 pm. (Memorial weekend - late June). Monday - Saturday, 10:00 am - 8:00 pm. Sunday Noon - 8:00 pm (Late June-Labor Day). Monday - Saturday, 11:00 am - 6:00 pm. Sunday, 1:00 - 5:00 pm. (Labor Day-early October)
❑ Admission: Adult/Teen $2.00, Elementary $1.00, Family $5.00
❑ Miscellaneous: Native American Museum Store. Marquette Mission Park adjacent is supposed site of grave of missionary Father Marquette and also site of archeological discoveries.

The museum is housed in Father Marquette's French Jesuit Mission Church and dedicated to his focus on Ojibwa Indians, the first inhabitants of this region. Learn traditions of the peoples through video presentation, dioramas, and frequent demonstrations by Native American interpreters.

MYSTERY SPOT

150 Martin Lake Road (US-2 west, 5 miles west of Mackinac Bridge)

St. Ignace 49781

❑ Activity: Amusements
❑ Telephone: (906) 643-8322
   www.uptravel.com/uptravel/attractions/9.htm
❑ Hours: Daily, 8:00 am - 9:00 pm (early May - Labor Day). Daily, 9:00 am - 7:00 pm (after Labor Day - late October)
❑ Admission: Adults $4.00, Children $3.50 (5-11).

O.K. - Illusion or reality. Reality or illusion. That's up for you to decide, but one thing's for sure...you'll sure have fun doing it. See the laws of physics as we know them...and why they don't apply to the "Mystery Spot". The kids will love this science lesson!

STRAITS STATE PARK

St. Ignace - 720 Church Street (I-75, exit onto US-2 east), 49781. *Activity:* Outdoors. (906) 643-8620. **www.dnr.state.mi.us/www/ parks/straits.htm**. *Admission:* $4.00 per vehicle. Great views from an observation platform of the Mackinac Bridge and the Straits of Mackinac. Camping/cabins, hiking trails, boating, fishing, swimming and winter sports. A visitor's center highlights Father Marquette exploration in the area.

TOTEM VILLAGE

1230 US Highway 2 West (US-2, 2 miles west of Big Mac Bridge)

St. Ignace 49781

- ❏ • Activity: Museums
- ❏ Telephone: (906) 643-8888
- ❏ Hours: Daily, (May – October)
- ❏ Admission: Adults $1.00, Children (5-18) $0.50

They've set this place up for picture taking. For example, pose your family beside a teepee or next to a giant totem pole. The focus is on scientifically studied lifestyles of the Indian culture and significant contributions of Upper Peninsula people. There's a model of the 1st American Lake Superior sailing ship, a replica of Fort Fond du Lac, a Scale model of the first Soo Locks, a trading post, an old-time sugar camp and live bobcats, foxes and reindeer.

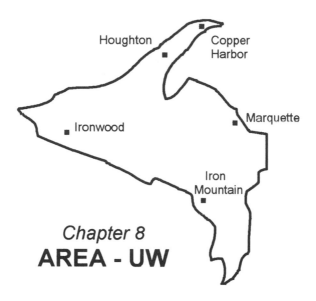

Houghton

Copper
Harbor

Ironwood

Marquette

Iron
Mountain

Chapter 8
AREA - UW

Our Favorites...

- Copper Harbor Lighthouse
- Copper & Iron Mines & Towns
- National & State Parks
- U.P. Children's Museum
- Michigan Iron Industry Museum

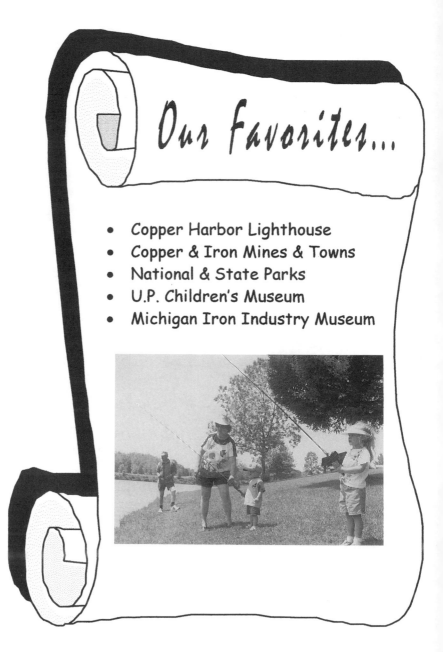

BARAGA STATE PARK

Baraga - 1300 US-41 south, 49908. *Activity:* Outdoors. (906) 353-6558. **www.dnr.state.mi.us/www/parks/baraga.htm**. *Admission:* $4.00 per vehicle. Along the Keweenaw Bay offers modern and rough camping, beach with swimming (water doesn't get much above 50 degrees though), boating, fishing, and hiking.

HANKA HOMESTEAD MUSEUM

Baraga - Arnheim Road (7 miles west of US-41), 49908. *Activity:* Museums. **http://museum.cl.msu.edu/mbpn/sum96v4/hanka.html**. (906) 353-7116, *Hours:* Tuesday, Thursday, Saturday & Sunday from 1- 4:00 pm. (Open Memorial Day to mid-October). Donations accepted. A 100 year old Finnish farming home restored to a 1920's appearance. Guided tours explain life for immigrants starting out in America.

BRIMLEY STATE PARK

Brimley - 9200 West 6 Mile Road, 49715. *Activity:* Outdoors. (906) 248-3422. **www.dnr.state.mi.us/www/parks/brimley.htm**. *Admission:* $4.00 per vehicle. Home to the Point Iroquois Lighthouse Station. Available is camping, boating, fishing and swimming.

COPPERTOWN USA MUSEUM

109 Red Jacket Road (2 blocks west of US-41)

Calumet 49913

❑ Activity: Museums
❑ Telephone: (906) 337-4354
   www.uptravel.com/uptravel/attractions/441.htm
❑ Hours: Monday - Saturday, 10:00 am - 5:00 pm (mid-June to mid-October). Sunday, 1:00 - 4:00 pm (in July & August)
❑ Admission: Adults $3.00, Seniors $2.00, Children $1.00 (12-18)

More than a copper museum, but rather a Visitor's Center (even includes a walk-in, simulated copper mine) for the Keweenaw Peninsula. See how copper mining has evolved from the early Native Americans who mined with stone hammers to the techniques used during the "Copper Rush".

IRON COUNTY MUSEUM

Museum Drive (off M-189 to CR-424)

Caspian 49915

❑   Activity: Museums
❑   Telephone: (906) 265-2617, **www.iron.org/museums-icm.html**
❑   Hours: Monday - Saturday & Holidays, 9:00 am - 5:00 pm.
     Sunday, 1:00-5:00 pm (June - August). Monday - Saturday, 10:00
     am - 4:00 pm. Sunday, 1:00 - 4:00 pm (May & September)
❑   Admission: Adults $5.00, Children $2.50 (5-18)

A historic, educational site that has 20 buildings including pioneers' cabins, a logging camp, train depot, and schoolhouse. The community was built here because of the Caspian Mine (during its peak production, it was the area's largest producer of iron ore). One of the homes featured was the home of Carrie Jacobs-Bond who was a nationally known composer of the 19th Century. Composing over 200 songs, her hits included "I Love You Truly" and "Perfect Day". This success allowed her to become the first female composer to earn a million dollars.

LAUGHING WHITEFISH FALLS SCENIC SITE

Cedar River - N7670 Highway, M-35. 49813. *Activity:* Outdoors. (906) 863-9747. One of the Upper Peninsula's many impressive waterfalls. Picnic area, foot trails, and 3 observation decks overlooking the falls. No camping. No services.

WELLS STATE PARK

Cedar River - N7670 Highway M-35. 49813. *Activity:* Outdoors. **www.dnr.state.mi.us/www/parks/plup.htm#wells.** (906) 863-9747. *Admission:* $4.00 per vehicle. Camping/cabins, hiking trails, boating, fishing, swimming, bicycle trails and winter sports.

CRAIG LAKE STATE PARK

Champion - (8 miles West of Van Riper State Park - on US-41 / M-28), 49814. *Activity:* Outdoors. (906) 339-4461. **www.dnr.state.mi.us/www/parks/craiglk.htm.** Craig Lake is a wilderness area (the most remote state park in the system) and access into the park is somewhat of an adventure. Only vehicles with high ground clearance are recommended due to the rocky conditions of the road. But if you're really into "getting away from it all" the park contains six lakes for fishing and a variety of wildlife such as black bear, deer, loons, beaver, and part of the Upper Peninsula moose herd.

VAN RIPER STATE PARK

Champion - M-41 (west of town), 49814. *Activity:* Outdoors. (906) 339-4461. **www.dnr.state.mi.us/www/parks/vanriper.htm.** *Admission:* $4.00 per vehicle. Camping, boating, and swimming are here but most come hiking to look for Canadian moose imported to this park by helicopters. Cabins and winter sports are also available.

COPPER HARBOR LIGHTHOUSE BOAT TOURS

(Copper Harbor Marina, ¼ mile west of Copper Harbor on M-26)

Copper Harbor 49918

❑   Activity: Tours
❑   Telephone: (906) 289-4966
    http://copperharbor.org/ads/lighthouse
❑   Admission: Adults $11.00, Children $6.00 (12 and under)

❑ Tours: Narrated, 60-90 minutes. Daily, Every hour, 10:00 am - 5:00 pm and are subject to weather conditions. (Memorial Day - September)

The only way to see the Copper Harbor Lighthouse (which is actually a part of the Fort Wilkins State Park) is by boat tour. During this narrated tour you'll have the chance to not only see the lighthouse (built in 1866), but also the first real attempts at creating a copper mine shaft (dates back to the 1840's).

DELAWARE COPPER MINE TOUR

(12 miles south on US-41)

Copper Harbor 49918

❑ Activity: Tours
❑ Telephone: (906) 289-4688,
❑ Admission: Adults $8.00, Children $4.00 (6-12)
❑ Tours: Self-guided tours. Daily 10:00 am - 5:00 pm. (mid-May to mid-June and September to mid-October). Guided tours depart every 20 minutes Daily, 10:00 am - 6:00 pm. (July-August)

This mid-1800's copper mine offers a 45 minute underground walking tour. Actual copper veins can be seen. Dress for 45-50 degree F. temperatures.

FORT WILKINS STATE PARK

Copper Harbor - US-41 east, 49918. *Activity:* Outdoors. (906) 289-4215. **www.dnr.state.mi.us/www/parks/ftwilkin.htm**. *Admission:* $4.00 per vehicle. The fort was built to protect copper miners from local tribes - completely made from wood. Tour the officer's quarters, then try some camping, hiking, boating, fishing, or winter sports. Visitor's Center at the fort.

KEWEENAW BEAR TRACK TOURS

First Street & Bernard (at the start of US-41), **Copper Harbor** 49918. Activity: Tours. (906) 289-4813. Hours: By appointment. Suggested to schedule a few weeks in advance of your trip. Open year-round. Admission: (Full Day Trips) Adults $20.00, Children $10.00 (12 and under). Half day trips are available at 50% off. Various trips into the beautiful Michigan wilderness are offered. Find the one that interests your family the most and prepare yourself for a guided tour day of family experiences. Be sure to check out the "Laughing Loon" gift shop.

BEWABIC STATE PARK

Crystal Falls - 1933 US-2 west, 49920. *Activity:* Outdoors. (906) 875-3324. **www.dnr.state.mi.us/www/parks/bewabic.htm**. Admission: $4.00 per vehicle. Camping, hiking trails, boating, fishing, and swimming available. Home to virgin woodlands and a wood bridge to the island.

DELTA COUNTY HISTORICAL MUSEUM AND LIGHTHOUSE

(Ludington Park, the east end of Ludington Street)

Escanaba 49829

❑ ▪Activity: Michigan History
❑   Telephone: (906) 786-3428 or (906) 786-3763
    www.cr.nps.gov/maritime/light/escanaba.htm
❑   Hours: Daily, 11:00 am - 7:00 pm. (June - Labor Day)
❑   Admission: $1.00 for lighthouse entrance, otherwise free.

Chronicles the development of the Upper Peninsula and Delta County, especially logging, railroads and shipping industries. An unusual display of a 1905 motor launch powered by only a one-cylinder engine is there also. Most folks make a point to go nearby to the restored 1867 Sandpoint Lighthouse. The keeper's house is furnished in period with winding stairs leading to the lighthouse tower's observation deck.

ADVENTURE COPPER MINE

200 Adventure Road (12 miles east of Ontonagon, off M-38)

Greenland 49929

❑   Activity: Tours
❑   Telephone: (906) 883-3371
     www.exploringthenorth.com/mine/venture.html
❑   Hours: Daily, 9:00 am - 6:00 pm. (Memorial Day weekend - end
     of color season)
❑   Tours: guided one hour, ¼ mile tour.
❑   Miscellaneous: Gift Shop with copper crafts. Camping with
     hookups. A jacket and walking shoes are recommended.

P ut on your hard hat for the beginning of your tour ride to the
     mine entrance. Turn on the miner's light as you follow the
path 300 feet underground walking through passages worked by
miners over 100 years ago. You'll see large clusters of pure copper
with silver threads and quartz and calcite crystals. Look down into
open mine shafts that run 100's of feet into the earth. The second
half of your tour you emerge from the depths of the mine onto an
overlook bluff for a great view of the distant hills and valleys.

MCCLAIN STATE PARK

Hancock - M-203 west, 49930. *Activity:* Outdoors. (906)
482-0278.   **www.dnr.state.mi.us/www/parks/plup.htm#mclain**.
Admission: $4.00 per vehicle. Camping/cabins, hiking, boating,
fishing, swimming and winter sports.

QUINCY MINE HOIST

201 Royce Road (along US-41 - part of Keweenaw Peninsula
National Park), **Hancock** 49930

❑   Activity: Tours
❑   Telephone: (906) 482-5569 or (906) 482-3101
     www.quincymine.com

❑ Hours: Monday - Saturday, 9:30 am - 5:00 pm. Sunday, 11:00 am - 5:00 pm. (Summer). Monday - Saturday, 10:30 am - 4:00 pm. Sunday, 12:30 - 4:00 pm (After Labor Day)
❑ Admission: (Surface & Underground Tour), Adults $12.50, Children $7.00 (6-13). (Surface & Tram Ride), Adults $7.50, Children $2.50 (6-13)
❑ Tours: Depart on the hour. Hard hats and coats are provided.
❑ Miscellaneous: Gift shop. As you can expect, this tour might not be suitable for younger children who don't like dark places, loud noises.

The "hoist" is where all the ore was hauled to the surface, and what you will see is the world's largest. The shaft started in the mid-1800's and operated until the 1960's, eventually reaching a depth of over 10,000 feet! As you can imagine, at this depth it can get quite "hot" (with temperatures averaging over 90 degrees F.). On the outside you can view the shafthouse which is over 150 feet tall and has hauled millions of pounds of copper to the surface. You can also travel over 2000 feet into the hill to view portions of the mine that were carved during the Civil War era.

ISLE ROYALE NATIONAL PARK

800 East Lakeshore Drive (only accessible by boat or seaplane)

Houghton 49931

❑ Activity: Outdoors
❑ Phone: (906) 482-0984, **www.nps.gov/isro**
❑ Hours: (mid-April to October)
❑ Miscellaneous: Isle Royale Queen offers summertime boat trips (4 ½ hours) and the Ranger III leaves Houghton in the summer (6 ½ hours). There's also a seaplane that floats over to the Isle.

The nation's only island national park is where roughed campers (no campfires permitted) or woodsy lodgers (only one on the entire island) gravitate. Backpacking hiking, canoeing, charter fishing trips or sightseeing trips are available. With 99 percent of the island still wilderness, many opt for marked trails like Greenstone, Minong, Mt. Franklin, Mt. Ojibwa, or the Rock Harbor Lighthouse. The trails are about 45 minutes in length along cliffs, paths of fir and wildflowers, and past many moose, wolves and beavers.

CORNISH PUMPING ENGINE AND MINING MUSEUM

Iron Mountain - (2 blocks west of US-2 on Kent Street), 49801. *Activity:* Museums. **www.ironmtntourism.org/atractions**. (906) 774-1086. *Hours:* Monday-Saturday, 9:00 am - 5:00 pm. Sunday, Noon - 4:00 pm. (May - October). *Admission:* Adults $4.00, Seniors $3.50 (over 62), Children $2.00 (10-18). A discounted combo admission is offered with the Menominee Range Museum. One of the largest steam pump engines built in North America (the flywheel is 40 feet in diameter and weighs 160 tons) plus displays of mining equipment and artifacts related to mining history.

MILLIE MINE BAT CAVE

Iron Mountain - (Just off East A on Park), 49801. *Activity:* Outdoors. (906) 774-5480. Always open. Free admission. Batcave...hummm...must be Batman's home right? Well, not really, but this IS the second largest (known in the North America) home for hibernating bats! The mine is 350 feet deep that has several rooms with a consistent temperature of 40 degrees...just perfect for the furry little creatures. You'll find a walking path, benches, and informational plaques. The bats come in for the winter in September and leave in April (if you're not scared...these are wonderful viewing times). Closed during snow months.

BLACK RIVER NATIONAL FOREST SCENIC BYWAY

Ironwood - County Road 513 (US-2 / M-28 to CR-513), 49938. *Activity:* Outdoors. (906) 667-0261. See the Black River with several beautiful waterfalls. Five waterfalls are 20 to 40 feet high and are named for their characteristics like Sandstone (red rock riverbed), Gorge, and Conglomerate (rock ledges). Paved sidewalks and a kid-friendly swinging bridge, and a pass by Ski

Flying Hill (only one in the states) where you might catch site of ski flying (jumping) events (especially late January).

OTTAWA NATIONAL FOREST

(Almost 1 million acres off US-2)

Ironwood 49938

❑ Activity: Outdoors
❑ Telephone: Visitor's Center (906) 932-1330 or (906) 358-4724
  www.fs.fed.us/r9/ottawa
❑ Hours: Dawn to dusk.

More than 50,000 acres of the expanse are designated wilderness with barely untouched lakes and trees. With more than 35 waterfalls with the forest, many plan to take the marked trails to catch a view. The 500 lakes and 2000 miles of rivers provide good fishing for trout and salmon. When the ground freezes, many try snowmobiling, ice fishing and cross-country skiing. In Watersmeet there are two facilities - The J.W. Tourney Forest Nursery and Visitors Center (US-2 and US-45). Great Lakes tree seed and stock are supplied here, as well as, exhibits, audiovisual programs and naturalist-led group walks and talks. Camping, hiking, boating and swimming are also available. Lake Gogebic State Park is included as part of the forest.

DA YOOPERS TOURIST TRAP

490 North Steel Street (US-41)

Ishpeming 49849

❑ Activity: Amusements
❑ Telephone: (906) 485-5595, **www.dayoopers.com**
❑ Hours: Monday - Friday, 9:00 am - 9:00 pm (Memorial Day - December). Times vary rest of the year.
❑ Free admission.

The UP life is "unique" to say the least. When talking to locals, we often heard that one of the greatest things about living up here is that you have time for a hobby (since you can only work 6 months a year). Well, "Da Yoopers" actually started as a singing group that promoted the "uniqueness" of this life around the state. They have fun "poking fun" and you'll see and hear it all at the "tourist trap". Not only can you learn how to really talk like a Yooper... but where else will you ever see a snowmobile that was built for "summer" use, a chainsaw the size of an 18-wheeler (in the Guinness Book...world's largest, really), or the world's largest firing rifle? We agree, be sure to pick up some "Da Yoopers" music before you leave to really get the most from your UP adventure.

TILDEN OPEN PIT MINE TOURS

(depart from Ishpeming Chamber of Commerce)

Ishpeming 49849

- ❑   Activity: Tours
- ❑   Telephone: (906) 486-4841
- ❑   Admission: $6.00/person
- ❑   Tours: (Reservations required). Daily @ 12:30 pm (mid-June to mid-August)
- ❑   Miscellaneous: For safety reasons no dresses, skirts, open-toed shoes, or children under age 10 are permitted on this tour.

One thing you'll know for sure after completing this tour is that the iron industry in Michigan is still very much a thriving business. We suggest to go to the Michigan Iron Industry Museum (see separate listing) first to see how it WAS mined. Then, see this huge pit (that is over 500 feet deep!) where the iron ore is mined and refined by some of the largest mining equipment in the world. (We really think it would be fun if they painted "Tonka" on the sides of the equipment!)

US NATIONAL SKI HALL OF FAME AND MUSEUM

Ishpeming - (US-41 between Second and Third Streets), 49849. *Activity:* Museums. (906) 485-6323. **www.portup.com/skihall/**. *Hours:* Monday-Saturday, 10:00 am - 5:00 pm and Sunday, Noon - 5:00 pm. *Admission:* Adults $3.00, Seniors $2.50, Students $1.00. Watch an 18 minute orientation tape, then explore the gallery of greats of American skiing. Also study the development of the sport through trophies, photos, old grooming equipment and a cable car.

HOUGHTON COUNTY HISTORICAL MUSEUM CAMPUS

5500 M-26 (after crossing the Portage Lake Lift bridge, head north on M-26), **Lake Linden** 49945

❑   Activity: Michigan History

❑   Telephone: (906) 296-4121, **www.habitant.org/houghton**

❑   Hours: Monday - Saturday, 10:00 am - 4:30 pm. (June - September)

❑   Admission: Adult $5.00, Student $2.00 (12-18), Youth $1.00 (6-11)

Eight historic buildings including themes of a Country Kitchen, Grandma's Room, Medicinal, Mining Room and Forestry Room. Kids will like trying to figure out what "bull ladle", "fanny", or "kibble" are. There's also a schoolhouse, log cabin, tool shop, church, railroad depot and Copperland sculptures.

LAKE GOGEBIC STATE PARK

Marenisco - N9995 State Highway M-64 (M-64 between US-2 and M-28), 49947. *Activity:* Outdoors. (906) 842-3341. **www. dnr.state.mi.us/www/parks/gogebic.htm**. *Admission:* $4.00 per vehicle. Enjoy shaded, waterfront camping on the shore of Lake Gogebic, the largest inland lake in the Upper Peninsula. Sandy beach, picnic area, boating, fishing.

GREAT NORTHERN ADVENTURES
Marquette 49855

- ❑ Activity: Outdoors
- ❑ Telephone: (906) 225-TOUR
  www.merchantfind.com/gna/gna.htm
- ❑ Hours: Year-round. Call or visit website for trip schedule.
- ❑ Admission: Vary by trip. Estimated prices (all daily/per person) $75.00 for Kayaking, $175.00 for Dogsledding. They also offer a two-day trip to the ice caves for $315.00 per person (includes all guide services, lodging, and food)

This listing is included in this book for adventurous family members (suggested 12 and older) who really want to get away from it all...and then go just a bit further! Trips vary (half day to 10 days) from journeying into the Michigan wilderness with just a dogsled and supplies (and yes, you'll set up camp...start a fire...etc.) to kayaking along the shores of Lake Superior or secluded lakes.   There are also trips that offer inn or motel accommodations (if you really would rather not sleep in a tent). Sure to create family memories that you'll talk about for years!

MARQUETTE COUNTRY TOURS

Marquette - 809 West College Avenue, 49855. *Activity:* Tours. (906) 226-6167. Admission varies by type of tour. Call for details. In addition to the hiking and canoe trips that are available, you have a chance to customize a tour for your family based on the sites (old mines, waterfalls, and historic areas) that you wish to see. Also available are 4-wheel drive vehicle trips.

MARQUETTE COUNTY HISTORICAL MUSEUM

Marquette - 213 North Front Street, 49855. *Activity:* Michigan History. (906) 226-3571. *Hours:* Monday - Friday, 10:00 am - 5:00 pm. *Admission:* Adults $3.00, Students $1.00 (over 12). A pioneer focus on mining and lumbering with changing exhibits of artifacts.

MARQUETTE MARITIME MUSEUM

Marquette - (East Ridge and Lakeshore Blvd.), 49855. *Activity:* Museums. (906) 226-2006. *Hours:* Daily, 10:00 - 5:00 pm, (day after Memorial Day - September). *Admission:* General $3.00 (over 12 only). Marquette and Lake Superior maritime heritage with antique charts, boats and models. Children love the hands-on exhibits and recreated dockside offices of a commercial fishing and passenger freight companies. Ever seen a fishing shanty kids?

MARQUETTE MOUNTAIN SKI AREA

Marquette - 4501 County Road 553, 49855. *Activity:* Outdoors. **www.marquettemountain.com**. (906) 225-1155 or (800) 944-SNOW, 8 runs, rental equipment, babysitting, and lessons are available. Great children's programs for all skill levels. Also now offering, Ski-by-the-hour rates as low as $4.00/hour (2-hour minimum), and Sunday Family Days.

PRESQUE ISLE PARK

Marquette - Lakeshore Blvd. 49855. *Activity:* Outdoors. (906) 228-0461 or (800) 544-4321. *Hours:* Daily, 7:00 am - 11:00 pm. **www.uptravel.com/uptravel/attractions/511.htm**. Free admission. A beautiful 300+ acre park that is located on a rock peninsula on Lake Superior. Some interesting trivia..."Presque Isle" means "almost an island". As you can imagine, the views are incredible with many lookouts, nature trails along bogs (in winter they are cross-country skiing or snowshoeing trails), and picnic facilities. An outdoor pool and waterslide (160') are also available (free admission) in the summer.

UPPER PENINSULA CHILDREN'S MUSEUM

123 West Baraga Avenue

Marquette 49855

- ❑ Activity: Museums
- ❑ (906) 226-3911, **www.marquette.org/index2.html**
- ❑ Hours: Tuesday - Thursday & Saturday, 11:00 am - 6:00 pm.
  Friday, 11:00 am - 8:00 pm. Sunday, 11:00 am - 6:00 pm
- ❑ Admission: Adults $4.00, Seniors $3.00, Children $2.00 (2-17)

A very family friendly place that features exhibits that were suggested by local area kids. Some of the fun programs available (subject to change) include:

- ❑ WHERE'S YOUR WATER? Crawl through the drain field and into an aquifer to explore life under a pond. Upon your return to the "real world", use microscopes and computers to examine water elements first hand.
- ❑ WONDER GROUND gives you a glimpse of the underground in a wonderful way.
- ❑ ALL ABOARD! RECYCLO-TORIUM, a fun filled creation station filled with different "stuff" to take apart, reassemble and just plain create.
- ❑ Don't forget MICROSOCIETY! Stroll down the kid-sized street and shop at all the wacky businesses along Main Street, USA.
- ❑ In the FANTASTIC FOREST you can climb into a tree habitat or into the inner workings of a tree.

MICHIGAN IRON INDUSTRY MUSEUM

73 Forge Road

Negaunee 49866

- ❑ Activity: Museums
- ❑ (906) 475-7857
  www.sos.state.mi.us/history/museum/museiron/index.html
- ❑ Hours: Daily, 9:30 am - 4:30 pm (May - October)

❑   Admission: Free

The theme is set for this museum with the "step back in time" approach. Walk on paths that wind you through a forest that gives you a sense of what the UP was like when it was still undeveloped. It's really neat to see how things in this region were changed (both below and above ground) by observing interesting time-line exhibits. The kids have several hands-on exhibits and also get to see a model of the Soo Locks and mining cars and other equipment.

MEAD LAKE MINE SITE

Ontonagon - (M-107), 49953. *Activity:* Outdoors. (906) 884-4735. **www.ontonagon.com**. Explore about 80 feet of this horizontal mine shaft (might be a bit dirty and wet for younger children). This mine is also home to thousands of bats (don't worry...they only come out a dusk). If you really want to be adventurous, visit at dusk to watch the "rush-hour" exit from the mine!

ONTONAGON COUNTY HISTORICAL MUSEUM

422 River Street

Ontonagon 49953

❑   Activity: Michigan History
❑   Telephone: (906) 884-6165, **www.ontonagon.com/mi/ochs**
❑   Hours: Monday - Saturday, 9:00 am - 5:00 pm. Closed Saturdays, January - April.
❑   Admission: General $2.00 (under 16)

County artifacts displays including photos, logging and mining equipment and Finnish items. Kids are amazed at the replica copper boulder found in 1843 and weighing over 3,700 pounds.

PORCUPINE MOUNTAINS WILDERNESS STATE PARK

412 South Boundry Road (M-107 west)

Ontonagon 49953

❑   Activity: Outdoors

❑   Phone: (906) 885-5275

  www.dnr.state.mi.us/www/parks/porkesvc.htm

❑   Admission: $4.00 per vehicle

❑   Miscellaneous: Lookout for black bears and black flies - they both love your food. Follow rangers posted instructions to prevent unwanted visitors.

Hiking will be most to your liking here especially along the shore of Lake of the Clouds or Mirror Lake. Stop in at the wilderness Visitor Center (open late-May to mid-October, 10:00 am - 6:00 pm) for a slide show and local info. Camping is rough (even in cabins) but auto campers are permitted at some sites. There's also beaches, boating, fishing, swimming, and winter sports offered.

OLD VICTORIA

Victoria Dam (4 miles southwest of town)

Rockland 49960

❑   Activity: Museums

❑   Telephone: (906) 886-2617

❑   Hours: Daily, 9:00 am - 6:00 pm. (Memorial Day-mid-October)

❑   Admissions: Donations.

❑   Miscellaneous: Picnic areas and hiking trails.

A restored settlement company town that thrived in the late 1800's. Miners from England came to work the copper mines and built many small homes, clubs and a barn for living. By the 1920's, Upper Peninsula mining sharply declined due to low copper prices and competition from out West. Guided tours explain the history of the village and its decline.

TWIN LAKES STATE PARK

Toivola - (M-26 South), 49965. *Activity:* Outdoors. (906) 482-
0278. **www.dnr.state.mi.us/www/parks/plup.htm#twinlakes**.
Admission: $4.00 per vehicle. Camping/cabins, boating, fishing,
swimming and winter sports.

IRON MOUNTAIN IRON MINE

(US-2 - 9 miles east of Iron Mountain - Look for "Big John!")

Vulcan 49852

❑   Activity: Tours
❑   Telephone: (906) 563-8077
    www.tm-arts.com/ironmine/ironmine.htm
❑   Hours: Daily, 9:00 am - 5:00 pm (Memorial Day - mid-October)
❑   Admission: Adults $6.00, Children $5.00 (6-12)

"But Mom and Dad, why do we need a raincoat...it's not
raining outside?". Well...you explain as you're buttoning
up raincoats... it's probably raining INSIDE! Begin your journey
by getting dressed properly for it with a raincoat and hardhat.
Then you'll take a train ride through tunnels (over ½ mile long)
into the mine on the same tracks that the miners used until 1945
(The mine actually produced over 22 million tons of iron ore). As
you travel into the mine (over 400 feet deep), your kids will start to
see the "rain" inside (the dripping water) and will be glad that they
are dressed properly. Learn the drilling methods that were used
like "Double Jack" or "Water Liner" and see demonstrations of
both.

INDIANHEAD MOUNTAIN SKI AREA

Wakefield - 500 Indianhead Road, 49968. *Activity:* Outdoors.
(800) 3-INDIAN or (906) 229-5181. **www.indianheadmtn.com**.
A favorite of many Michiganders (state's largest vertical drop of
over 600 feet), this resort offers 22 runs, rentals, on-slope lodging,
babysitting, and lessons. (mid-November to mid-April).

Seasonal & Special Events

JANUARY

WINTERFEST

CW - Grand Haven, Spring Lake, Ferrysburg, Downtown. (800) 303-4097. Celebrating the Arts, Theater and Music through family activities and Children's Day. Winter sporting events like cardboard toboggan races and Polar Ice Cap Golf. (last weekend in January for one week)

TIP-UP TOWN, USA

NE - Houghton Lake. (800) 248-LAKE. Chilly festival. Ice fishing with tip-up rigs (hence, the name of the town), parade and games such as ice softball or snow eating contests. (3rd week in January)

WINTERFEST

NE - Mackinaw City. (800) 666-0160. Various activities each week.   Highlights include a professional snow sculpting contest, the Mackinaw Mush Sled Dog Race, Mackinaw City 300 Snowmobile Race, Battle of the Straits Gumbo Cook-off and the annual Snow Ball formal dance. (3 weeks during the month. January)

INTERNATIONAL ICE SCULPTURE SPECTACULAR

SE - Plymouth, Downtown. (I-275 to Ann Arbor Road west to Main Street). (734) 459-6969. **www.oeonline.com/plymouthice**. Up to 500,000 people walk the streets of downtown Plymouth to gaze at hundreds of blocks of carved ice (each several hundred pounds). Probably more ice to see here than anywhere and they even have a section for kids' make-believe carvings of delightful characters. Cozy shops and restaurants line the streets, plus many food vendors are on hand. Open 24 hours. Free Admission. (mid-January week)

SLED DOG ENDURO & WINTER FLURRY FESTIVAL

UE - St. Ignace. 6 dog, 10 dog, and mid-distance races. Winter games and Kiddie Mutt Races are fun for kids. (Late January weekend)

MICHIGAN TECH WINTER CARNIVAL

UW - Houghton. (held on Campus of Michigan Tech), 49921. (906) 487-2818. A celebration of snow and winter that dates back nearly 80 years. But, be sure you are dressed for the festivities as temperatures can reach -20 F. or colder. See huge snow and ice sculptures along US-41 that bring the winter season alive. The campus dorms function as a place where you can "warm up". (Carnival last 4 days. late-January to early-February)

FEBRUARY

ICE HARVEST

CE - Flint, Crossroads Village, Genesee County Parks. (800) 648-PARK. Visitors help cut ice from Mott Lake for the Village Ice House. The event is dependent upon the weather because only traditional tools and techniques are used. Admission. (Second Saturday in February)

SNOWFEST

CE - Frankenmuth. National and international snow sculptors work on over 13 tons of snow during the Michigan Snow Sculpting Championship and Ice Carving Championship. Some sculptures are more than ten feet tall and created from 6-ton blocks of snow. The streets of Frankenmuth are lined with ice carvings, a children's village-petting zoo, train rides, snow slides; fireworks, German food and entertainment. (February)

WINTER CARNIVAL

NE - Cheboygan. (231) 627-3181. Snowmobile drag racing, snow football, snow sculpting, and chili cook-off. (February)

PERCHVILLE USA

NE - East Tawas. (800) 55-TAWAS. Ice and shorelines. Ice fishing contests for all ages, ice demolition derby, all-you-can-eat perch dinners, and the annual Polar Bear Swim where adults cut a giant hole in the frozen bay, jump in and swim. Children's ice/snow games. (1st weekend of February)

SNOLYMPICS WINTER PICNIC

UE - St. Ignace. Golf chipping and Fishing contests, kids games, Broomball Tourney, Scavenger Hunt, Marshmallow Roast and Cook-off. (3rd Saturday in February)

UP 200 SLED-DOG CHAMPIONSHIP

UW - Marquette to Escanaba. (800) 544-4321. Mushers race their teams across 200 miles of the Winter Upper Peninsula. Visitors can race through steaming stacks of pancakes and syrup served throughout the day. (mid-February)

MARCH

MAPLE SUGARING WEEKEND

CE - Midland, Chippewa Nature Center. (517) 631-0830. With a naturalist along, tour the 1000 acre center, looking for maple sap. Learn how the sap is turned into syrup in the Sugar Shack. Donation admission. (Begins the 3rd Saturday in March)

CLARE IRISH FESTIVAL

CW - Clare. (888) AT-CLARE. Admission charged to some events. Everyone's Irish. Parade, leprechaun contest, Irish stew, music and dancing. (2nd weekend in March)

ST. PATRICK'S DAY PARADE

CW - Grand Rapids, Downtown. (616) 631-6953. Parade with marching bands, clowns, pipers and floats presented by the Ancient Order of Hiberians. (March)

SUGARBUSH

CW - Grand Rapids, Blandford Nature Center, 1715 Hillburn NW, 49504. (616) 453-6192. Observe maple sap being gathered, taken inside the Sugar House, and boiled into maple syrup. Finally it is bottled and available for sampling and purchase. (Weekends in March)

POW WOW

SE - Ann Arbor. (734) 763-9044. For several decades now, more than 1000 champion Native American singers, dancers, artisans and drummers gather for competitions. (March)

POW WOW DANCE FOR MOTHER EARTH

SE - Ann Arbor, Crisler Arena, 333 East Stadium Blvd., (734) 763-9044. More than 1000 Great Lakes Native American dancers, drummers, and singers gather for competitive dancing and crafts. Nearly 12,000 people attend this event. Admission charged. (mid-March for a long weekend)

MAPLE SYRUP FESTIVAL

SE - Bloomfield Hills, Cranbrook Institute of Science, (1221 North Woodward Avenue). (248) 645-3200. See maple sap extracted from trees and then taken to the sugar shack to be made into maple products. (Usually a late weekend in March)

SUGARING & SHEARING FESTIVAL

SE - Jackson, Ella Sharp Museum. (517) 787-2320. Maple tree tapping at a turn-of-the-century farm. Watch sap being processed and help make maple sugar candy. (last Saturday in March)

ST. PATRICK'S DAY PARADE

SE - Ypsilanti. Travels from the Water Tower to Historic Depot Town. (734) 483-4444. An annual tradition, the parade features authentic costumes and antique autos. (Begins 2:00 pm, March 13th)

APRIL

BRUNCH WITH THE BUNNIES

CE - Flint. Crossroads Village & Huckleberry Railroad, 6140 Bray Road. (800) 648-PARK. Bring the family for a fun-filled brunch, including treats and children's activities. (Easter weekend, usually April)

MAPLE SYRUP FESTIVAL

CW - Shepherd. (517) 828-6486 or (517) 828-5726. Breakfast foods, amusement rides, historic recreations, music, parades, stage coach rides, historical museum tours, and the highlight - sugarbush tours and demos. (Last weekend in April)

EGG HUNT

SE - Ann Arbor, Domino's Farms, (US-23 at Ann Arbor-Plymouth Road east). (734) 930-5032. Come Easter, it's the annual egg hunt when youngsters scour the grounds for plastic eggs that contain candy, stickers, or coupons redeemable for prizes. The Easter Bunny "pops" in and there's also face-painting, hayrides, clowns, and entertainment. (Easter weekend, usually April)

WOLDUMAR HISTORIC ENCAMPMENT

SE – Lansing. Woldumar Nature Center, 5539 Old Lansing Road, (517) 322-0030. Nature Center facilities and grounds open with a Civil War and Scottish Kiltsmen encampment. Tours of the Moon Log Cabin also. Free admission. (Last Saturday in April)

MAPLE SYRUP FESTIVAL

SE - Mason, Snow's Sugarbush. (517) 676-1653 or (517) 676-2442. (First half of April)

BUNNYVILLE

SE - Royal Oak, Detroit Zoo, (8450 West 10 Mile Road). (248) 541-5835. Celebrate Easter with a zoo theme and prizes and entertainment. (Easter – usually in April)

BLOSSOMTIME

SW - Benton Harbor & St. Joseph. (616) 925-6301. 20 plus neighboring ⸱ Southwest Michigan communities celebrate Michigan's fruit-growing country making pilgrimages into the countryside to see the orchards in bloom. Carnival, youth parade, and the finale Grand Floral Parade with it's 100-plus flowered floats and their queens. (Last Sunday in April for one week)

MAPLE SYRUP FESTIVAL

SW - Vermontville. (517) 726-0394. Michigan's oldest maple-syrup festival. Parade, petting zoo, carnival and maple-sugar treats sold. (Last weekend in April)

MAY

ALMA HIGHLAND FESTIVAL AND GAMES

CE - Alma, Alma College, downtown. (517) 463-8979 or (517) 463-5525. **www.mach7.com/highlandfestival**. More than 600 costumed bagpipers and drummers march onto the athletic field for performances and competitions. Dancers perform the sailor's hornpipe and Highland fling. Highland shortbread and briddies (pastries stuffed with ground meat). Competitions include border collie sheep-herding and tossing capers. Admission over 5 years old.

MOTHER'S DAY CELEBRATION

CE - Flint, Crossroads Village & Huckleberry Railroad, (6140 Bray Road). (800) 648-PARK. Free village, train and Genesee Belle cruise admission for Mom. Special buffet dinner offered (reservations recommended). (Mother's Day - May)

FEAST OF THE STE. CLAIRE

CE - Port Huron, Riverfront. **www.bluewater.org**. (800) 852-4242. Battle re-enactments of British and American soldiers with other features of trading, music, wares and cooking. (Memorial Day Weekend - May)

GREAT LAKES SPORT KITE CHAMPIONSHIPS

CW - Grand Haven, Grand Haven State Park Beach. (800) 303-4097. Sponsored by the Mackinaw Kite Company, this event fills the air with brightly colored, high-flying kites everywhere. One of the largest kite festivals in the Nation, you'll find up to 40,000 spectators, pilots flying kites (some craft up to 40 foot long), kite ballet events and lessons for beginners. (3rd long weekend in May)

GRAND QUACKER DUCK RACE

CW - Grand Haven, Waterfront Stadium. (616) 846-2015. "Adopt" a rubber duck for $5.00 each and then be the best cheerleader for your duck to win the race. Nice big prizes for winners and profits go to Hospice. Family activities late morning until the race at 1:00 pm. (3rd Saturday in May)

SHEARING FESTIVAL

CW - Ionia, 6720 Ainsworth Road, 48846. (616) 527-5910. Exotic, rare farm featuring llamas, alpacas, sheep, angora goats and more. See shearing techniques used on each animal, how raw fibers are hand spun to be used making garments. Try you hand too. (2nd Saturday in May)

GREEKTOWN ARTS FESTIVAL

SE - Detroit, Greektown, (Monroe and Beaubien Streets). (877) GREEK-TOWN. Contemporary craftspeople demonstrations offer the public a chance to learn about the artists' ideas, techniques and materials. Also Greektown's famous food. (3rd weekend in May)

EAST LANSING ART FESTIVAL

SE - East Lansing, Downtown between Abbott and Mac Streets, 48823. www.ci.east-lansing.mi.us. (517) 337-1731. Especially for kids are the performing dancers, storytellers, clowns and jugglers. Creative art project areas for kids include face painting and making a contribution to the Chalk Art Mural. Shuttles available from many parking sites nearby. (3rd weekend in May)

STRAWBERRY FESTIVAL

SE - Hamtramck, St. Florian's Parish. (313) 871-2778. Local cooks create all kinds of strawberry desserts. Dancing, Polish music. (1st weekend in May)

WIZARD OF OZ FESTIVAL

SE - St. Johns, Downtown. (517) 224-7248. Features a parade, celebrity dinner and brunch, and several of the Munchkins will be available for autographs. Free admission. (mid-May weekend)

WAYNE COUNTY AIR SHOW

SE - Ypsilanti, Willow Run Airport, (I-94, exit Belleville Road north to Tyler Road west to Beck Road north). (734) 482-8888. Two afternoons of appearances by thrilling precision flight teams like the Blue Angels, wing walkers, aerobats and flyby drills. Many military and civilian aircraft are on display to peek in. The Yankee Air Museum also hosts an open house. (Around Memorial Day Weekend - May)

TULIP TIME

SW - Holland. (800) 822-2770. **www.tuliptime.org**. 8 miles of tulips (6 million red, yellow and pink blooms), Klompen Dancers, fireworks and top entertainment. To start the festival, the town crier bellows "the streets are dirty" and youngsters begin cleaning with brooms and pails. Volksparade is next with the Kinder Parade of 5000 children dressed in costume. There are Dutch treats like pigs in blankets and pastries galore, a Muziekparade and Kinderplasts - music, clowns, puppets, petting zoo , arts & crafts for kids. (Begins Mother's Day weekend for one week - May)

JUNE

FREE FISHING WEEKEND

STATEWIDE - Inland and Great Lakes Waters. (800) 548-2555. All weekend long, all fishing license fees will be waived for resident and nonresident anglers. All fishing regulations will still apply. (2nd weekend in June)

BAY CITY RIVER ROAR

CE - Bay City, Saginaw River. (517) 893-5596. Pro outboard performance races, top name entertainment, tunnel boats racing and on display. (Last weekend in June)

BAVARIAN FESTIVAL

CE - Frankenmuth, Downtown. (800) FUN-TOWN. During this festival, Michigan's Little Bavaria looks truly like old-time Germany with flower boxes full of blooms, "oompah" bands and dancers and costumes. Nearly 50,000 visitors attend yearly. Specialty foods include strawberry shortcake, brats, sauerkraut, funnel cakes, dozens of cheeses and sausages. (1st and 2nd weekends of June)

GRAND PRIX HYDROPLANE SUMMER NATIONALS CHAMPIONSHIP AND OFFSHORE RACING

CE - Muskegon, Muskegon Lake docks. (800) 585-3737. $13-19.00 per day. More than 100 teams compete in various categories of skill. Top speeds of the boats is 175 mph. Mart Dock area downtown has festival events and food and entertainment. Friday Noon – 5:00 pm is the Kids Korner. (2nd long weekend in June)

SAND SCULPTURE CONTEST

CW - Grand Haven, Grand Haven City Beach. (616) 842-4910. Different skill level categories compete for the best sand sculptures, usually with a general theme. Sculpting in the morning, judging and announcements of winners in the afternoon. (Last Saturday in June)

WALK THROUGH HISTORY

NE - Grayling, Wellington Farm Park, (I-75 south to exit 251, turn right, left at Military Road). (888) OLD-FARM. Walk through American History from the 1700's to 1932. Displays, women and men folk chores demos, music, encampments and lots of hands-on experiences. (Father's Day Weekend - June)

SCREAMIN' ON THE STRAITS PERSONAL WATERCRAFT RACES

NE - Mackinac City, Straits of Mackinac. (800) 666-0160. Personal watercraft compete for top speeds in various class races. Short distance races one day and long distance "Enduro Race" the next day. (Third weekend in June)

LILAC FESTIVAL

NE - Mackinac Island. (800) 4-LILACS. Lilacs were first planted by French missionaries a couple of hundred years ago and the bushes still bloom full of white and purple flowers each year. Dancers fill the streets and food specialties from local hotels line the streets at the Taste of Mackinac. The Grand Lilac Parade has more than 100 horses pulling lilac-theme floats with clowns and marching bands in between. Their famous fudge is available at every turn. (June)

NATIONAL STRAWBERRY FESTIVAL

SE - Belleville, Wayne County Fairgrounds and downtown, (I-94 Belleville Road exit south into town). (734) 697-3137. If they're ripe, local farms can be visited heading in or out of town (Rowe's or Potter's). The festival draws 100,000 berry lovers, mostly families. A family circus, kids carnival and games, pony rides, and a parade Saturday. (Father's Day Weekend in June)

AIR MICHIGAN

SE - Detroit, Willow Run Airport. (734) 482-8888. Catch daring tricks like wing walkers and acrobatics teams, also see some of the world's fastest flyers. (Last weekend in June)

MICHIGAN CHALLENGE BALLOONFEST

SE - Howell, Howell High School area, (I-96 exit 133). (800) 686-8474. **www.michiganchallenge.com**. 60,000 or more folks will share space with you watching skydiving, stunt kites, music, fireworks, and spectacular balloon launch flight competitions.

There's also a carnival for the kids and bright balloon glows in the evening. Admission by carload ($8.00) or by entire weekend per person (slightly more). (3rd or 4th weekend in June)

CEREAL FEST

SW - Battle Creek, Downtown along Michigan Avenue, (I-94 exit 98B). (800) 397-2240 or (616) 962-2240. *Hours:* Thursday parade @ 6:00 pm. Children's activities Saturday, 8:00 am - Noon (games, free samples/literature). Farmers Market, Festival Park. The World's Longest Breakfast Table began in 1956 (*celebration was set up for 7000 people - 14000 showed up!*). They could see it was a hit and so competitors Kellogg's, Post, and Ralston Foods team up each year to serve over 60,000 people. Over 600 volunteers serve complimentary cereals, milk, Tang, Pop Tarts, donuts and Dole bananas on more than 300 tables lining one street. It's really a treat for the whole family and very well organized. We were pleasantly and promptly served within minutes and the variety of food choices was abundant. If you haven't already, be sure to stop by Kellogg's Cereal City USA, just a block away. (2nd week of June)

INTERNATIONAL FREEDOM FESTIVAL

SE - Detroit/Windsor, Detroit Waterfront & Downtown Museums/Windsor Downtown Waterfront. (313) 923-7400. **www.theparade.org**. Take the kids over the bridge or through the tunnel to Canada for the carnival rides, Canada's largest parade (July 1), or the Great Bed Race. On the U.S. side you'll find a children's carnival, food fair, tugboat race, international tug-of-war with Windsor, and finally fireworks on July 4th (said to be the largest pyrotechnic show in North America). (mid-June through July 4th)

JULY

HONORING THE EAGLE POW WOW

CE - Flint, Crossroads Village & Huckleberry Railroad, 6140 Bray Road. (800) 648-PARK. The Genesee Valley Indian Association invites you to participate in a traditional ceremony or Pow Wow. (3rd weekend in July)

RIVERDAYS FESTIVAL

CE - Midland, Chippewassee Park and area surrounding the Tridge. (517) 839-9661. 17th and 18th century voyageurs reenactment, Valley Fife & Drum Corps music and pageantry. Paddlewheel cruises aboard the Princess Laura or get "hands-on" experience paddling the 32 foot canoe. Milk Jug Raft Race, Pancake Breakfast, Dinners, children's activities and concerts. (Third weekend in July for 4 days)

NATIONAL BABY FOOD FESTIVAL

CW - Fremont, Downtown. (800) 592-BABY. Five days of baby contests and people acting like baby contests. Try entering a Gerber (headquartered here) baby food eating contest (*1st one to down 5 jars wins*) or enter a baby in the baby crawl race (imagine what parents hold as prizes to get their babies to move towards the finish line!). A baby food cook-off, top live entertainment, a midway, and 2 downtown parades. (Third long weekend in July)

COAST GUARD FESTIVAL

CW - Grand Haven. (888) 207-2434. A Coast Guard tradition filled with family entertainment day and night leading up to the final Saturday. Saturday starts with the biggest and best parade in all of West Michigan, a carnival on Main Street, all leading up to the fantastic fireworks late at night. (Begins last weekend in July for 10 days)

MUSKEGON AIR FAIR

CW - **Muskegon**, Muskegon County Airport. (800) OK-AIR-SHOW. **www.muskegon-air-fair.com**. Solo aerobatics, barnstorming Red Baron Squadron and racing ground vehicles, and parachute teams. *Admission:* $4-10.00. (3rd weekend in July)

MICHIGAN BROWN TROUT FESTIVAL

NE - **Alpena**, Downtown and Alpena Mall. (800) 4-ALPENA. The Great Lakes' longest continuous fishing tournament. Anglers vie for top prizes and all can enjoy Art On the Bay, a Kid's Carnival, Fish Pond, and free concerts. (mid-to-end of July)

ALPENFEST

NE - **Gaylord**, Downtown. (800) 345-8621. The featured activity is a Swiss tradition of the burning of the Boogg - where residents place all their troubles on slips of paper and throw them into a fire. Many parades and the world's largest coffee break. (3rd week in July)

FOREST FEST

NE - **Grayling**, Hartwick Pines State Park, (I-75 & M-93). (517) 348-2537. Renaissance Forester performance of logging songs, visit by Smoky Bear, displays of DNR fire-fighting equipment, a tree giveaway, pine walks and Logging Museum (Last weekend in July)

AU SABLE RIVER INTERNATIONAL CANOE MARATHON & RIVER FESTIVAL

NE - **Grayling to Oscoda**, Downtown and along Au Sable River. (800) 937-8837. Called the world's toughest spectator sport - why? Probably because it's tough to follow canoes by land and a good chunk of the race is through the night until daybreak. Because the kids might only be able to catch the beginning or end of this canoe race, downtown areas are prepared to fill the time with family activities like Youth Canoe Races, Children's Fishing Contest, a

Festival Parade and Dance, and a tour of Camp Grayling - the nation's largest National Guard training facility. (Last full weekend in July)

NATIONAL FOREST FESTIVAL

NW - Manistee, Downtown. **www.manistee~edo.chamber.** (800) 288-2286. Visit the open houses of the Lymon Building and Water Works with local history artifacts, parades, dances, midway, boat parade and fireworks. (4th of July)

NATIONAL CHERRY FESTIVAL

NW - Traverse City. (231) 947-4230. Cherry treats, three parades, two air shows, turtle races, band contests, mountain-bike rides, live performances and beach volleyball to begin with. There's also a Very Cherry Luncheon, Cherry Pie Eating Contest, cherry grove tours and fireworks above Grand Traverse Bay. (Begins July 3rd or 4th for eight days)

ANN ARBOR STREET ART FAIR

SE - Ann Arbor, Main and State Streets, downtown. (734) 995-7281 or (734) 662-3382 (Guild). 1000+ artisans from across the nation set up booths. There are face-painting experts, beginner watercolor stations with try-it easels, Family art activity center, magicians, jugglers, and lots of American and ethnic food. (3rd week in July)

SPIRIT OF DETROIT THUNDERFEST

SE - Detroit, Detroit River. **www.thunderfest.com.** (800) 359-7760. 500,000 plus fans gather to watch aerodynamic turbine or piston-powered hydroplane racing. Speeds can exceed 200 mph. Admission. (Long weekend after July 4th)

MICHIGAN TASTFEST

SE - **Detroit**, New Center on West Grand Blvd., (between Woodard and the Lodge Freeway). **http://comnet.org/tastefest**. (313) 872-0188. World-wide flavored smorgasbord of food and entertainment, a Kid Zone, walking tours. (1st week on July)

HOT AIR JUBILEE

SE - **Jackson**, Reynolds Municipal Airport. (517) 782-1515. **www.jacksonmich.com/jubilee**. Launches mornings & evenings, flight demo teams, stunt kites, Kids Kingdom, aircraft displays and carnival. (3rd weekend in July)

CIVIL WAR ASSOCIATES' RE-ENACTMENT

SE - **Newport**, Nike Park. (734) 242-3366. Re-enactments of artillery and cavalry battles, period craftspeople in costume demonstrate their skills. (2nd weekend in July)

SALINE CELTIC FESTIVAL

SE - **Saline**, Mill Pond Park. 48176. **www.salineceltic.org**. (734) 429-4907. A free shuttle to the park brings you Highland athletic competitions, children's activities, thematic reenactments, Celtic music and dancing and food. (2nd Saturday in July)

SUMMER MUSIC GAMES

SE - **Ypsilanti**. (734) 483-4444. Top-ranked drum corps from around the nation compete in events such as precision drills, choreography, costume and quality of music. (July)

TEAM US NATIONALS BALLOON CHAMPIONSHIP AND AIR SHOW

SW - **Battle Creek**. W.K. Kellogg Airport, (I-94 exit Helmer Road). (616) 962-0592. **www.bcballoons.com**. 200 plus balloons (some shaped like Tony the Tiger, flowers, bears or fruit) take off in competitions, a top-level air show, fireworks choreographed to music, and many ground displays of aircraft. Parking fee. (Eight days starting the Saturday before the 4th of July)

COVERED BRIDGE FESTIVAL

SW - Centreville. Parade, kids activities and scenic covered bridges. (616) 467-5532. (2nd weekend in July)

INTERNATIONAL CHERRY PIT SPITTING CHAMPIONSHIP

SW - Eau Claire, Tree-Mendus Fruit Farm, (East on M-140 on Eureka Road). (800) 957-4735. The world record is almost 73 feet! Can you compete or do you just want to watch? Playground and petting corral too! (July 3rd)

VENETIAN FESTIVAL

SW - St. Joseph, St. Joseph River. (616) 983-7917. Two parades, one on land, and the other a lighted boat parade on the river. Live entertainment, fireworks, and food fair. (3rd long weekend in July)

WORLD LOGROLLING & GREAT LAKES LUMBERJACK CHAMPIONSHIPS

UW - Gladstone. (906) 789-7862. The most prestigious event in the world of logging. Local, national, and international contestants compete in events such as springboard, Jack & Jill sawing, pole climbing, hot sawing, and the standing block chop. (July 4th weekend)

UPPER PENINSULA CHAMPIONSHIP RODEO

UW - Iron River. (888) 879-4766. Eat a chuck-wagon breakfast and then watch barrel racing and other cowpoke competitions. (3rd long weekend in July)

4TH OF JULY CELEBRATIONS

Independence Day is celebrated with parades, carnivals, entertainment, food and fireworks.

- ❑   **CE - Bay City**. Bay City Fireworks Festival. 888-BAY-TOWN. Three days around the 4th.
- ❑   **CE - Bridgeport**. Valley of Flags, Junction Valley Railroad. (517) 777-3480. Rides through display of flags. Five days around the 4th.
- ❑   **CE - Flint**. Crossroads Village and Huckleberry Railroad. (800) 648-PARK. Parade through park and American flags everywhere.
- ❑   **CW - Grand Haven** Area. (800) 250-WAVE.
- ❑   **NE - Mackinaw City**, A Frontier Fourth, Historic Mill Creek. (906) 847-3328. 1820's style Independence Day with games, music, sawmill demonstrations, patriotic speeches and reading of the Declaration of Independence.
- ❑   **NE - Mackinac Island**, A Star Spangled Fourth, Fort Mackinac. (906) 847-3328. 1880's celebrations include cannon firings. Admission to Fort.
- ❑   **NE - Mackinac Island**, Old Fashioned Mackinac, Grand Hotel. (800) 33-GRAND.
- ❑   **SE - Ann Arbor/Ypsilanti** Area. (734) 544-3800. (4th of July)
- ❑   **SE - Detroit**. International Freedom Fest. (313) 923-7400. Late June-early July. More than 100 festivals.
- ❑   **SW - Jackson**, Cascade Falls Park. (517) 788-4320.
- ❑   **SW - Marshall**, 4th of July Celebration. Cornwell's Turkeyville USA and downtown. (800) 877-5163.
- ❑   **SW - Saint Joseph** Pavilion. Patriotic Pops. (616) 934-7676.

AUGUST

COLONIAL LIFE WEEKEND

CE – Flint. Genesee County Parks, 5045 Stanley Road, 48506. (800) 648-PARK. Re-enactment of Revolutionary War Battles, drills and skills. Admission. (Last weekend in August)

WEST MICHIGAN GRAND PRIX

CE - Grand Rapids, Downtown streets. 49503. (616) 336-PRIX. SCCA Pro Racing / Trans-Am event races. Tickets available through TicketsPlus. (Last weekend in August)

NATIONAL PICKLE FESTIVAL

CE - Linwood, Downtown, (east of M-13). (517) 697-3790. Cucumber pickles are ripe and moving out by the truckload this time of year. Entertainment, a pickle parade with Petunia Pickle as mascot plus 100+ floats, a kiddy bike parade, food, and carnival. $3.00 admission button. (3rd weekend in August)

OLD GAS TRACTOR SHOW

CE - Oakley, Corner of Brennan & Ferden Roads. (800) 255-3055. Step back in time as unique tractors and steam engines demonstrate old-fashioned threshing, sawmilling, and bailing techniques...only using steam power. (3rd weekend of August)

P.R.I.D.E.

CE - Saginaw, Morley Plaza, downtown. (517) 771-2409. Music from dozens of cultures along with their crafts and food available to purchase. Countries included are Ireland, Greece, Mexico, etc. (Held the 1st Friday - Sunday August weekend)

WHITE CLOUD'S HOMECOMING & POW WOW

CW - White Cloud, Downtown. (231) 689-6607. There's a parade and firemen's water battles as part of the homecoming but most kids really look forward to the Pow Wow. In the spirit of sharing, Native Americans join together in song, dance, crafts and momentos. Watch the traditional activities and then listen to elders tell children stories of wisdom passed on through the ages. (1st weekend in August)

ANTIQUE TRACTOR AND STEAM ENGINE SHOW

NE - **Alpena**. (800) 4-ALPENA. Return to yesteryear to see a hay press, sawmill, thresher motors, antique chain saws, stone crushers and a shingle mill. Food available. (2nd weekend in August)

THE FLAT BELT FESTIVAL

NE - **Grayling**, Wellington Farm Park, (I-75 to exit 251). (888) OLD-FARM. Park farmers demonstrate preparations for the upcoming harvest including threshing, blacksmithing, preping tractors, sawmill operations, and mill grinding grain to flour. (Last weekend in August)

IRONWORKERS FESTIVAL

NE - **Mackinac City**, Mackinac Bridge. Ironworkers from around the world come here annually to test their skills in the column climbing. The prize is the coveted gold belt buckle. Also a celebration of the building of the Mackinac Bridge in 1957. (800) 666-0160. (August)

DETROIT GRAND PRIX

SE - **Detroit**, Belle Isle. (313) 393-7749. **www.grandprix.com**. Free admission on Friday for trials. 1000's of fans watch Indy cars and check out "Indy Lites" race-related activities. (1st weekend in August)

AFRICAN WORLD FESTIVAL

SE - **Detroit**, Hart Plaza. (313) 494-5800. Sponsored by the Museum of African American History, this outdoor festival features cultural and educational programs, music, global cuisine, and storytellers at the Children's Village. Free. (3rd long weekend of August)

MICHIGAN STATE FAIR

SE - Detroit, State Fairgrounds, (Woodward and Eight Mile Road). (313) 369-8250. Open 10:00 am - 10:00 pm, this fair has a midway, baby animal birthing areas, champion animal contests, fair food, and free concerts daily by nationally famous artists. Held the last week of August through Labor Day. (August / September)

MICHIGAN FESTIVAL

SE - East Lansing, Citywide, mostly MSU campus. (800) 935-FEST. Subtitled "a big block party", there's plenty of events including one block of sandy beach made for volleyball and beach games, The Festival of Michigan Folklife (eighteenth century crafts and chores), American Indian Pow Wow, and Kids Mania. Most kid's activities are at Landon Field, near Sparty (MSU mascot) with crafts, kid's performers and a talent show. Food vendors are everywhere. Admission for people 11 or older. (mid-August weekend)

RODEO

SE - Hanover, 12770 Roundtree Road, (US-12 to Moscow Road, follow signs). (517) 563-8249. Old-fashioned rodeo with a couple hundred competitors and a couple hundred spectators. Tours of the buffalo ranch, ranch food, horseback riding, and hayrides are available. Admission. (mid-August weekend)

MICHIGAN RENAISSANCE FESTIVAL

SE - Holly, Festival grounds near Mount Holly, (I-75 north exit 106). **www.members.aol.com/renfestmi**. (800) 601-4848. Beginning in mid-August and running for seven weeks, the "Robinhood-ish" woods of Holly take you back to the sixteenth century. See knights in shining armor, strolling minstrels or Henry VIII characters. If you like, your family can dress as a lord or lady. Don't dress the kids too fancy though, all the food served is eaten with only your hands and fingers (ex. Giant turkey legs, cream soups served in bread bowls). Watch a mock jousting tourney, run from the friendly dragon, see jugglers and jesters, listen to storytellers, and best of all, ride on human-powered fair rides (it's hilarious). Admission $6-14.00 depending on age. Discount coupons available at area supermarkets. (mid-August weekend for seven weekends through September)

CIVIL WAR MUSTER

SE - Jackson, Cascades Park, 1992 Warren Avenue, 49203. (517) 788-4320. Midwest's largest Civil War Battle re-enactment with Union and Confederate soldiers, artillery and infantries. (Last weekend in August)

NATIONAL FOLK FESTIVAL

SE - Lansing. (517) 337-1731. Celebrating traditional visual and performing arts with musicians, dancers, craftspeople, storytellers, parades and lots of ethnic food. (August)

CORN-FUSING CROSSROADS, THE FARMERS PUZZLE

SE - Monroe, Heiss Road, (3 miles west of Telegraph, off I-24 or I-25). (734) 242-7053. Fridays open at 4:00 pm, Weekends open 10:00 am - 1 hour before dark. *Admission:* $4.00 Adults, $3.00 Children (6-10). Walk through a Corn Maze and have bushels of fun trying to find your way out. Crafts, refreshments, petting farm, pumpkins. (mid-August - November 1st)

OLD FRENCH TOWN DAYS

SE - Monroe, Hellenburg Park. (734) 242-3366. Military re-enactments, tomahawk throws, canoe races, crafts demonstrations and music. (Weekend before Labor Day)

CARDBOARD REGATTA

SE - Port Huron, Black River. (800) 852-2828. The flimsy and the festively decorated are both here to compete in a short regatta (most disintegrate quickly once in water). Kids will get a good laugh at the decorations and the "floating" disasters. Free. (mid-August)

WAR OF 1812 RE-ENACTMENT

SE - Rockwood, Lake Erie Metropark. (734) 242-3366. (mid-August weekend)

RUBY CIDER MILL AND TREE FARM

SE - Ruby, 6567 Imlay City Road, (I-69 west exit 96). (810) 324-2662. A cider mill, carnival rides, wax museum (presidential), a Christmas gift shop, and a petting zoo await you. (Weekends August through October)

MICHIGAN FIBER FESTIVAL

SW - Allegan, Allegan County Fairgrounds. (616) 945-2816. Meet llamas, rabbits, alpacas, goats, and sheep who all grow great coats that are sheared and processed. Come learn spinning, weaving, and see border collies herd sheep. 100's of merchant booths too. (3rd weekend in August)

NATIONAL BLUEBERRY FESTIVAL

SW - South Haven, Lake Michigan shores. (616) 637-5171. Visit the "World's Highbush Blueberry Capital" with every blueberry food concoction, sand-sculpting contests and beach volleyball. (2nd long weekend in August)

UPPER PENINSULA STATE FAIR

UE - Escanaba, (Fairground - east side of Escanaba – US-2), 49829. (906) 786-4011. *Admission:* Adults $3.00, Children $1.00 (5-11). (*Additional charge for grandstand shows*). As summer draws to a close in Michigan, you can choose to celebrate the seasons harvest at one of 2 state fairs (*one in Detroit, the other in Escanaba*). All the usual fun is here from tractor pulls, motorcycle racing, live entertainment, great food, and rides for the whole family. Can't you just smell the barbecue? (August)

SEPTEMBER

GRANDPARENT'S DAY TRAIN

CE - Bridgeport, Junction Valley Railroad, 7065 Dixie Highway, 48722. (517) 777-3480. Grandparents Day (Sunday) in September When accompanied by paying grandchildren, grandparents are given a discount rate of $2.50 per ride. Bring young and old to ride on the largest quarter size railroad in the world. (September)

CROSSROADS VILLAGE

CE - Flint. (800) 648-PARK. Reenactment of historic rallies by farmers, reformers and women's rights groups. (Labor Day Weekend - September)

BALLOON FEST

CE - Midland, Midland County Fairgrounds. (517) 832-0090 (RE/MAX office). 3rd weekend in September, Friday - Sunday. "Lift-off" to the United Way campaign with daily morning launches of 50 or so balloons. "After Glows" both Friday and Saturday nights. Skydiver shows. Free admission. (September)

UNCLE JOHN'S CIDER MILL

CE - St. Johns, 8614 North US-27. www.ujcidermill.com. (517) 224-3686. Apples in September, pumpkins in October. Walk along the nature trail, take a tractor ride tour through the orchards, play in the fun house or check out the petting zoo and train rides. Small admission per activity. (Weekends in September and October)

RED FLANNEL FESTIVAL

CW - Cedar Springs, Main Street and Morley Park, downtown, (US-131 exit 104). (616) 696-2662 or (800) 763-3273 Shoppe. Lumberjacks and clowns wore them - the original trapdoor red flannels made in this town since the early 1900's. They're still made here (purchase some at Cedar Specialties Store). An historical museum in Morley Park is usually open and features the history of red flannels (ex. Why the trapdoor?). A warning to visitors: be sure to wear red flannel (pajamas, long johns, shirts) as you walk the downtown streets or else the Keystone Cops might arrest you! There's plenty of red flannel (many still with trapdoors) for yourself or your teddy bear to purchase. They're so adorable on our teddy! (September)

THE GREAT TRAIN ROBBERY

CW - Coopersville, Coopersville/Marne Railway. (616) 837-7000. Last 2 Saturdays in September. Departures at 1:00 and 3:00 pm. A passenger train is robbed by desperadoes on horse back and the excursion ends with a rewarding Chuck Wagon Barbecue. (September)

MACKINAW FUDGE FESTIVAL

NE - Mackinaw City, Downtown. (800) 666-0160. "Fudgies" from this state and neighboring states and countries come to taste and judge the area's famous fudge. Numerous "fudge-related" events include eating contests (got milk?). (Last long weekend in September)

PAUL BUNYAN DAYS & OCTOBERFEST

NE - Oscoda. (800) 235-4625. Lumberjacks and loggers go blade-to-blade in the chainsaw competition plus other contests. (3rd weekend in September)

KNAEBE'S MMMUNCHY KRUNCHY APPLE FARM

NE - **Rogers City**, 2622 Karsten Road, 49779. (517) 734-2567. Saturdays. Watch them press cider, then slurp some along with homemade donuts, apple pies or caramel apples. In October they have goat and pony rides for kids. (September / October)

LABOR DAY BRIDGE WALK

NE - **St. Ignace to Mackinaw City**. This annual crossing draws an average of 50,000 participant walkers. Starting in St. Ignace, the walkers head south across the Mackinac Bridge to the other side in Mackinaw City. This is the only time civilians are allowed to walk over the bridge. If you complete the 5 mile walk, you'll receive a Bridge Walk Certificate and enjoy a celebration in town. Labor Day. (800) 666-0160. (Labor Day - September)

PARKER MILL

SE - **Ann Arbor**, 4650 Geddes, (east of US-23). (734) 971-6337. Weekends. Free admission. This restored 1800's gristmill is one of the country's few remaining completely functional mill and log cabin. Picnicking is recommended. (September / October)

FESTIVAL OF THE ARTS

SE - **Detroit**, University Cultural Center. (313) 577-5088. International arts festival held in a 20-block area and has a gigantic children's fair, street performances and great varieties of food. Admission. (Weekend after Labor Day)

DEXTER CIDER MILL

SE - **Dexter**, 3685 Central Street, Downtown. (734) 426-8531. Since 1866, it is the oldest operating mill in Michigan. Cider and donuts available. (Almost daily September - November)

APPLEFEST

SE - Fenton, Spicer Orchards, (US-23 to Clyde Road exit). (810) 632-7692. Take a hayride out to the orchards for apple picking, pony rides, Victorian Carriage House (storage for 10,000 bushels, a sorting machine, cider mill and shops) highlight this free event (Weekends in September and October)

CASCADES PARK

SE - Jackson. (517) 788-4320. Giant fireworks, live concerts. (Labor Day Weekend - September)

RIVERFEST

SE - Lansing, Riverfront Park. (517) 483-4499. Highlights are the Electric Float Parade, live music performances, children's activities and a great carnival. (Labor Day Weekend)

ALBER'S ORCHARD

SE - Manchester, 13011 Bethel Church Road. (734) 428-7758. A family-owned business since 1890, they freely let you view the old-fashioned cider pressing and taste the fresh, cold cider as you browse through their shop. (September)

APPLE CHARLIE'S ORCHARD AND MILL

SE - New Boston, 38035 South Huron Road. (734) 753-9380. Open mid-August to January. Call for seasonal hours. Apples, cider press, petting farm, hayrides and a country store with farm gifts and freshly-made donuts. (September / October)

PLYMOUTH ORCHARDS AND CIDER MILL

SE - Plymouth, 10865 Warren Road, (Ford Road west to Ridge Road, follow signs). (734) 455-2290. Petting farm, hayrides to orchards to pick apples, lots of fresh squeezed cider or cinnamon-sugar donuts or caramel apples available to eat there or take home. (September)

COUNTRY FAIR WEEKENDS

SE - Ypsilanti, Wiard's Orchards, 5565 Merritt Road, (I-94 exit 183 south to Stony Creek south, follow signs. (734) 482-7744. Apple orchards, cider mill, fire engine rides, pony rides, wagon rides out to the apple-picking or pumpkin patch areas, face-painting and live entertainment. (September / October)

JOLLAY ORCHARDS

SW - Coloma, 1850 Friday Road, (I-94 exit 39). (616) 468-3075. Hayrides through enchanted/decorated orchards to u-pick apples. Make your own warm caramel apples and bakery with pies baked in a brown paper bag. (September)

ZIEGER CENTENNIAL FARM

SW - Three Oaks, 5692 West Warren Woods Road, (I-94 exit 4). (616) 756-9707. Fall playland with farm animals like horses, cows, turkeys and sheep to pet, hayrides, horse rides, cow milking at 4:00 pm, and a corn field maze. Month-long in the fall. (September / October)

FALL HARVEST FESTIVALS

Join the rural farm environments at these locations as you help perform the tasks of harvest and the celebration of bounty.

- ❑ **SE - Jackson**, Ella Sharp Museum, 3225 Fourth Street. (517) 787-2320.
- ❑ **SE - Dearborn**, Henry Ford Museum & Greenfield Village, 20900 Oakwood Blvd. (313) 271-1620.
- ❑ **NE - Alpena**, Jesse Besser Museum. (1st Saturday in October)

OCTOBER

PUMPKIN TRAIN

CW - Coopersville, Coopersville & Marne Railway. (616) 837-7000. Twice a day in the afternoon. Take a train with the Great Pumpkin. On board entertainment and refreshments. Pick your own pumpkin from the giant pile. Admission. (Weekends in October)

PUMPKINFEST

CW - Remus, 5100 Pierce Road, (south of M-20), 49340. (517) 967-8422. A Centennial Farm with plenty of animals and harvest crops. Country Store with cider, donuts, etc. Swinging Hay ropes, tractors, hayrides to pumpkin field. (Month long in October)

GREAT LAKES LIGHTHOUSE FESTIVAL

NE - Alpena, Old and New Presque Isle Lighthouses. (800) 4-ALPENA. Plan to make it annually to tour and climb the famous short & spooky Old Presque Isle Lighthouse or the three times as tall - New Lighthouse. Keeper's quarters are open too. U.S. Coast Guard exhibits recall tales of disasters and valiant rescues. (October)

PUMPKINFEST

NE - Grayling, Wellington Farm Park, (I-75 to exit 251). (888) OLD-FARM. Visit the pumpkin patch, watch cider-making, corn-husking, wood-carving, milling and blacksmithing demos. Every weekend, beginning the (2nd weekend in October)

PUMPKIN FANTASY WORLD

NE - Herron, The Farm, 11715 Cripps Road. (517) 356-9462 or 727-8004. Take a hayride to the Great Pumpkin Patch and enjoy the country living on a real farm. Cider and donuts available. (Entire month of October).

NORWEGIAN PUMPKIN ROLLING FESTIVAL

NW - Williamsburg, 11274 Munro Road, (M-72 to Elk Lake Road north, west via Townline Road, then south to Munro. (231) 264-8371. The mill is powered by horse-driven gears while circling the mill. Festival activities include a pumpkin rolling contest, apple relays, pumpkin watercolor painting and Norwegian food and entertainment. Free admission. (1st weekend in October)

ANDY T'S FARMS

SE - St. Johns, 3131 South US-27. (517) 224-7674. Open, daily 9:00 am - 8:00 pm. Family fun farm with fresh veggies and fruit (esp. apples and pumpkins), U-pick tours, hayrides, a petting barn, holiday decorations and bakery. (October)

GOOSE FESTIVAL

SW - Fennville. You're invited to witness the annual migration of Canada Geese. Some 300,000 geese pass through the palate of fall colors in this area. Grand parade, music, games and food. (mid-October long weekend)

NOVEMBER

CHRISTMAS FANTASYLAND TRAIN RIDE

CE - Bridgeport. Junction Valley Railroad, 7065 Dixie Highway, 48722. (517) 777-3480. Beginning the weekend after Thanksgiving through the third weekend of December. 6-10:00 pm. $5.50 per person. 2 mile evening rides through land aglow with 100,000 lights. Travel through Candlestick Trail, Candy Cane Pass, Santa Claus Lane, Soldier Alley, Valley Station Lit Highway, and Railway to Heaven. Elves will guide you to Santa and kids get to decorate their own ornament as a keepsake of their visit. (November - December)

CHRISTMAS LIGHTS

SE - Ann Arbor, Domino's Farms. (734) 930-5032. 800,000 outdoor lights, indoor tree display and nightly live entertainment. There are webs of lights shaped like animals arching over your car as you travel the farm complex roads. Nightly 6-10:00 pm. Carload admission around $5.00. Begins Thanksgiving weekend through December. (November / December)

AMERICA'S THANKSGIVING DAY PARADE

SE - Detroit. (along Woodward Avenue from the Cultural Center to downtown). (313) 923-8259. Buy a ticket for a grandstand seat ($15) or rent a room downtown along Woodward or get there early (6:00 am) for free space streetside.   Signaling the traditional kickoff to the holidays, you'll see floats, marching bands, giant balloon characters, and finally, at the finale, Santa and his sleigh. The parade starts at approximately 9:15 am. (November)

INDOOR AMUSEMENT PARK

SE - Detroit. Cobo Center. (313) 923-8259. This is the fundraiser that supports the Thanksgiving Day Parade. Admission is free, but individual rides charge fees or you can get an all day pass for around $14.00. Along with basic amusement rides, you'll also find Santa and Mrs. Claus. (Thanksgiving Day to - mid-December)

CHRISTMAS TREE FESTIVAL

SE - Ida. Matthes Evergreen Farm, (13416 Lulu Road). (734) 269-2668 or (734) 269-6244. Thanksgiving weekend. Open until Christmas for you-pick trees. Farm tours by hayride, cut-your-own tree, pre-cut trees, snacks, crafts, Santa Claus, wagon rides, pony rides and entertainment. The scent of evergreen is heavy in the air. (November)

FESTIVAL OF TREES

SE - Lansing. Lansing Center. (517) 372-4636. Plenty of holiday theme trees, wreaths and gingerbread houses on display. Admission. (November)

WONDERLAND OF LIGHTS

SE - Lansing. Potter Park Zoo. (517) 371-3926. Thousands of lights create a "Wildlife Wonderland" of unique zoo animal displays. Evenings beginning at dark from Thanksgiving through December. (November)

WILDLIGHTS

SE - Royal Oak. Detroit Zoo. (8450 West 10 Mile Road). (248) 541-5835. Evenings beginning Thanksgiving weekend through December. This annual holiday lighting of nearly 300,000 sparkling lights and lighted animal displays is a delight for kids and the animals. Warm refreshments available. Admission. (November / December)

WAYNE COUNTY LIGHTFEST

SE – Westland. Hines and Merriman, (I-96 exit Merriman). (734) 261-1630. Nearly one million lights of arcs and tree-lined straights billed as the Midwest's largest holiday light show. More than 35 displays and a refreshment shelter, gifts, and visits with Santa. Admission $5.00 per car. Runs between (mid-November & January 1 - closed Christmas night).

CHRISTMAS OPEN HOUSES

Museum homes are decorated for the holidays, mostly with Victorian themes. Visits from old Saint Nick, cookies and milk, and teas are offered for kids and parents. A great way to see local history with the focus on old-fashioned toys and festivities instead of, sometimes boring to kids, minute details of miscellaneous artifacts.

Christmas Open Houses (cont.)

- ❑ **SE - Jackson**, Ella Sharp Museum, 3225 Fourth Street. (517) 787-2320.
- ❑ **SE - Ann Arbor**, Waterloo Farm Museum. (517) 596-2254.
- ❑ **SE - Wyandotte**, Ford-Macnichol Home and Wyandotte Museum. (734) 324-7297.

HOLIDAY MUSICALS

Admission charged.

- ❑ **CE -** "Visions of Sugar Plums" - Flint Youth Theatre at Bower Theatre. (810) 760-1138. Friday evenings, Saturday afternoon and evenings. Ages 4 and up only. 2nd and 3rd weekend.
- ❑ **SE -** The Nutcracker Ballet - Detroit Opera House. (313) 874-7464. Dates TBA. Music supplied by the Detroit Symphony Orchestra.
- ❑ **SE -** Ann Arbor Symphony Holiday Concert. Michigan Theatre. Ann Arbor. (734) 994-4801. Favorite holiday music and a family sing-along.
- ❑ **SE -** Handel's Messiah. Ann Arbor Symphony Orchestra. (734) 994-4801.
- ❑ **SW -** "A Christmas Carol". Saugatuck. (616) 857-1701. After the show, climb aboard for a ride in a horse-drawn buggy through town.

CHRISTMAS AT CROSSROADS

CE - Flint, Crossroads Village. (800) 648-7275. Long weekends throughout December. 3:30 - 9:30 pm. Over 400,000 lights light up Crossroads Village and trackside displays. Craft demos, live entertainment in the Opera House, and festive traditional buffets. (December)

LONGWAY PLANETARIUM HOLIDAY SHOWS

CE - Flint. (810) 760-1181. Friday evenings at 8:00 pm, Saturday afternoon and evening, Sunday afternoon throughout December. Night sky shows with traditional (Nutcracker Fantasy) and contemporary (The Alien Who Stole Christmas) themes. Admission. (December)

SANTA EXPRESS

CW - Coopersville, Coopersville & Marne Railway. (616) 837-7000. Twice each weekend afternoon, the first three weeks in December. Santa and his helpers ride along and play games and sing songs to get everyone in the holiday spirit. Admission. (December)

GIANT NATIVITY SCENE

CW - Grand Haven, Waterfront Stadium. Daily. (800) 303-4097. Watch the story of the first Christmas come alive by the water. Donations. (December)

MUSICAL FOUNTAIN NATIVITY

CW - Grand Haven, (Grandstand at Harbor and Washington Streets on the riverfront). (800) 303-4096. Evening performances. (all month long) Donations. A 40 foot nativity scene on Dewey Hill offers evening performances focused on the "spirit" of the holiday. (December)

KWAANZA

SE - Detroit, Museum of African American History, (315 East Warren Avenue). (313) 494-5800. Weeklong during Kwaanza. Kwaanza (first fruits) is an African celebration of the harvest and the fruits of the community's labor. Each day has a special focus: unity, self-determination, collective work and responsibility, cooperative economics, purpose, creativity and faith. (December)

FIRST NIGHT

SE - Detroit, Birmingham Principal Shopping District. (248) 433-3550. First Night is an alcohol-free festival of arts for children and adults. Many booths have kids crafts, storytelling, musical entertainment and dancing, kid-friendly food and a big Midnight celebration. Admission. (December 31 - Beginning mid-day New Year's Eve)

NITE LITES

SE - Jackson, 200 West Ganson Street, Jackson County Fairgrounds, (I-94 exit 139). (800) 245-5282. A one-mile drive with 100,000 lights of "Candyland" (a candy cane treat is included with admission). They even have a drive up animated manger scene. Admission per vehicle under $5.00. Wednesday - Sunday weekly beginning the week of Thanksgiving through Christmas. (December)

FEST EVE

SE - Lansing and East Lansing. Downtown and Michigan State University Campus. (517) 371-6698. Alcohol-free new year activities and live entertainment plus midnight fireworks. New Years Eve. (December)

NEW YEAR JUBILEE

SE - Ypsilanti, Depot Town. (734) 483-4444. Alcohol-free evening of entertainment and fun for families. More than 45 performances in town churches and buildings. (December - Begins mid-day on New Year's Eve)

ZOOLIGHTS FESTIVAL

SW - Battle Creek. Binder Park Zoo. 1000's of lights and specially theme-lighted animal displays only viewed month-long in December. Evenings 5-9pm. Admission. (December)

MIDNIGHT AT THE CREEK

SW - Battle Creek, Downtown. (800) 397-2240. Ring in the New Year with a family-oriented evening of activities, storytellers, kid-friendly food and beverage, and musical performances of all different types. (December 31)

CHRISTMAS PICKLE FESTIVAL

SW - Berrien Springs, Downtown, (I-94 to US-31 south). (616) 473-6921. Do you know about a German tradition at Christmas? The first child to find a glass pickle hidden in the tree gets an extra present! This is the town's inspiration for a holiday parade, street lighting, and pickle tastings. Pickle and non-pickle foods and gifts. (1st week of December)

1839 Historic Courthouse Museum, 142
4th of July Celebrations, 213
AAA Canoe Rentals, 49
Adrian & Blissfield Railroad, 92
Adventure Copper Mine, 182
African World Festival, 215
Air Michigan, 206
AJ's Family Water Park, 36
Alber's Orchard, 222
Albert E. Sleeper State Park, 5
Algonac State Park, 122
Alma Highland Festival And Games, 201
Aloha State Park, 56
Alpenfest, 209
Alpine Valley Ski Area, 136
America's Thanksgiving Day Parade, 226
Amway Visitor's Center, 27
Andy T's Farms, 225
Ann Arbor Hands-On Museum, 87
Ann Arbor Street Art Fair, 210
Ann Arbor Youth Chorale, 88
Antique Tractor & Steam Engine Show, 215
Apple Charlie's Orchard And Mill, 222
Apple Mountain Ski Area, 13
Applefest, 222
Au Sable River Int'l Canoe Marathon, 209
Au Sable River Queen, 67
Automobile Hall Of Fame, 98
Bald Mountain State Park, 116
Balloon Fest, 219
Baraga State Park, 177
Battle Creek Battlecats, 140
Bavarian Festival, 205
Bavarian Inn Restaurant, 9
Bay City River Roar, 204
Bay City State Park, 3
Bear Cave, 143
Beaver Island Boat Company, 75
Belle Isle, 106
Bewabic State Park, 181
Big Al's Restaurant, 14
Binder Park Zoo, 139
Bittersweet Ski Area, 152
Black River Nat'l Forest Scenic Byway, 184
Blandford Nature Center, 32
Blossomtime, 201
Blue Water Area, 18
Bottle Cap Museum, 59
Boyne Highlands, 77
Boyne Mountain, 73
Brighton State Park, 93

Brimley State Park, 177
Bronner's Christmas Wonderland, 10
Brunch With The Bunnies, 200
Bunnyville, 201
Burt Lake State Park, 62
Butterfly House, 62
Calder Dairy Farm, 94
Call Of The Wild Museum, 58
Cannonsburg Ski Area, 28
Captain Nichols' Perch Boats, 154
Cardboard Regatta, 218
Carnegie Center Of The Arts, 157
Cascades, 115
Cascades Park, 222
Castle Rock, 171
Cereal Fest, 207
Charlton Park Village & Museum, 37
Cheboygan County Hist'l Museum, 56
Cheboygan State Park, 56
Chelsea Milling - "Jiffy Mix", 95
Children's Museum, 30
Childs' Place Buffalo Ranch, 113
Chippewa Nature Center, 15
Christmas At Crossroads, 228
Christmas Fantasyland Train Ride, 225
Christmas Lights, 226
Christmas Open Houses, 227
Christmas Pickle Festival, 231
Christmas Tree Festival, 226
City Of Douglas, 145
Civil War Assoc. Re-Enactment, 211
Civil War Muster, 217
Clare Irish Festival, 199
Clear Lake State Park, 55
Clinch Park Zoo, 81
Coast Guard "Mackinaw" Tours, 56
Coast Guard Festival, 208
Coe Rail Scenic Train, 134
Colonial Life Weekend, 213
Colonial Michilimackinac State Park, 64
Cook Energy Info Center And Dunes, 143
Coopersville & Marne Railway, 28
Copper Harbor Lighthouse Boat Tours, 179
Coppertown USA Museum, 179
Corn-Fusing CR, Farmers Puzzle, 217
Cornish Pumping Engine & Mining Mus., 184
Cornwell's Turkeyville USA, 151
Corsair Ski Area, 57
Country Fair Weekends, 223
Covered Bridge Festival, 212
Craig Lake State Park, 179

Cranbrook Art And Science Museums, 110
Crawford County Historic Museum, 59
Crossroads Village & Huckleberry RR, 8
Crossroads Village, 219
Crosswinds Marsh Wetland, 134
Crystal Mountain Ski Area, 80
Curiosity Kids' Museum, 156
Da Yoopers Tourist Trap, 185
Dahlem Environmental Center, 114
Deer Acres, 17
Deer Forest, 144
Deer Ranch, 171
Delaware Copper Mine Tour, 180
Delft Factory & Wooden Shoe Factory, 37
Delhi Metropark, 110
Delta College Planetarium, 4
Delta County Hist'l Mus.& Lighthouse, 181
Dennos Museum Center, 82
Detroit Children's Museum, 103
Detroit Grand Prix, 215
Detroit Historical Museum, 103
Detroit Institute Of Arts, 104
Detroit Lions Football, 131
Detroit Neon Soccer, 90
Detroit Pistons Basketball, 90
Detroit Red Wings Hockey, 108
Detroit Rockers Soccer, 91
Detroit Science Center, 105
Detroit Shock Women's Basketball, 91
Detroit Symphony Orchestra, 102
Detroit Tigers Baseball, 107
Detroit Vipers Hockey, 91
Detroit Zoo, 132
Dexter Cider Mill, 221
Diamond Jack's River Tours, 109
Diana Sweet Shoppe, 19
Dinosaur Gardens Prehistoric Zoo, 68
Dodge No. 4 State Park, 134
Domino's Farms, 88
Dossin Great Lakes Museum, 106
Double JJ Resort, 50
Dow Gardens, 15
Dr. Liberty Hyde Bailey Museum, 154
Drayton Plains Nature Center, 135
Dreamfield Farm, 49
Duck Lake State Park, 48
Dune Rides, 152
Dutch Village, 40
East Lansing Art Festival, 203
Echo Valley, 147
Egg Hunt, 200
Fair Lane, 101

Fall Harvest Festivals, 223
Father Marquette Nat'l Memorial/Mus, 170
Fayette State Historic Park, 161
Feast Of The Ste. Claire, 202
Fenner Nature Center, 116
Fest Eve, 230
Festival Of The Arts, 221
Festival Of Trees, 227
First Night, 230
Fish Ladder Sculpture, 30
Fisherman's Island State Park, 75
Flat Belt Festival, 215
Flint Children's Museum, 8
Flint Cultural Center, 6
Flint Generals Hockey Club, 7
Flint Symphony Orchestra, 8
Forest Fest, 209
For-Mar Nature Preserve & Arboretum, 5
Fort Custer Recreation Area, 139
Fort Mackinac State Park, 62
Fort Wilkins State Park, 180
Four Bears Waterpark, 133
Frankenmuth Cheese Haus, 11
Frankenmuth Historical Museum, 11
Frankenmuth Riverboat Tours, 12
Frankenmuth Woolen Mill, 12
Free Fishing Weekend, 204
Fridge, 135
Full Blast & Battle Creek Youth Center, 140
Fun Country Water Park, 77
Garlyn Farm & Zoological Park, 165
Genesee Recreation Area, 6
Gerald Ford Museum, 33
Giant Nativity Scene, 229
Gilmore Classic Car Club Museum, 146
Goose Festival, 225
Grand Haven / Spring Lake Trolley, 28
Grand Haven State Park, 29
Grand Island Shipwreck Tours, 163
Grand Lady Riverboat Cruises, 36
Grand Mere State Park, 153
Grand Prix Hydroplane Summer Nationals, 205
Grand Quacker Duck Race, 202
Grand Rapids Art Museum, 31
Grand Rapids Choir of Men & Boys, 32
Grand Rapids Civic Theatre, 31
Grand Rapids Griffins Hockey, 31
Grand Rapids Hoops Basketball, 31
Grand Rapids Rampage Football, 32
Grand Rapids Symphony, 32
Grand Rapids Youth Symphony, 32
Grandparent's Day Train, 219

Grayling Fish Hatchery, 59
Great Lakes Lighthouse Festival, 224
Great Lakes Shipwreck Museum, 166
Great Lakes Sport Kite Championships, 202
Great Northern Adventures, 188
Great Train Robbery, 220
Greater Lansing Symphony Orchestra, 111
Greektown Arts Festival, 203
Greenmead Historical Park, 121
H.H. Dow Historical Museum, 16
Hackley Hose Company No. 2, 44
Hanka Homestead Museum, 177
Harbor Steamer, 29
Harbor Trolley, 29
Harrisville State Park, 61
Hart-Montague Trail State Park, 43
Hartwick Pines State Park, 60
Hayes State Park, 127
Heath Beach, 122
Henry Ford Mus. & Greenfield Village, 98
Hiawatha National Forest,161
Highland Recreation Area, 135
Historic Mill Creek, 65
Historical Museum Of Bay County, 4
Historical Society Of Saginaw County, 22
Hoeft State Park, 69
Holiday Musicals, 228
Holland Museum, 38
Holland State Park, 38
Holly Recreation Area, 114
Honoring The Eagle Pow Wow, 208
Hot Air Jubilee, 211
Houghton County Hist'l Museum, 187
Huron City Museum, 14
Huron Lightship Museum, 19
Huron-Manistee National Forests, 73
Iargo Springs, 67
Ice Harvest, 197
Idler Riverboat, 156
Impression 5 Science Center, 118
Indian Lake State Park, 163
Indianhead Mountain Ski Area, 193
Indoor Amusement Park, 226
Interlochen State Park, 77
International Cherry Pit Spitting , 212
International Freedom Festival, 207
International Ice Sculpture Spectacular, 196
Ionia State Recreation Area, 14
Iron County Museum, 178
Iron Mountain Iron Mine, 193
Ironworkers Festival, 215
Island Lake Recreation Area, 92

Isle Royale National Park, 183
J & K Steamboat Line, 146
Japanese Cultural Center & House, 20
Jeepers! At Wonderland Mall, 121
Jesse Besser Museum, 55
John Ball Park Zoo, 33
Johnny Panther Quests, 22
Jollay Orchards, 223
Junction Valley Railroad, 5
Kalamazoo Aviation Museum (Air Zoo), 150
Kalamazoo Civic Youth Theatre, 149
Kalamazoo Nature Center, 148
Kalamazoo Symphony Orchestra, 149
Kalamazoo Valley Museum, 149
Kal-Haven Trail State Park, 155
Kellogg Bird Sanctuary, 139
Kellogg's Cereal City USA, 141
Kensington Metropark, 123
Kentwood Station Restaurant, 41
Keweenaw Bear Track Tours, 180
Kilwin's Candy Kitchens, 79
Knaebe's Mmmunchy Krunchy Apple Farm, 221
Kwaanza, 229
Labor Day Bridge Walk, 221
Lafayette Coney Island, 108
Lake Gogebic State Park, 187
Lake Hudson State Park, 128
Lake Michigan Recreation Area, 78
Lakelands Trail State Park, 130
Lakeport State Park, 15
Lansing Lugnuts, 117
Laughing Whitefish Falls Scenic Site, 178
Leelanau State Park, 78
Legs Inn, 57
Leila Arboretum & Kingman Museum, 142
Lilac Festival, 206
Lionel Trains Visitor's Center, 96
Little Switzerland Resort & Campground, 48
Little Traverse Historical Museum, 79
Longway Planetarium Holiday Shows, 229
Ludington City Beach, 41
Ludington State Park, 41
Mac Wood's Dune Rides, 43
Mackinac Bridge Mus/ "Mighty Mac" Bridge, 65
Mackinac Island Horse-Drawn Carriage Tours, 63
Mackinaw City Transportation Tours, 66
Mackinaw Fudge Festival, 220
Manistee County Museum, 78
Maple Sugaring Weekend 198
Maple Syrup Festival 199, 200, 201
Marquette Country Tours, 188
Marquette County Historical Museum, 188

Marquette Maritime Museum, 189
Marquette Mountain Ski Area, 189
Marquis Theater, 126
Marshall M. Frederick's Sculpture Gallery, 23
Marvin's Marvelous Mechanical Museum, 112
Maybury State Park, 126
McClain State Park, 182
McCourtie Park 133
Mead Lake Mine Site, 191
Mears State Park, 49
Memory Lane Arcade, 13
Meridian Township's Central Park, 127
Metamora-Hadley State Park, 15
Metro Beach Metropark, 125
Michigan Ausable Valley Railroad, 57
Michigan Botanic Garden & Meijer Park 35
Michigan Brown Trout Festival, 209
Michigan Challenge Balloonfest, 206
Michigan Festival, 216
Michigan Fiber Festival, 218
Michigan Historical Center, 117
Michigan Iron Industry Museum, 190
Michigan K-Wings Hockey, 147
Michigan Maritime Museum, 155
Michigan Railroad History Museum, 6
Michigan Renaissance Festival, 216
Michigan Space Center, 115
Michigan Speedway, 94
Michigan State Capital, 119
Michigan State Fair, 216
Michigan State University, 111
Michigan Tastfest, 211
Michigan Tech Winter Carnival, 197
Michigan Women's Hist'l Center, 120
Michigan's Adventure Amusement Park, 47
Michihistrigan Mini-Golf, 162
Midland Center For The Arts , 16
Midnight At The Creek, 231
Milan Dragway, 123
Millie Mine Bat Cave, 184
Miss Port Austin, 18
Mitchell State Park, 74
Monroe County Historical Museum, 124
Morley Candy Makers, 97
Mother's Day Celebration, 202
Motorsports Museum & Hall Of Fame, 126
Motown Historical Museum, 107
Mount Baldhead, 153
Mount Brighton Ski Area, 92
Museum Of African-American History, 102
Museum Of Ojibwa Culture, 172
Museum Ship - Valley Camp, 168

Music Hall Center - Detroit Youtheater, 108
Musical Fountain, 29
Musical Fountain Nativity, 229
Muskallonge Lake State Park, 165
Muskegon Air Fair, 209
Muskegon Civic Theatre, 44
Muskegon County Museum, 44
Muskegon Fury Hockey, 45
Muskegon State Park, 49
Muskegon Winter Sports Complex, 48
Mystery Hill, 128
Mystery Spot, 172
National Baby Food Festival, 208
National Blueberry Festival, 218
National Cherry Festival, 210
National Folk Festival, 217
National Forest Festival, 210
National Pickle Festival, 214
National Strawberry Festival, 206
Negwegon State Park, 61
New Year Jubilee, 230
Newaygo State Park, 48
Nite Lites, 230
North Higgins Lake State Park, 70
Norwegian Pumpkin Rolling Festival, 225
November, 225
Nub's Nob, 77
Old French Town Days, 217
Old Gas Tractor Show, 214
Old Mission Peninsula Lighthouse, 82
Old Victoria, 192
Onaway State Park, 67
Ontonagon County Historical Museum, 191
Orchard Beach State Park, 78
Original Wooden Shoe Factory, 39
Ortonville Recreation Area, 130
Ostego Lake State Park, 59
Ottawa National Forest, 185
P.J. Hoffmaster SP/Gillette Dune Center, 45
P.R.I.D.E., 214
Paint Creek Cider Mill Restaurant, 131
Palms Book State Park (Big Spring), 163
Parker Mill, 221
Paul Bunyan Days & Octoberfest, 220
Perchville USA, 198
Petoskey State Park, 80
Phyllis Haehnle Memorial Sanctuary, 115
Pictured Rocks Cruises, 164
Pictured Rocks National Lakeshore, 164
Pinckney Recreation Area, 130
Pirate's Cove Adventure Golf, 80
Pirate's Cove Adventure Golf, 81

Planet Walk, 120
Platte River State Fish Hatchery, 73
Plymouth Historical Museum, 130
Plymouth Orchards And Cider Mill, 222
Pontiac Lake Recreation Area, 134
Porcupine Mountains Wilderness SP, 192
Port City Princess, 46
Port Crescent State Park, 17
Potter Zoo And Zoological Gardens, 117
Pow Wow, 199
Pow Wow Dance For Mother Earth, 199
Prehistoric Forest, 128
Presque Isle County Historical Museum, 69
Presque Isle Lighthouse Museums, 68
Presque Isle Park, 189
Proud Lake State Park, 124
Pumpkin Fantasy World, 224
Pumpkin Train, 224
Pumpkinfest, 224
Queen's Inn Restaurant, 41
Quincy Mine Hoist, 182
R.E. Olds Transportation Museum, 120
Rainforest Café, 90
Red Flannel Festival, 220
Rifle River Recreation Area, 70
River Of History Museum, 169
River Raisin Battlefield Visitor's Ctr, 125
Riverdays Festival, 208
Riverfest, 222
Riverwalk Theatre Shows, 121
Rodeo, 216
Rolling Hills County Park, 136
Rooftop Landing Reindeer Farm, 136
Rosie's Dinerland, 50
Roxy's Depot Restaurant, 157
Ruby Cider Mill And Tree Farm, 218
S/S Keewatin, 145
Saginaw Art Museum, 22
Saginaw Children's Zoo, 21
Saline Celtic Festival, 211
Sand Lakes Quiet Area, 82
Sand Sculpture Contest, 205
Sandy Beach Campground, 52
Sanilac County Historical Museum, 20
Sanilac Petroglyphs, 3
Santa Express, 229
Saugatuck Dunes State Park, 39
Schoolhouse Café, 78
Screamin' On The Straits Races, 206
Seney National Wildlife Refuge, 170
Seven Lakes State Park, 113
Shanty Creek Resort, 73

Shearing Festival, 203
Shelby Man-Made Gemstones, 51
Shiawassee National Wildlife Refuge, 22
Shrine Of The Pines, 27
Silver Lake State Park, 44
Silver Ridge Resort, 6
Skyline Ski Area, 61
Sled Dog Enduro & Winter Flurry Fest, 197
Sleeping Bear Dunes National Lakeshore, 76
Sleepy Hollow State Park, 116
Snolympics Winter Picnic, 198
Snowfest, 197
Soo Locks Park, 167
Soo Locks Tour Train, 169
South Higgins Lake State Park, 70
SW Michigan College & Cass County Mus, 146
Spirit Of Detroit Thunderfest, 210
Spirit Of Ford, 100
Spring Valley Trout Farm, 111
SS Badger, 42
St. Patrick's Day Parade, 199, 200
Stagecoach Stop USA, 129
Star Of Saugatuck, 153
Sterling State Park, 125
Stevens Family Circle, 61
Straits State Park, 173
Strawberry Festival, 203
Sugar Loaf Resort, 75
Sugarbush, 199
Sugaring & Shearing Festival, 200
Summer Music Games, 211
Tahquamenon Falls State Park, 166
Tall Ships "Malabar" & "Manitou", 80
Tawas Point State Park, 57
Team US Nationals & Balloon Air Show, 211
Thompson's Harbor State Park, 69
Three Oaks Spokes Bicycle Museum, 23
Tibbits Opera House, 144
Tilden Open Pit Mine Tours, 186
Tip-Up Town, USA, 196
Toonerville Trolley & Riverboat Ride, 162
Totem Village, 173
Tower Of History, 169
Traverse City State Park, 82
Tulip Time, 204
Twin Lakes State Park, 193
Twin Points Resort, 42
Uncle John's Cider Mill, 219
University Of Michigan College Sports, 89
University Of Michigan Museums, 89
UP 200 Sled-Dog Championship, 198
Upper Peninsula Championship Rodeo, 212

Upper Peninsula Children's Museum, 190
Upper Peninsula State Fair, 218
US National Ski Hall of Fame & Mus, 187
USS Silversides, 46
Van Andel Museum Center, 34
Van Buren County Historical Museum, 146
Van Buren State Park, 156
Van Riper State Park, 179
Venetian Festival, 212
W.C. Wetzel State Park, 114
Wagner Falls Scenic Site, 165
Walk Through History, 205
Walker Tavern State Historic Complex, 93
War Of 1812 Re-Enactment, 218
Warren Dunes State Park, 154
Waterloo State Park, 96
Wayne County Air Show, 204
Wayne County Lightfest, 227
Wells State Park, 179
West Michigan Children's Museum, 46
West Michigan Grand Prix, 214
West Michigan Whitecaps Baseball, 35
Wexford County Historical Museum, 75
White Cloud's Homecoming, 214
White Pine Village, 42
White River Light Station Museum, 52
Whitehouse Nature Center, 139
Wild Swan Theater, 87
Wilderness State Park, 55
Wilderness Trails Animal Park, 4
Wildlights, 227
Wilson State Park, 37
Windmill Island, 39
Winter Carnival, 198
Winterfest, 196
Wizard of Oz Festival, 203
Wolcott Mill Metropark, 131
Woldumar Historic Encampment, 201
Wolf Lake Fishery Interpretive Center, 151
Wonderland Of Lights, 227
World Logrolling & Lumberjack, 212
Yankee Air Force Museum, 91
Yankee Springs Recreation Area, 152
Yogi Bear's Jellystone Park, 83
Young People's Theater, 88
Young State Park, 76
Zieger Centennial Farm, 223
Zoolights Festival, 230

<u>NOTES</u>

NOTES

<u>NOTES</u>

GROUP DISCOUNTS AND FUNDRAISER OPPORTUNITIES!

Dear Coordinator:

We're excited to introduce our new book to your group! This new guide for parents, grandparents, teachers and visitors is a great tool to discover hundreds of fun places to visit around Michigan. **KIDS ♥ MICHIGAN** is one resource for all the wonderful places to travel either locally or across the state.

We are two parents who have researched, written and published this book. We have spent over 1000 hours collecting information and personally visited all of the most unique places listed in this guide. This book is kid-tested and the descriptions include great hints on what kids like best!

After you have reviewed your copy of **KIDS ♥ MICHIGAN**, please consider the following options: *(Please visit* **www.kidslovepublications.com** *for latest information)*

- ❑ **Group Discount/Fundraiser** – Purchase the book at the price of $10.00 and offer the 23% savings off the suggested retail price to members / friends. Minimum order is ten books. Greater discounts (up to 38%) are available for fundraisers. Call for details.

- ❑ **Available for Interview/Speaking** – The authors have a treasure bag full of souvenirs from favorite places in Michigan. We'd love to share ideas on planning fun trips to take children while exploring Michigan. The authors are available, by appointment, at (614) 898-2697. The minimum guaranteed order is 50 books. There is no additional fee involved.

Call us soon at (614) 898-2697 to make arrangements!
Happy Exploring!

Attention Parents:

All titles are "Kid Tested" (*the authors and kids personally visited all of the most unique places*) and wrote the books with warmth and excitement from a parent's perspective. Find tried and true places that children will enjoy. No more boring trips! Listings provide: Names, addresses, telephone numbers, <u>internet addresses</u>, directions, and descriptions.

KIDS LOVE INDIANA ™

❖ **Discover places where you can "co-star" in a cartoon or climb a giant sand dune.** Almost 600 listings in one book about Indiana travel. 10 geographical zones, 193 pages.

KIDS LOVE MICHIGAN ™

❖ **Discover places where you can "race" over giant sand dunes, climb aboard a lighthouse "ship", eat at the world's largest breakfast table, or watch yummy foods being made.** Almost 600 listings in one book about Michigan travel. 8 geographical zones, 237 pages.

KIDS LOVE OHIO ™

❖ **Discover places like hidden castles and whistle factories.** Almost 1000 listings in one book about Ohio travel. 9 geographical zones, 291 pages.

KIDS LOVE PENNSYLVANIA ™

❖ **Explore places where you can "discover" oil and coal, meet Ben Franklin, or watch you favorite toys and delicious, fresh snacks being made.** Over 900 listings in one book about Pennsylvania travel. 9 geographical zones, 268 pages.

ORDER FORM

Kids Love Publications
7438 Sawmill Road, PMB 500
Columbus, OH 43235
(614) 898-2697

Visit our website: **www.kidslovepublications.com**

Quantity	Title	Price (ea.)	Total
	"Kids Love Indiana"	$12.95	
	"Kids Love Michigan"	$12.95	
	"Kids Love Ohio"	$12.95	
	"Kids Love Pennsylvania"	$12.95	
Special Combo Pricing - Please Indicate Quantity & Titles Above			
	Combo #2 - Any 2 Titles	$21.95	
	Combo #3 - Any 3 Titles	$29.95	
	Combo #4 - All 4 Titles	$36.95	

Note: All Combo Pricing is for different titles only. For multiple (10+) quantity discounts <u>of one title</u> please refer to the Group Sales information page in this book.

Subtotal	
Sales Tax (Ohio Residents Only) - 5.75%	
Shipping	FREE
TOTAL	

(Please make check or money order payable to: KIDS LOVE PUBLICATIONS)

Name_____

Address_____

City_____State_____

Zip_____Telephone_____

All orders are shipped within 2 business days of receipt by U.S. Mail. Your satisfaction is 100% guaranteed or simply return your order for a prompt refund. If you wish to have your books personally autographed (for a special gift, etc.) please include a legible note indicating what you wish to be written in your book(s). Thanks for your order and Happy Exploring!

George ♥ Michele